IEE Computing Series 7
Series Editors: D.A.H. Jacobs
S.L. Hurst
M.W. Sage

Software engineering
environments

Software engineering environments

Edited by
Ian Sommerville

Peter Peregrinus Ltd on behalf of the Institution of Electrical Engineers

Published by Peter Peregrinus Ltd., London, United Kingdom

© 1986: Peter Peregrinus Ltd.

British Library Cataloguing in Publication Data

Software engineering environments.—(IEE
   computing series; 7)
   1. Computer programs
   I. Sommerville, Ian II. Institution of
   Electrical Engineers III. Series
   005.3 QA76.6

ISBN: 0 86341 077 4

Printed in England by Billing and Sons Ltd.

Contents

Foreword

This book is the proceedings of a conference on the topic of Software Engineering Environments which was held at the University of Lancaster, England from 2nd to 4th April 1986.

This was the second conference on this topic to be held in the UK, the first conference being at the University of York in 1985. The support received emphasised the increasing interest and work being carried out in this area - there were four times as many papers submitted as could be accepted and papers were submitted from the UK, the USA, Australia, France, Germany and Italy. Over 140 people attended the conference at Lancaster.

The main themes of the conference were software engineering environments in use, formal methods and software engineering environments, and the user interface to complex environments. This is reflected in these proceedings but as papers were not restricted to these topics, the papers reflect a broad spread of interest in the field.

A great many people assisted in the arrangements for this conference. I would particularly like to thank my fellow members of the Programme Committee, namely Howard Nichols, Doug Shepherd, Tom Cox, John Smart, Bernie Cohen, Ian Wand and Tim Lyons; the authors for the timely submission of their papers; the local organisers, John Mariani and John Gallagher who made such a success of the conference and the Alvey Directorate for their financial support. Particular thanks are due to Ray Welland who took over as Programme Committee secretary at a critical time and did an immense amount of work whilst I was ill.

Finally, I would like to dedicate this book to Bob Berry of the University of Lancaster who died unexpectedly whilst the conference was being arranged. Bob did all of the initial arrangements for the conference and it is largely due to his conscientious efforts that the conference was a success.

Ian Sommerville,
University of Strathclyde, May 1986.

Preface

It is a historical truism that the most significant improvements in individual productivity are achieved by providing skilled individuals with powerful tools to do their work. For example, one man with a mechanical digger can move more earth in a day than 50 men whose only tool is a simple shovel so it is reasonable to conjecture that the key to improvements in software productivity is the development of powerful tools to support the software engineer. However, in the same way as earthmovers alone are not enough to build roads, tools working in isolation are not enough. It is only when powerful, integrated collections of software tools are available and widely used that we shall see significant increases in the productivity of software engineers.

Such tool collections are called Software Engineering Environments and, realistically, are very difficult and expensive to build. They represent an important phase in the transition of software development from a craft activity, which is labour intensive, to a capital-intensive engineering science. In future, software engineers will carry out their work using very powerful personal computers which run a software engineering environment providing support for all of the activities involved in developing computer software systems.

What then is a software engineering environment and how is it distinct from other collections of software tools which assist with the process of programming? In short, a software engineering environment is a collection of tools which is, firstly, *integrated* and which, secondly, supports all of the activities involved in the development of software. Hence the name *Integrated Project Support Environment (IPSE)* which is sometimes used instead of Software Engineering Environment.

Tool integration within an environment can and should be achieved at more than one level. The most essential level is the database level where all tools should record and retrieve information through a common database management system. Hence, the sharing of data between tools should be straightforward and not constrained by data representation issues. The second level of integration is at the level of tool invocation and control where one tool may automatically invoke another in response to some event (a compiler calls an editor to allow the user to fix a syntax error, say) and the final level is at the user interface level where all tools should share a consistent approach to user interface design.

Complete life cycle support where tools exist to assist with all of the software development activities implies that there are tools in the environment to support requirements analysis and definition, software specification, software design, programming, software testing and validation, documentation, software management and software maintenance. Currently, no such environment exists and, indeed, we are only just starting to explore how tools to support some of these activities may be constructed. The environments discussed in this book, go some way towards meeting this ideal but all of their developers would admit that we still have a long way to go before a complete software engineering environment may be built.

The papers in this book have been divided into a number of sections each of which addresses a particular theme. These are:

1. Existing environments which are either in use in industry or about to come onto the market shortly as software products.

2. The database and operating system mechanisms which are needed to support software engineering environments.

3. Tools which support some of the non-programming phases of software development which might be included in complete integrated environments.

4. The user interface to software engineering environments.

5. Experimental environments which address research topics likely to emerge as products in the next generation of environments. These include environments to support formal methods of software construction and environments designed using formal methods.

Chapters 1 to 3 discuss existing environments. Chapter 1 (an invited paper) covers the ISTAR environment which is unusual in that it is built on a set of independent cooperating databases rather than single database system. By contrast, Chapters 2 and 3 discuss environments built on the traditional model around a single database system. Chapter 2 describes the EPOS environment which is widely used in Germany and Chapter 3 describes work going on at GEC Software in the UK to develop a practical IPSE.

The next three chapters address the substructure essential to a successful software engineering environment. The paper by Ian Campbell (invited paper) describes PCTE which is a pan-European project to develop a portable basis for a number of different environments. The papers by Crawley and by Blair et al. discuss investigations into the use of an object-oriented model to construct a filestore and a complete operating environment as a basis for IPSE construction.

Section three is made up of three papers which discuss tools to support activities involved in the software process. The first paper in this section discusses a system which is intended to support the CORE methodology of requirements analysis and definition and this is complemented by Eagling's paper on supporting SSADM, a methodology which can take over where CORE leaves off. By contrast, the final paper by Carré addresses software testing and discusses a tool which simplifies the systematic testing of software systems.

It is now accepted that one of the key features of an environment as far as its general usability is concerned is the user's interface to that environment. The first paper on this topic (Chapter 10) discusses a theoretical approach to interface design which evaluates a design according to a set of predefined principles. This is followed by a paper which discusses an elegant and ambitious interface management system which has been designed as part of the ASPECT IPSE. The third paper on this topic also discusses the user interface part of an Alvey IPSE project, namely ECLIPSE, and demonstrates how a user-interface metaphor and standardisation in using that metaphor can lead to consistency across the user interfaces of the tools making up a software engineering environment.

As would be expected, the final section which covers experimental environments is the largest section in the book. The section is introduced by a paper by Roy Campbell (invited paper) which describes the SAGA environment which includes specific support for formal software specification. This is followed by a paper on the ASPECT IPSE which discusses how formal specifications may be used, in an effective way, to define tool interfaces. The third paper discusses the Flex environment and shows how a consistent approach to the treatment of all objects (including procedures) can lead to effective software reuse and Chapter 16 describes an environment being built at McGill University, Canada which is intended to support the programming language Modula-2. Finally, the last chapter speculates on the future and how developments in hardware and software technology will lead to more effective environments to support software production.

This book will be of interest to three classes of reader. These are advanced students studying topics such as software development environments or software engineering, practitioners who are involved in constructing environments and software tools and research workers who are investigating how advanced environments may be built. In general, readers should have some appreciation of the problems involved in software engineering environments but no specialised programming language or mathematical knowledge is required to understand the majority of the papers.

The papers here are indicative of the state-of-the-art in software engineering environments. It is clear that we have arrived at a stage where the feasibility of constructing such an environment is no longer in doubt and it only remains for this exciting technology to migrate from the research laboratory to the marketplace.

Chapter 1

An introduction to ISTAR

Vic Stenning

1. INTRODUCTION

ISTAR is an environment for use on computer systems development projects. It addresses the three critical "dimensions" of such a project - technical development, project management and configuration management - in a coordinated way, and is thereby able to support all members of the project team throughout the project life cycle.
The environment is not specific to any particular development method or programming language, but rather provides a controlled overall structure within which particular methods and languages can be employed as required.
This paper discusses the contractual approach on which ISTAR is based, describes the structure and organisation of the environment, and summarises the available tools and facilities.

2. OBJECTIVES

Concern here is with Integrated Project Support Environments (IPSEs). The scope of an IPSE can conveniently be identified by contrast with a program development system and a programming support environment.
Program development systems have traditionally been supplied by computer manufacturers. They provide only those facilities that are essential to implement programs in some chosen programming language. Thus they would typically offer facilities for editing, compiling, linking and debugging.
Programming support environments recognise that actual implementation in some chosen programming language is only one small part of the complete process of software development. (The term "development" is used consistently here to encompass not only initial development but also subsequent maintenance and evolution during the operational life of the software and system.) They therefore provide facilities to support all development activities throughout the complete life cycle, from initial concept formulation and requirements analysis, right through operational use and into controlled phasing out and replacement. In some cases this system life cycle can last for tens of years. Version control and configuration management are obvious issues that must be addressed by a programming support environment.

Project support environments go beyond programming
support environments in that they provide support to all
project staff, not just to development staff. Thus they
should provide facilities for project management, quality
assurance, document preparation, and so on. Ideally, a
project support environment should offer facilities for
complete system development, not just software. Thus one
would expect to see support for total system design methods,
with smooth transition into individual design methods for the
hardware and software elements.

ISTAR is a full integrated project support environment.
In addition to the general requirements for life cycle support
and project team support, a number of specific objectives were
identified for the product. It should be portable across a
wide range of machines, and in particular should be suitable
for both shared development machines and single user
workstations. Indeed, there must be a smooth transition path
from use of shared machines to use of workstations, and this
obviously involves a stage of using the two together. It
should be open-ended, in that user organisations should be
able to incorporate new tools without recourse to the
environment supplier. It should support use of existing tools
without modification. And it should be able to support
projects that are geographically distributed across several
sites.

3.   THE CONTRACTUAL APPROACH

3.1 The Contract

ISTAR is organised to support a powerful but general
approach to software and systems development - the contractual
approach. This approach is based upon the hierarchical
decomposition of work units into smaller work units that is
typically employed for any complex project.

With the contractual approach, each identified task
within a project is organised as an individual contract. This
contract takes as input a precise specification of the task to
be performed, and produces as output the deliverables that are
required from the task. Where those responsible for a
contract can identify various sub-tasks which would help to
achieve the goal, and are able to precisely specify those
sub-tasks, then sub-contracts can be let to perform those
sub-tasks. The whole structure is of course recursive, and
the sub-contracts may themselves have sub-contracts, and so
on. The net result is that any task typically involves a
complete hierarchy of contracts, where each of those contracts
has the same basic form (Fig.1). Within this hierarchy, when
a given contract lets a sub-contract, we refer to the former
as the "client" and the latter as the "contractor".

As noted above, the main interface between a client and a
contractor is that the client supplies a specification to the
contractor, and the contractor returns deliverables to the
client. However, for coordination purposes the client will
typically need to be informed of the contractor's progress and
any problems that are encountered. Further, the client may

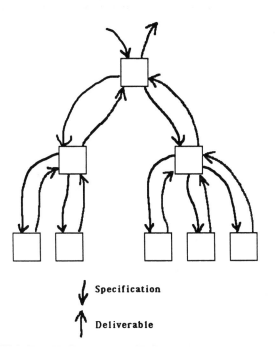

Fig 1. A contract hierarchy.

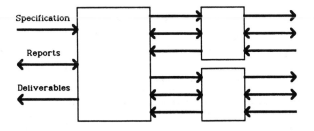

Fig 2. A client-contractor interface

need to pass to the contractor information that is outside the
scope of the specification, for example some informal response
to a problem report. Thus there may be a flow of reports in
both directions between client and contractor, and the
complete client-contractor interface has three components:
specification, deliverables, and reports (Fig.2).

3.2   The Contract Specification

A contract specification is regarded as having three
distinct parts

- a task specification, which precisely defines the task to be
  performed (what rather than how)

- a set of verification criteria, which define an objective
  test to show that the task has been performed satisfactorily

- and a set of management constraints that govern the
  performance of the task. These may cover, for example, the
  required timescale for the task, resources to be employed,
  standards to be applied, and so on.

Of course, the nature of the contract specification will
vary with the task to be performed, and different kinds of
specification will be appropriate at different levels of the
hierarchy. Thus, for a top level step that encompasses a
major product development the task specification would
typically concentrate on the market requirement and the
verification criteria might call for acceptance testing
according to established procedures. However, for a low-level
step the task specification might provide a detailed interface
specification for a software module to be implemented in
Pascal, and the verification criteria might define a specific
set of tests to be performed on the implemented module.

3.3   Amendment and Cancellation

It cannot be assumed that all contracts will proceed
smoothly and produce their deliverables as specified and
within the management constraints. Some contracts will take
longer than planned, or consume more than the allocated
resources. It might prove impractical or impossible to
produce deliverables that meet the specification. Or the need
to revise the contract specification may arise externally.
    Therefore it must be possible to amend contract
specifications. However, such amendments can only be made by
the client. Should a problem arise within a contract then
this must be reported to the client (using the normal
reporting facilities) who may choose as a result to amend the
contract's specification. The contractor may use reports to
suggest or negotiate contract amendments, but cannot
unilaterally make such amendments. By contrast, the client
can make an amendment at any time - and of course must take
the responsibility for doing so.
    Occasionally, due to changing circumstances or

insurmountable problems, it may become pointless to continue
with a contract. In this case the client may choose to
completely cancel the contract.

3.4 Specification Issues

All main aspects of the contractual approach have now
been introduced - the letting of contracts, exchange of
reports, return of deliverables, amendment of contracts, and
cancellation. However, two further points should be made
concerning contract specifications.

First, although the specification must be precise, it
need not be detailed. Thus, for example, a contract
specification may call for a feasibility study to be
performed, but may not detail the options to be investigated.
The "rules of the game" are that any deliverables that meet
the specification and satisfy the acceptance criteria are
legitimate. Thus it is the client's responsibility to provide
an appropriate specification of sufficient detail to ensure
that the returned deliverables will be satisfactory. Of
course, the client could misjudge the level of detail that is
needed, and as a consequence receive an unsuitable
deliverable. In this event it is necessary to produce a more
detailed specification, removing the area of freedom that
allowed the unsatisfactory deliverable, and then issue the
appropriate contract amendment (or perhaps even let a
completely new contract).

The second point on the contract specification concerns
the acceptance criteria. It would have been possible to
regard the definition of acceptance criteria as part of the
task specification. However, by choice the acceptance
criteria are separated out, both to emphasise their importance
and to indicate that an objective means of assessment should
be defined before a contract is let, rather than while it is
proceeding. Of course, it may later prove necessary to modify
the acceptance criteria, but this must then be treated as a
contract amendment.

4. USING THE CONTRACTUAL APPROACH

The contractual approach reflects a common way of
organising projects that is completely general. It
corresponds to the "work breakdown" approach that is typically
employed (consciously or unconsciously) for any non-trivial
project. The objective in following this approach is primarily
to instil a basic level of project hygiene and to ensure that,
at all times, all the people involved in a project know
exactly what they are trying to do.

To appreciate the generality of this approach, first
consider an organisation that typically conducts its projects
in phases: feasibility study, requirements analysis, system
specification, and so on. Within ISTAR the complete project
would be a contract, and this contract would then let one sub-
contract for each phase. These sub-contracts would themselves
let sub-contracts as appropriate.

Of course, it is frequently the case that the different

phases are not strictly sequential. Rather, the work on a
given phase can often be initiated as soon as the previous
phase has produced useful output. This again can be
accommodated within the contractual approach. Each
sub-contract is now required to produce not just a single
deliverable, but rather a set of deliverables. The
sub-contract for a new phase is initiated as soon as the
previous phase produces a useful deliverable. This
sub-contract must then be amended as further relevant
information becomes available, but with proper planning these
amendments can be handled without disruption. Only in the
case where there is a genuine change of requirement or design
need there be any significant re-working, and in these cases
such re-working is inevitable. Obviously this parallel
working with overlapping phases requires more coordination
than the sequential case, and as always this coordination must
be the responsibility of the client contract.

Within a given phase it is often possible for work to
proceed in parallel. The classic example is where a system
can be decomposed into component parts and, once specified,
each of these components can be developed independently. With
the contractual approach, the decomposition into components,
and the specification of these components, is performed within
a coordinating contract (or by a sub-contract on behalf of
that contract). The coordinating contract then lets
sub-contracts for the production of the individual components,
with all these sub-contracts proceeding in parallel. Any
interfacing problems that subsequently arise must be handled
by the coordinating contract, and this may of course involve
amendments to various sub-contracts. Eventually the required
deliverables will be returned by all the sub-contracts, and
these can be combined to yield the desired system.

Discussion thus far has been on the basis of sequential
phases, possibly with parallel development within the phases.
However, the contractual approach is obviously not limited to
such an arrangement, and in general any required combination
of sequential and parallel working can be employed. This is
achieved by letting sub-contracts at the appropriate times and
with the appropriate management constraints, particularly on
timescales. The degree of parallel working is constrained
only by practical considerations of retaining overall control
and avoiding excessive amounts of rework.

Consider now some extensions to the basic scenario.
Suppose that, in order to assist with requirements analysis or
design, it is decided to construct a rapid prototype. This is
obviously handled by letting a sub-contract, with the
deliverable either being the prototype itself or the results
of building and experimenting with the prototype, whichever is
most appropriate.

Now suppose there is a need to construct a product and,
because of time constraints, to simultaneously develop a user
guide for that product. This might best be handled by
separate contracts, one for product development and one for
the user guide, with deliverables from the former being fed to
the latter as they become available. In this case it might be
appropriate for the specification of the user guide contract

to be expressed in terms of "reflecting the current state of knowledge of the product", so that the contract would not need amending every time more information became available.

Finally, suppose that it is desired to develop a new product and simultaneously develop a set of acceptance tests for that product, both being based upon the same initial specification. Again separate contracts will be let, one for the product and one for the acceptance tests, but there are in fact several possible ways of proceeding. However they all involve initially defining some "working" acceptance criteria for the production contract. One possibility would be to allow the production contract to proceed to completion on the basis of these working criteria, and then let a separate contract to run the independent acceptance tests. Should any of these tests fail the production contract could be amended to reflect the detected problems, and the tests re-run on the subsequent deliverable. Other approaches are also possible, and these could be equally viable.

Obviously the above discussion has not been exhaustive. The intention was simply to illustrate the generality of the contractual approach and its relationship to some recognised project organisations. As stated earlier, the objective of this approach is primarily to encourage basic project hygiene and to ensure that the people working on a project know precisely what they are trying to do.

5.   THE ORGANISATION OF ISTAR

ISTAR is based upon the contractual approach, and its organisation directly reflects that approach. This perhaps has its greatest impact in the area of the database. Rather than having one large "environment database", ISTAR employs a large number of small databases, one for each contract. As a new contract is let, the database to hold information pertaining to that contract is created automatically. The relationships between the individual databases, reflecting the contract hierarchy, are maintained by ISTAR.

It is on the basis of these small databases that an ISTAR system can be geographically distributed. Individual databases within the same contract hierarchy can be held on different machines. A single contract database must be held in its entirety on a single machine, but related databases - for example, the databases for two contracts where one is a sub-contract of the other - can reside on different machines. Thus the complete contract hierarchy within a given ISTAR system can be dispersed over an entire network.

All the basic operations of the contractual approach, as summarised at the beginning of section 3.4, are directly supported as ISTAR primitive operations. All these contractual operations (except reporting) involve a "handshake" exchange between client and contractor. Thus a new contract is let by a client assigning the contract to some user of the environment, and that user must subsequently acknowledge the assignment. That particular user thereby accepts overall responsibility for the contract, although other users may work on the contract as required.

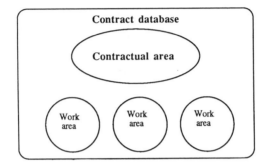

Fig 3. Structure of a contract database

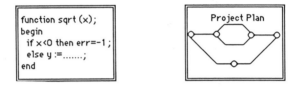

Fig. 4. Transfer items

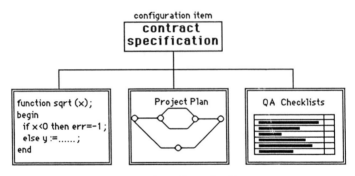

Fig. 5 A configuration item

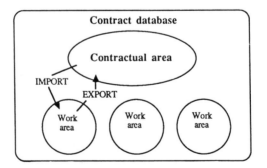

Fig. 6. Import and export

The contractor can subsequently make deliveries, and these are acknowledged by the client. Similarly the client may either amend or cancel the contract, and again these operations require acknowledgment from the contractor. And, of course, reports can be sent in either direction at any time for any extant contract.

6. TRANSFER ITEMS AND CONFIGURATION ITEMS

Internally, an individual contract database is partitioned into a number of distinct areas. Specifically, each contract database has precisely one "contractual" area and an arbitrary number of "work" areas (Fig.3). As these names suggest, the contractual area is used primarily for coordination with other contracts, while the work areas are used for performing work within this contract.

Two types of information unit are particularly important within ISTAR, namely the transfer item and the configuration item. A transfer item is a single self-contained unit of information of a given type: META-IV specification, Pascal source, project plan, document, or whatever (Fig.4). A configuration item is a set of transfer items (Fig.5).

Information is held in the contractual area in the form of configuration items, and it is configuration items that are moved between contract databases. (Such moves are achieved by copying, so that following such a move the configuration item exists both in the source database and in the destination database.) Thus, when the contract is established, its specification is installed as a single configuration item in the contractual area. Similarly, any subsequent amendments are also installed as single configuration items within this area, with a relationship to the original specification and earlier amendments. And a deliverable from the contract must be established as a configuration item in this area before the actual delivery to the client can be made.

Similar arrangements apply for any sub-contracts that may be let. Thus, the specification of a sub-contract will be established as a single configuration item in the contractual area before the sub-contract is assigned. Deliverables from the sub-contract will be installed in this area as they arrive. And so on.

Once established in the contractual area, configuration items and their member transfer items are normally immutable. Work within the contract does not modify established configuration items, but rather produces new configuration items - the contract deliverable, for example, or a new sub-contract specification. This is done by first creating an empty configuration item in the contractual area, and then developing various transfer items in various work areas and "exporting" these transfer items to the contractual area. In order to produce a new transfer item it may be necessary to consult or employ some existing transfer item - from the contract specification, for example - and these can be imported into work areas as required (Fig.6).

Thus configuration items are held in contractual areas and moved between contract databases, while their member transfer items are imported from the contractual area into work areas, or exported from work areas into the contractual area.

Within the contractual area, both configuration items and transfer items within configuration items can exist in many distinct versions. A simple naming scheme is adopted, whereby there are distict variant "threads" for each item, with many successors within each thread. A particular version of an item is then identified by specifying the variant and the successor, thus: STACK_SPEC(UNBOUNDED,5). Various naming defaults can then be employed when accessing existing versions, for example to access the latest version or some preferred version. Although the naming scheme is deliberately kept very simple, the data management facilities recognise a richer versioning structure, involving arbitrary trees, and record this structure by means of relationships within the contractual area. These relationships can then be queried and used where appropriate by users or tools.

The discussion thus far has perhaps suggested that configuration items can only move up or down the contractual hierarchy, between client and contractor. However this is not in fact the case. Rather, a configuration item can be moved on request from any database to any other database, subject only to access right restrictions. Such moves are normally recorded at both databases, with the source recording the destination and the destination recording the source. Thus detailed records of the movement of configuration items are maintained.

This general facility for moving configuration items between databases is employed extensively within ISTAR. For example, when there is a need for a component library this is achieved by establishing a contract to operate the library. Library components are of course configuration items. New components may be submitted to the library from any source, and the source of each component is recorded. Contracts may take components out of the library as required, and all usage of a given component is again recorded. Defect reports can easily be sent to the original donor and all users of a given component, and any new version can readily be distributed to all interested users.

7.   WORKBENCHES

The many tools within ISTAR are not simply organised as one large toolkit. Rather, the tools are grouped into collections of related tools, termed "workbenches". Each workbench typically operates on just a few transfer item types that are in some way related. For example, a simple workbench that supports development in some programming language might operate on two transfer item types: source module in that programming language, and executable program.

As might be expected, a workbench typically operates in its own work areas within the contract. Thus a Pascal workbench would operate in Pascal work areas, a VDM workbench in VDM work areas, and so on. The workbench would support import and export of transfer items of the relevant types, and analysis and production of items of these types. Each kind of work area - Pascal, VDM, or whatever - has a well-defined "data model" that governs the organisation of data within such work areas. This data model is defined solely to meet the needs of the workbench, and is independent of the data model for the contractual area or that of any other work area.

Indeed, achieving this independence of data models was a major objective of the contractual area and work area arrangement. A work area is completely self-contained and insulated from the outside world, to which it interfaces solely by (workbench specific) import and export operations. This means that workbenches can be developed independently and incorporated into ISTAR without danger of clashing with existing workbenches. This is obviously important to user organisations that wish to extend the system, and is particularly important when incorporating existing tools that impose their own requirements on the organisation of data. In the latter case, a new kind of work area is introduced, with a data model conforming to the requirements of the existing tool. The tool is then incorporated into a workbench that operates on this kind of work area.

Transfer items are typed, in the sense that they will be processed only by workbenches designed to operate on items of that type. In this context, it should be noted that the contractual area and the contractual operations are completely independent of transfer item types. A useful analogy is that of shipment of standard containers on lorries or ships. A workbench can process the contents of a transfer item, but as part of the export operation this transfer item is loaded into a standard container that is then labelled with the type of the transfer item. These containers can be held in contractual areas, and moved between databases, without any need to examine their contents. However, when these contents are required in some other work area the container is unloaded into that work area as part of the import operation. Of course, such unloading will only be performed by a workbench capable of processing transfer items of that particular type.

8.   THE USER INTERFACE

All ISTAR workbenches and tools interact with the user via a common user interface system. This user interface provides a range of facilities, to be used by workbenches as appropriate

- full screen editing
- multiple windows
- pop-up menus and windows
- forms with protected fields
- syntax-directed editing

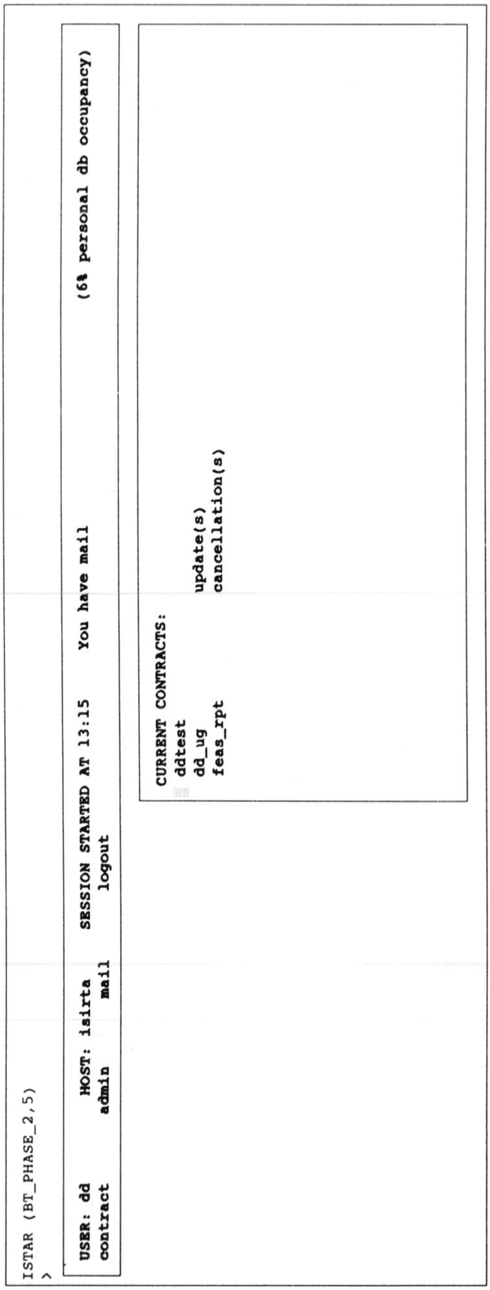

```
ISTAR (BT_PHASE_2,5)
>

 USER: dd        HOST: isirta    SESSION STARTED AT 13:15    You have mail        (6% personal db occupancy)
 contract        admin    mail           logout


                 CURRENT CONTRACTS:
                 ddtest             update(s)
                 dd_ug              cancellation(s)
                 feas_rpt
```

Fig. 7 A log-in display

In addition, an extended version of the user interface system supports graphical display (see section 10.5). The user normally directs the system by means of menu selection. Direct entry of commands is also possible. Since there is a single common user interface package, all editing commands are common throughout the system and for the different modes of editing. Thus, screen editing, forms editing and syntax-directed editing all employ the same basic set of commands.

9.   THE USER'S VIEW OF THE SYSTEM

As might be expected, the user's overall view of ISTAR is dominated by the contractual structure.

When a user first logs in to the system, the log-in display presents basic information on all contracts in which that user has some involvement. Specifically, the display lists the established contracts for which the user has some responsibility, highlights for each such contract any significant events that are awaiting acknowledgment, and also indicates any new contract assignments to this user. Recall that a user can have some responsibility on a given contract either because that contract was initially assigned to that user, or because that user was subsequently given a task to be performed within the contract. A significant event for a contract is the arrival of an amendment, a deliverable from a sub-contract, any kind of report, an incoming configuration item from another database, or a cancellation order.

As an example, the large window in the log-in display shown in Fig.7 indicates that the user is currently responsible for three contracts, called "ddtest", "dd_ug", and "feas_rpt". This latter contract has been cancelled by its client, and this user has not yet acknowledged the cancellation.

Typically, having examined the log-in display the user will select a contract on which to work. Selection of "ddtest" from Fig.7 leads to the display of Fig.8, where the window dedicated to "ddtest" indicates that this contract has been opened.

Because ISTAR offers a large number of workbenches they have been grouped into five categories. Selection of the "function" option within the "ddtest" window pops up a menu listing these categories. Selection of a category, such as "technical development", then pops up a menu listing the workbenches in this category. An individual workbench can then be selected from this menu to operate on a work area within contract "ddtest". A workbench would typically employ the whole screen for its interactions, with similar usage of windows and pop-up menus, and on exit from the workbench the display would revert to that shown in Fig.8.

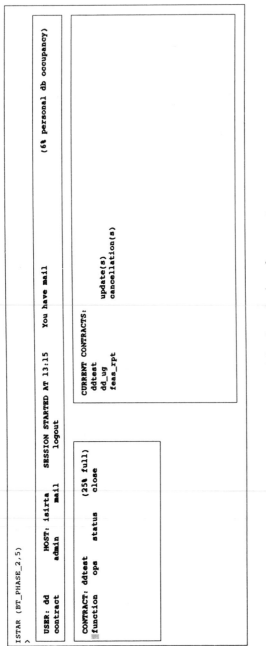

Fig. 8. Display following selection of a contract

10. AVAILABLE WORKBENCHES

An ISTAR workbench typically operates within a single work area and interacts with the remainder of the system by importing and exporting transfer items. Workbenches normally employ a number of discrete tools, but the boundaries between the individual tools are often obscured from the user. The objective of a workbench is not to present a set of disjoint tools, but rather to provide a coordinated range of facilities for performing work of a given kind. Thus a complete workbench, including its component tools, is designed and presented to users as a single coherent whole.

As mentioned in the previous section, ISTAR workbenches are grouped into five categories: general, project management, technical development, configuration management, and tool development. These categories are discussed individually below.

10.1 General

The "general" category includes three workbenches: text, documentation, and timesheet completion. (A personal mail facility is also provided by ISTAR, but this facility is generally available throughout the system, rather than provided by a specific workbench.)

The text workbench offers simple word processing facilities, and is used for preparing transfer items of type "text". This is a common transfer item type, since most specifications and deliverables feature a text item that summarises their more formal content.

The documentation workbench offers similar word processing facilities, but recognises the concept of a document that has chapters and sections. These partial documents can be held in several versions, and a complete document can be assembled from selected versions. A spelling checker is also provided.

Inclusion of text processing and mail facilities reflects the philosophy that all personnel on a project should regard ISTAR as their normal working environment. Much of the work on any project is concerned with preparation of documents, and personal mail is now in common use. ISTAR therefore provides facilities in these areas so that users can remain within the environment, with no need to invoke some other system or tool.

The timesheet completion workbench supports the filling and submission of weekly timesheets. This workbench is closely related to the resource management system, which is discussed below.

10.2 Project Management

The project management category includes two workbenches: contract management and resource management.

The contract management workbench directly supports the management of an individual contract and its sub-contracts. Specifically the workbench includes tools for work breakdown structuring, estimation, scheduling, detailed task definition,

and progress monitoring. These tools are used in combination
to support the activities of coordination, planning and
monitoring.
   The work breakdown tools supports the decomposition of a
given task into its component sub-tasks and the identification
of dependencies between those sub-tasks. The estimation tool
provides estimates of the effort profile for a task, using the
COCOMO model. The scheduling tool produces plans for
completion of a task, based upon its work breakdown structure
and a knowledge of available resources. The task definition
tool allows a task within a work breakdown structure to be
specified in detail, covering task specification, verification
criteria and management constraints (section 3.2). And the
monitoring tool produces performance reports for a task based
upon reported progress and actual resource usage of its
component sub-tasks.
   The workbench can produce both textual and graphical
reports, with the latter being used, for example, for the
presentation of PERT networks.
   The contract management workbench is in many ways
comparable to a "conventional" management toolkit, albeit a
particularly good one. It would therefore have been possible
to build this workbench from some existing set of tools,
exploiting ISTAR's ability to run such tools without
modification. However, it was decided to build new tools
specifically for ISTAR, because we wanted the management
workbench to be very closely coordinated with the overall
contractual structure. Thus, for example, the scheduling tool
interacts closely with resource management centres (see
below), new sub-contracts can be let directly from the task
definition tool, the monitoring tool monitors progress on
sub-contracts as well as on local tasks within this contract,
and so on.
   The resource management workbench is used to control the
deployment of people and other resources across contracts,
where these contracts may be in different project hierarchies.
Any individual resource that is to be managed within ISTAR is
affiliated with a specific resource management centre. These
centres are created in the normal way, by letting contracts,
and a given ISTAR system can have as many centres as required.
Thus, for example, when a given organisation is sub-divided
into groups - a communications group, a user interface group,
and so on - there could be one centre corresponding to each
group.
   Each centre maintains records of the types and current
allocations of the resources under its control. When a
contract requires a resource of a particular type it obtains
this resource from an appropriate centre, which then records
the new allocation.
   The resource management workbench interacts closely with
the project management workbench and the timesheet completion
workbench (section 10.1). The scheduling tool requests
information on resource availability from resource management
centres, and subsequently forwards bookings for resources
whose use has been scheduled. The task definition tool
notifies appropriate resource management centres when each

task is activated, and of any subsequent change to the status of the task (e.g. when it is completed). The timesheet collection tool forwards completed timesheets to the appropriate resource management centre for validation against active tasks, and the centre then forwards validated entries to the monitoring function of the appropriate contracts. And if a contract shows signs of falling behind schedule the monitoring tool may request data on resource allocations in order to perform a forward projection.

10.3 Technical Development

The technical development category includes workbenches for CORE, SDL, VDM, Pascal and Unix/C(*).

CORE is a method of requirements analysis that places considerable emphasis on a "whole world" view (rather than modelling just a system's interfaces or internal operation) and on extensive analysis of the emerging "world model". It is a genuine method with a well-defined procedure to be followed. The ISTAR workbench supports all steps of the method and provides a very extensive range of analyses, going beyond those that are conventionally associated with manual use of the method to incorporate some powerful checks that are only feasible with an automated tool operating on a model residing in a database.

SDL (System Description Language) is the CCITT-recommended specification notation for concurrent systems. A system is modelled as a set of "blocks" that communicate with each other and with their environment by exchanging "signals" over "channels". Blocks can recursively be decomposed into sub-blocks. At the lowest level the blocks contain processes that receive and send the signals of the block. An SDL process has a discrete set of "waiting states" where it is awaiting an incoming signal. When such a signal arrives the process performs a transition to a new waiting state; during this transition the process would normally perform some computation and perhaps send some signals. The ISTAR workbench supports progressive decomposition with consistency checking, definition of processes at the lowest level, and code generation directly from the process definitions. The latter two facilities are actually provided by the SX1 tool, developed by British Telecommunications, which has been integrated into the ISTAR workbench.

VDM (Vienna Development Method) is a formal development method for sequential programs, with strong emphasis on abstract data types. The method supports both initial specification and sequential refinement from this initial specification, if required with formal verification at every step. The ISTAR workbench currently provides only limited support for the method; specifically it supports syntax-directed editing of the method's specification language (META-IV) and simple type and signature checking of this language.

As discussed in section 7, the design of ISTAR allows existing tools to be incorporated into workbenches without modification. This was exploited in the case of the SDL

workbench, where SX1 was incorporated, and is also exploited
in the case of workbenches that support implementation
languages. Thus, both the Pascal and Unix/C workbenches are
based upon pre-existing compilers and other tools. The Pascal
workbench supports syntax-directed editing and compilation.
The Unix/C workbench is simply one that provides direct access
to the facilities of Unix; because of the close association in
this case between language and operating system there is no
separate "C workbench". An Ada workbench is currently under
development.

The technical development workbenches that are currently
available reflect the initial interest in one particular
application area, namely that of real-time systems. However,
the overall design of ISTAR is in no way specific to that
application area, and other areas could be supported by
providing appropriate workbenches in the technical development
category. For example, consideration is being given to a
workbench for SSADM, a method that is typically employed for
the design of DP systems.

10.4 Configuration Management

There are two workbenches in the configuration management
category, namely component management and build.

It should be emphasised that the basic configuration
management facilities of ISTAR - version identification,
freezing of items, tracking of item usage and movement - are
not the responsibility of any individual workbench. Rather,
these facilities are "built in" to the underlying structure,
and are pervasive throughout the system.

Thus the configuration management workbench does not
implement the basic versioning and control mechanisms, but
rather is more concerned with administrative issues.
Specifically the workbench supports such operations as setting
and querying preferred versions, querying version histories,
establishing and querying relationships between items, and so
on. It should be noted that all such operations are available
to other workbenches, and indeed these operations would
normally be performed by tools as part of their normal
function rather than explicitly by the user. However, the
configuration management workbench provides a direct user
interface to these operations, should this in some
circumstances be required.

The configuration management workbench also provides
support for component libraries, as discussed at the end of
section 6, and for the submission and control of problem
reports. The facilities in these areas are heavily dependent
upon the more general configuration management facilities, and
these functions are therefore included in this workbench for
reasons of user convenience.

The build workbench supports the construction of new
transfer items by applying tools to existing transfer items.
An obvious special case is the production of some required
"system" by integration of its component sub-systems.
However, the workbench is not limited to this special case.
In ISTAR it is common for a contract deliverable to be formed

by combining deliverables from sub-contracts, and this applies
whether the required deliverable is a program, a
specification, a document, or whatever. In all these cases
the build workbench would be used to construct the
deliverable.

Basically, the workbench is given a "construction plan"
for the required construction process and a "bill of parts"
identifying the specific transfer items to be input to that
process. The workbench then constructs the required transfer
item(s) and also generates a precise record of the build.
This record serves both to show the dependencies between
transfer items and also as a possible input to subsequent
builds. For example, suppose that a new version of one of the
input transfer items is produced and it is required to re-run
the build using this new version as an input but with all
other inputs remaining unchanged. This can be done simply and
reliably by using the record from the previous build.

10.5 Tool Development

The tool development category includes three workbenches:
APCR, interface definition, and ARLO. As the name suggests,
the workbenches in this category support the development of
new ISTAR tools and workbenches. These workbenches are
therefore of interest to those who wish to extend the system
to support a particular method or address a particular need.

The APCR (analyser/prompter/checker/reporter) workbench
is used to develop new workbenches to support specific
"structured" methods. There are a large number of such
methods - SADT, SA/SD, and so on - each with their own
particular features but all with a great deal in common.
Essentially, any structured method involves construction of a
model of the desired system using a small number of entity
types and relationship types. Typically such models are
presented graphically, with entities of different types being
represented by boxes of different shapes and relationships
being represented by lines between boxes. A particular method
defines the entity and relationship types to be employed and a
sequence of stages for constructing the model, typically with
specific checks to be performed at each stage.

In ISTAR, all structured methods are supported in the
same way. The model is held explicitly in a database, with
entities and relationships in the database corresponding to
those in the model. Checks on the model are implemented by
running analysis programs on the database, and reports are
generated from the database.

The APCR workbench generates other workbenches to support
particular structured methods. The user of the APCR workbench
is prompted for a definition of the method to be supported, in
terms of its entity and relationship types, the stages of the
method, and the prompts and checks associated with each stage.
The APCR workbench then generates a new workbench that
supports the various stages of the defined method.

An example of the use of the APCR workbench is provided
by the CORE workbench, which was generated in this manner.
Further, the method used for defining structured methods is

itself a structured method, and the facilities of the APCR
workbench were therefore used to generate the workbench - in
much the same way that compilers are bootstrapped and
eventually used to compile themselves.

With most structured methods it is desirable to present
various "views" of the model in graphical form. This can be
done by using the graphics facilities of the extended user
interface system. However, this requires the production of a
"filter" that extracts the appropriate information from the
database and presents it to the user interface system in a
generic form. At present such filters are implemented by
writing a program, making extensive use of a database query
language, or by using ISTAR's report generator. Typically,
new filters are produced by modifying some existing filter,
rather than by starting "from scratch". It would be possible
to largely automate filter production, and a workbench to do
so may be produced in the near future.

The graphics presentation facilities are not restricted
to use in conjunction with the APCR kit, but are generally
available. For example, the contract management workbench
uses the graphics interface for presenting PERT networks, and
the SDL workbench uses the interface for presenting block
hierarchies.

The interface definition workbench relates to the forms
and syntax-directed editing capabilities of the user interface
system. For each kind of form to be edited the user interface
system requires a table defining the form. Similarly,
syntax-directed editing requires tables defining the syntax of
the language and required layout. When introducing a new form
or language the interface definition workbench is used to
generate the required tables from, respectively, a forms
definition notation or an augmented BNF notation.

The ARLO workbench can be used to rapidly develop new
workbenches and individual tools. ARLO is an interpretive
language specifically designed for easy development of
interactive tools. Using the language it is possible to
quickly produce a working prototype or production tool and
then incrementally improve and extend the tool as desired.
ARLO is also useful for incorporating existing tools into an
ISTAR workbench. A major problem with such tools is that they
do not operate on ISTAR databases, but rather on files. This
problem, and the problem of user interface consistency, can be
addressed by wrapping the existing tool in an "envelope".
This envelope initially interacts with the user and the
appropriate ISTAR database, sets up access to the required
files, and then invokes the existing tool. Upon return the
envelope updates the ISTAR database as appropriate, dependent
upon the completion status of the tool. ARLO is a convenient
language in which to implement such envelopes.

The workbenches in the tool development category are
delivered to users as an integral part of the system. This is
in keeping with the overall objective that user organisations
should themselves be able to extend the system to meet their
own particular needs.

11. STATUS

The ISTAR system, including the workbenches discussed in section 10, is available from Imperial Software Technology as a commercial product.

The system is currently implemented under Unix. It will run under any "real" Unix (as opposed to "Unix-like"), including System V and BSD 4.2. It has been ported to several machines, including VAX, Pyramid, AT&T 3B2, and 68000-based workstations. Ports to other machines with a real Unix are straightforward. A port to VAX/VMS(**) is scheduled during 1986.

Communications facilities are not implemented as part of ISTAR itself. Rather, the system is interfaced to whatever communications facilities are available. The only requirement is that the communication medium should be able to transfer a file (i.e. a large block of data) from one machine to another with a reasonable level of reliability. The current implementation communicates using any combination of Ethernet TCP/IP, RS232 using UUCP, and physical transfer of magnetic media. ISO protocols will be supported as soon as a suitable Unix implementation becomes available.

For its graphics, ISTAR uses GKS.

12. FINAL REMARKS

ISTAR is a rich environment, and inevitably the latter parts of this introduction have concentrated on the available workbenches and tools. However, the path to success with ISTAR does not lie with making optimum use of some individual facility. Rather, it is important to make effective use of the system as a whole, and particularly to exploit the overall contractual structure.

Thus any consideration of ISTAR should not begin at the level of individual tools or facilities, or with details of the database system or the user interface. It should instead begin with consideration of the contractual structure and the way in which this can be deployed to achieve overall project control and visibility and to ensure a basic level of hygiene. This in itself can make a major contribution in the areas of quality and productivity, and is also an essential prerequisite to the introduction of better methods and tools that can offer further improvements.

ISTAR addresses the concerns at both levels - overall structure and hygiene, and individual methods and tools - but it is important that these concerns are taken in the right order: first overall structure, then methods, then tools. This was the order in which ISTAR was designed, and it is the order that should be followed in any consideration or use of the system.

13.   TRADEMARKS

   (*)   Unix is a trademark of AT&T Bell Laboratories
   (**) VAX and VMS are trademarks of Digital Equipment
         Corporation

14.   ACKNOWLEDGMENTS

   ISTAR is a collaborative development by Imperial Software
Technology and British Telecommunications PLC, and many people at
both organisations have contributed to its design and
implementation.

Chapter 2
Development and project management support with the integrated software engineering environment, EPOS

P. Lempp

ABSTRACT

In recent years several programs have been established and projects started to achieve integrated project support environments (IPSEs) in order to overcome the notorious deficiencies of non-integrated tool boxes and tool systems. This paper gives an overview of the Engineering and Project-management Oriented Support System EPOS, a full "second-generation" IPSE based on a consistent project data base. The paper touches most fundamentals but the main emphasis is placed on aspects especially important for the production of medium to large-scale systems: integrated project management, product assurance support and assistance in decentralized development within a workstation concept. Experiences from industrial applications are summarized and some topics of future R&D work, the enhancement towards a third generation IPSE, are discussed.

2.1 INTRODUCTION

The complexity of today's software/hardware systems requires computer support during development, not only for the technical aspects but for project management and product assurance as well. In the last decade tools have been created to support work-intensive activities, to manage the enormous amount of information in a project and to reduce manual error sources.

However, the assistance of these tools varies to a large extent: independent tools from different suppliers provide support only for parts of the development process, whereas tool boxes contain tools in at least some sort of order. A major step forward has been the tool systems with their adapted tools, a database and a consistent user interface. But efficient project control cannot be achieved by using different tool systems for project control and technical development. Hence, software engineering environments today have to be integrated project support environments (IPSEs). Several European and world-wide activities which have been started in recent years emphasize the necessity to design (and use) these advanced environments.

2.2   SHORT SYNOPSIS OF EPOS

2.2.1 Objectives

EPOS is an integrated project support environment for technical or commercial software/hardware projects. It has been developed with the understanding in mind that
- contradictory to the emphasis of support of pure programming support environments, programming and test are not the most important phases in the project. It is rather in the early phases of the life cycle that the support has to be improved. Therefore EPOS provides <u>computer support for all phases</u> of the project life cycle, from initial requirements capture to long-term maintenance (see e.g. Biewald et al (2))
- the success of projects is not only dependent on the achievement of the technical staff. On the contrary, for medium to large-scale projects in particular, it is important to have a good project management and an efficient product assurance support. The <u>integrated computer support</u> of EPOS for managerial issues in a project will be elaborated later on in this paper
- in embedded systems, computer systems for process control and the like, it is not decided at the time the requirements are established whether a function is to be implemented in software or in hardware. With hardware becoming more flexible and available in a large variety, the choice of when to use hardware and which parts should be implemented in software is made during the design phase only. EPOS allows the specification of <u>software and hardware components</u> as well as the interrelations between them (see e.g. Dais et al (4))
- different projects demand different approaches and different target languages. Since there is not one single design method, an appropriate method must be chosen according to the nature of the application. Issues which influence this choice are restrictions or dominant viewpoints of either functions, the data flow, data structures, events in automation systems or hardware devices. The programming language to which the design has to be transformed also depends on a variety of factors, not all technically based. EPOS solves these conflicts by providing <u>support for different methods</u> as well as by being <u>target language independent</u> (see Göhner (5), Lempp and Zeh (8)).

2.2.2 Fundamentals

A (slightly simplified) project model is illustrated in fig. 2.1. It shows the four major work areas
- technical development
- project management
- product assurance and
- maintenance,

which are interrelated to a high degree. The computer support for these work areas in a project is accomplished first by the provision of three description languages ("specification languages", namely EPOS-R, EPOS-S and EPOS-P). These differ in formality according to the purpose for which they are. used (requirement capture, system design, project management and product assurance, respectively).

Using these object oriented languages with predefined "specification object types" and relations (Chen (3)) the relevant data of all work areas is modelled in a common data base.

Evaluation and analysis program packages evaluate the contents of this data base, textual and especially graphical documentation is provided as well as (semi-automatic) transformations from one representation into another (e.g. code generation).

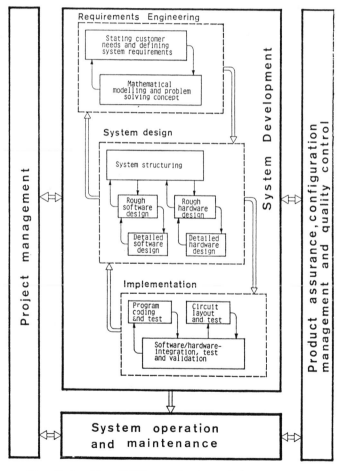

Fig.2.1   The EPOS project model

2.3   PROJECT MANAGEMENT FRAMEWORK

2.3.1 Project Planning Support   -   with Close Links to Requirements Engineering Tasks

Even during the preparation of the system requirements document not only the technical requirements but also the management framework for the project is outlined - e.g. total cost, final deadline, standards to be observed, configuration management guidelines etc.

Fig. 2.2 shows in a simplified way the tasks to be accomplished in project planning after this system requirements document has been agreed upon:
- the definition of subprojects and work-packages as the basis for a work breakdown structure of the project as well as for cost estimation and resource planning
- the planning of the project organization, i.e. the companies, departments, team members etc. involved in the project

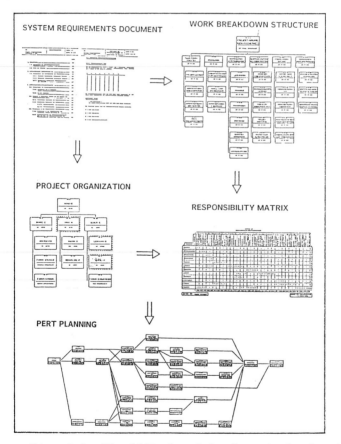

Fig. 2.2   Simplified model of project planning

- the assignment of work-packages to the project team members on one side and the planning of competences of the team members on the other
- the schedule estimation and the estimation of money to be spent per time span (cash flow) with milestones and/or PERT charts.

For the description of this project planning data the formal specification language EPOS-P provides different types of so-called management objects. The instances of these objects contain informal text descriptions but especially the structure information and formal attributes like quantifying data - e.g. costs, time spans etc. The final result of this planning is a model of all relevant structures and relations of the project in the EPOS database: technical requirements closely linked to management structures like the work breakdown structure, the project organization structure, the schedule and financial planning, account departments, etc. Fig. 2.3 gives an overview of the most important relations between system requirements, project organization and the work breakdown structure/PERT planning.

Two main categories of relations - each consisting of a whole set of single relations - can be distinguished:

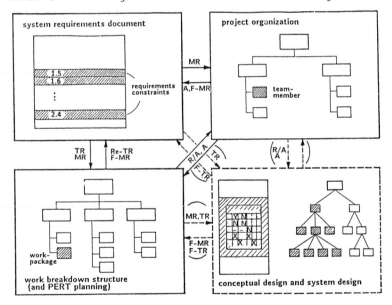

LEGEND: R/A Responsibility/Assignment   F-TR Fulfilment of Technical Requirements
          A   Data Access Rights   Re-TR Reference to Technical Requirements
          TR   Technical Requirements   F-MR Fulfilment of Management Requirements
          MR   Management Requirements

Fig.2.3   Major relations between system requirements, work breakdown structure, project organization and (later on) the design

1) requirements of either technical or managerial nature
   (e. g. the selection of the design method and the estimation of costs, respectively) as well as work-package
   references to these requirements or fulfilment of requirements
2) responsibility of project team members for subprojects,
   work packages, etc. and special data access rights of
   team members to parts of the EPOS data base.

One of the advantages of this modelling with EPOS can
be seen in the completeness, consistency and plausibility
analysis possible early in the life cycle. E.g. it can
easily be checked whether all system requirements are at
least considered in one work-package; another check is
whether there are any inconsistencies between attributes on
one side and section and requirements consideration on the
other.
        Other computer-support during project planning in-
cludes a variety of documentations (some of them have been
shown in fig.2.2 already), calculations and information
reduction.

2.3.2 Project Monitoring Support - based on Objective Data

The conceptual design, the system design, the coding
etc. can be monitored in an efficient way. In fig. 2.3 some
of the important relations used for monitoring have been
included in parentheses and with dotted lines, respectively. Again one relation shown stands for a set of single
relations.
        These relations are used to monitor the project and to
ensure a consistent order. The work authorization according
to the PERT plan and the acceptance of completion of a
work-package only when all associated requirements are
fulfilled and - in case of a software component - code
parts or an automatically generated program exist are just
two examples of advantages offered by this integrated
support.
        For the assessment of the project status there are two
different approaches possible that supplement each other.
On one hand (conventional but computer supported) progress
reports from team members, on the other hand the computer-
assisted evaluation of the (objective) technical development data in the data base.
        The first kind of computer support for project monito-
ring in EPOS based on (subjective) reports will be sketched
in an example only. The management support system EPOS-M
generates planning/factural comparisons using the progress
information, status reports, data about expenses and
updated estimates provided by the responsible staff. Here
computer support is mainly documentation, calculation and
consolidation of data for the different management levels.
An example of such a document, a bar chart (Gantt chart),
showing project progress and plan deviations is given in
fig. 2.4.

BAR CHART

NO	ACTIVITY	SHORT-NAME AV	DURATION (DAYS)	TOTAL FLOAT												NO
					AUG	SEP	OCT	NOV	DEC	JAN	FEB	MAR	APR	MAY	JUN	
1	PRECISE-TASK-DESCRIPTION	3.9	21	0												1
2	CONCEPT-DEFINITION	3.4	42	0												2
3	EVALUATION-CONCEPT	4.2	14	84												3
4	CORE-AND-DDL-DEFINITION	4.4	56	0												4
5	EVALUATION-DB-CORE	4.3	7	0												5
6	CORE-IMPLEMENTATION	4.5	28	36												6
7	ACCESS-LAYER-1	3.6	43	14												7
8	ACCESS-LAYER-2	3.7	57	0												8
9	ADMINISTRATION-ROUTINES	3.8	42	0												9
10	COMPLETE-TEST	3.9	28	0												10
11	COMPILATION-FINAL-REPORT	4.1	14	42												11
12	PILOT-APPLICATION	3.10	56	0												12

EPOS84 PROJECT MANAGEMENT

TOP-ACTIVITY; COMMERCIAL-DATABASE-SYSTEM
PROJECT STATUS OF 02.09.85

LEGEND: PLANNED/WORK-AUTH. / DELAYED / IN-DEVELOPM. /-EVAL. / EARLY/LATE START/FIN. / APPROVED / CRITICAL PATH
WITH CALENDER/HOLIDAYS OF 01.08.85 - 0 ADDITIONAL HOLIDAYS - 5 WORKING DAYS PER WEEK

Fig.2.4 Example of an actual/nominal comparison of schedules at a special point in time in form of a bar chart (Gantt Chart)

With this (conventional) support the project-management is able to keep track of
- finished project phases
- reached milestones
- approved activities
- changes in the status of an activity (e.g. from planned to work-authorized).

For the progress assessment between these fixed status changes the computer-assisted evaluation of the corresponding technical development data in the common data base provides reliable (objective) statements. One example of a graphical preparation of this data is shown in fig. 2.5 in a (hierarchy) "progress chart".

A part of a design has been plotted which corresponds to a workpackage in the work breakdown structure or an activity in the Gantt chart. The project leader can determine the progress made since a given reference date - e.g. since the last time he invoked this program. In addition, the hierarchy diagram indicates where work at the design is completed and which parts of the design need more effort to be put in.

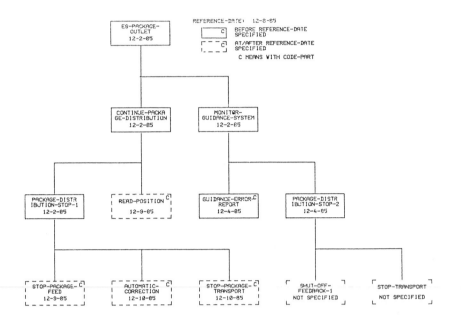

Fig.2.5 Progress   chart   showing   advances   since   a
reference date

In the diagram design objects which have been already
specified before the reference date are enclosed by solid
lines, objects entered in the data base during the reference time span are drawn with dotted lines - highlighting
the new results. Objects boxed only at the corners have
been introduced with a name but have not been specified
yet. This indicates further work is to be carried out at
this part of the design. A 'C' in the upper right corner of
an object stands for the code section the object is associated with - an indication of completion of the work at this
leaf of the object tree.

A special placing algorithm draws the objects at the
same location every time the diagram is requested, independently of the changed number of objects. Diagrams drawn at
different points in time can thus be compared easily and
trends become visible (Lempp (7)).

2.4   PRODUCT ASSURANCE FRAMEWORK

2.4.1 Version/Variant Control

In EPOS a development project is seen as a process in which a software/hardware system exists in a sequence of representations resulting from each other by transformations. These transformations can be either manual (as e.g. from the system requirements to the conceptual design) or automatic (e.g. from the design to program code). Within one representation a structure of objects is modelled, which can exist in different versions - as different changes in time - and/or variants - as different forms at the same time. All objects are assigned a version identification part and a variant identification part. The version identification part includes a multiple-digit version number in addition to creation attributes of the change/new entry like date and author, previous version(s), etc. The variant identification consists of one or more variant identifiers and corresponding attributes.

Variants of a part of a representation can be interpreted as different viewpoints of this part. Fig. 2.6 shows how the variant attributes are used in the common data base to switch from one possible variant (e.g. VARIANT-A) to another.

The granularity of the version/variant control ranges from single unstructured information objects as the smallest items ('atoms') to parts of a representation or representations themselves consisting of a structure of specification objects (e.g. a module). On the one extreme the developer gets assistance in keeping track of his (atomic) changes, whereas on the other extreme the configuration management will trace versions/variants of configuration items which are normally structured objects.

2.4.2 Configuration Management

The configuration management support does not only include administration of versions/variants of configuration items, but also procedural aspects of identifying baselines and formal control of changes of these baselines.

A baseline is an (intermediate) project result, "frozen" at some point in time to form a fixed reference configuration. Before fixing a baseline, extensive consistency and completeness analysis can therefore be performed with administrative checks, e.g. to verify that all activities and change proposals leading to this new baseline are completed. The data access rights to the baseline items are switched to read-only.

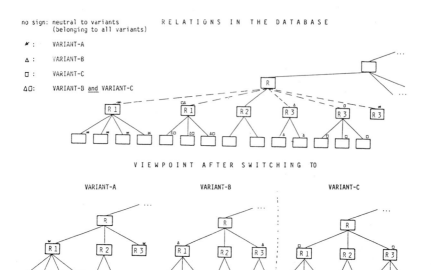

Fig. 2.6   Variants as different viewpoints within the
data base

If new requirements or errors in the baseline necessi-
tate changes of a baseline, the system enforces a configuration management procedure which mainly consists of first
specifying a formal request (change proposal). This can be
at least partly evaluated with computer assistance, identifying related objects to the proposed change. The decision
of the management (e.g. of a configuration control board)
will be entered in the data base together with - if accepted - a technical and managerial framework for incorporating the change(s). With this framework set up the baseline
can be modified again, a history of all changes being kept.
     The baseline status accounting includes the documen-
tation of all baselines, all change proposals and their
current status as well as details on the responsible
project team member(s). After completion of the change
activity a new baseline can be fixed.

2.4.3 Quality Assurance

EPOS comprises both aspects of quality assurance: the
constructive and the analytical one. Constructive quality
planning includes a technical development planning which
minimizes the chance of omissions and errors. EPOS enforces
structured development and, through the methodological
restriction to use only proven constructs out of the nearly

infinite possibilities, the chances of errors are reduced and the development becomes comprehensible. Two examples illustrate this:
- for synchronization between tasks in real time systems there are only a limited number of syntactic constructs. These nevertheless provide all the necessary properties.
- the design specification language EPOS-S allows only control flow specification according to the rules of structured programming. Hard-to-comprehend jumps are avoided from the beginning.

The semi-automatic or totally automatic transformations from one representation - e.g. formal specification - to the next representation - e.g. source code in a programming language - has advantages against manual errorprone ones too. The supervising schema for change control to baselines has been mentioned. Here the strict (formal) control limits unforeseen implications of a change.

For the analytical part of quality assurance and quality control, EPOS attempts not to emphasize testing after the entire development is accomplished, but rather to provide analysis and verification support throughout the whole life cycle starting in early phases. There are not only consistency and completeness checks and simulation possibilities within each representation but also formalized checks between different ones. E.g. it is possible to trace all requirements from the system requirements document to their fulfilment in later representations always keeping references to the appropriate work-package and the project team member(s) responsible for the work. Fig. 2.7 shows an analysis indicating incomplete and omitted fulfilment of requirements. Latest developments include verification possibilities based on assertions in the design (Baur and Lauber (1)).

2.5 SPECIAL ISSUES IN MEDIUM TO LARGE-SCALE PROJECTS

2.5.1 Problems

All issues discussed so far are relevant to projects of all sizes. Additional problems arise especially in medium or large-scale projects. First, with several project teams in different departments and/or companies, it is not sufficient to provide one single (central) computer with a project data base. The computer support has to be available on workstations at the team members' desks. Second, because the system to be developed is large and complex and it is designed by only loosely interrelated project teams, additional support is necessary for modular development with closely controlled interfaces.

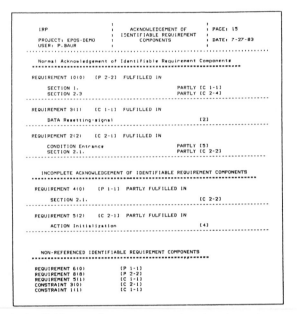

Fig. 2.7 EPOS analysis report showing incomplete and missing fulfilment of requirements.

2.5.2 Decentralized Development with EPOS Workstations

EPOS runs not only on minicomputers and mainframes (VAX 11/7xx, SIEMENS 7xxx, IBM 370) but also on workstations (INTEL 286/310 or IBM AT). These workstations will be connected by some communication media (e.g. a wide area network area / local area network). The computer support depends on the facilities of the workstation communication. In the simplest case there is only file transfer between the workstations. The most basic mechanism would even work with magnetic tapes sent by mail between the companies involved.

Besides the physical structure of decentralized hard-ware the logical view of the (local) data bases is still a hierarchical one. Fig. 2.8 illustrates the usual inter-dependencies between work breakdown structure, project organization and physical workstations with a small example.

The problem of appropriate partitioning and good defi-nition of independent work packages is not solved by any workstation concept on distributed data bases. Here the basic idea is that all relevant project data is stored in a (central) project data base which serves also as the refe-rence for project progress assessment and configuration control. Information can be "distributed" to the next level in the hierarchy of workstations and "integrated" from the local data bases in the workstations to the central project data base. Distribution and integration are controlled by the system.

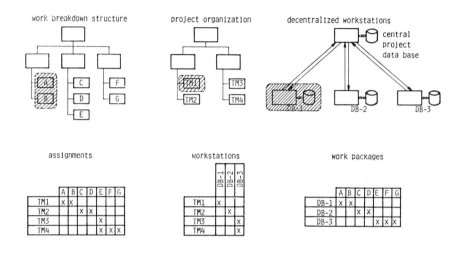

Fig. 2.8 Relations between work breakdown structure, project organization and decentralized workstations

In the databases, it can be seen which parts and versions have been integrated already. Hence, whenever a synchronization of the data bases is requested, only minimal data has to be transfered. It has to be noted that the cycle of integration of the latest development data is a management decision and depends on the project. Weekly or bi-weekly updates have often proved to be sufficient.

If the workstations are transparently connected by a network, consistency checks which require reading the project data base can be performed. Otherwise additional analysis for consistency is provided during the integration, especially the enforcement of the modular design planned in the work breakdown and product structure.

2.5.3 Modular Development and Interface Management

Development with different project teams demands a clear definition of work-packages and an appropriate modular approach. The definition of modules together with their interfaces consisting of exported and imported functions and/or data is part of the support EPOS provides to cope with this problem. Clearly arranged documentation of the interface in both graphical and tabular form assists in the comprehension of module interconnections. Fig. 2.9 shows an example of a module exporting functions to other modules.

Different analysis tools - which will be extended in the future - uncover violations against the principle of information hiding and check consistency of interfaces. When changes of an interface are necessary the implications on other modules are listed by the system.

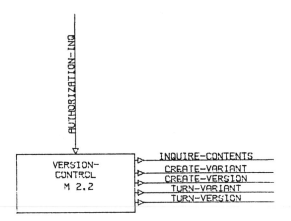

Fig.2.9 Exported objects of a module forming the interface to other modules

2.6 EXPERIENCES GAINED IN INDUSTRIAL PROJECTS

The EPOS system has been in development at the University of Stuttgart (IRP), Germany, since the mid-seventies. After internal use it was made available to industrial users in 1980 and after pilot projects has been used in several hundreds of industrial and military applications since 1981. A German software house and its partner companies in other countries are responsible for installation and maintenance. Currently about 150 installations have been delivered worldwide.

Every year, during the extensive discussions between the users and the R&D group of the University at the annual user group meetings, one is surprised to learn about the wide range of projects EPOS has been used in: from small assembler programs for products with a large number of items to large systems, which are designed by different companies with different development computers in different programming languages. The application areas range from complex, safety-critical real-time systems to the development of commercial software. The automation systems have been mostly integrated software/hardware systems, the commercial applications have usually been pure software systems.

EPOS has been used in the development of new systems, in the extension of existing systems - which were originally developed without the aid of EPOS - and even in the follow-up documentation of unstructured program systems (Göhner (5)).

Evaluating the experience reported from these projects one can see clearly that the application of EPOS has been successful. The systematic and structured guidance through the whole life cycle for one - and the extensive computer support in automatic checkings, documentations, calculations etc. for another - support all project team members and lead to overall cost savings due to increased productivity. Even if it is hard to exactly measure the advantages quantitatively the investments and training show to pay off. This is particularly true if one includes the maintenance phase in the product life cycle.

For the management task it has been especially stated that the computer support throughout the project makes the development visible as well as comprehensible. The integrated support has also initiated the tendency that customers not only will ask for informal progress reports but will demand EPOS specifications on a regular time basis to check the achievements.

2.7 FUTURE WORK

Although being applied successful in a large variety of applications, some bottlenecks and limitations in EPOS become obvious. The important aspects for the future are being examined by the R&D team at the university. One issue is the interactive design with (mostly) graphical means, whereas today EPOS provides extensive graphical outputs but allows only textual input. Another issue is the examination of whether additional formalized method support for the requirements engineering phases can be provided. A central issue for all phases and representations is the extension of measurement capabilities to support standard and specific metrics, a R&D subproject which will be extensified in the future.

The main stroke of R&D will attempt to lead to a third generation IPSE (Talbot (10), Snowdon et al (9)) with not only passive support but also active guidance throughout the project using IKBS techniques to provide experiences and even concepts from other projects.

2.8 REFERENCES

1.   Baur, P. and Lauber, R., 1985, 'Design Verification for (Safety-Related) Software Systems', Preprints, SAFECOMP 1985, Como, Italy.

2. Biewald, J., Göhner, P., Lauber, R., and Schelling, H., 1979, 'EPOS - a Specification and Design Technique for Computer Controlled Real-Time Automation Systems',
    Proc. 4th ICSE, Munich, IEEE Comp. Soc., Los Alamitos, CA, 245-250.

3. Chen, P., 1976, 'The Entity-Relationship Model, Toward a Unified View of Data',
    ACM Trans. on Database Systems, 1, 9 - 36.

4. Dais, S., Kiencke, U. and Schelling, H., 1984, 'EPOS for Microcomputer Programs', (in German),
    Bosch-Zünder, 5, 5.

5. Göhner, P., 1985, 'Integrated Computer Support for the Development and Project Managment of Software/Hardware Systems',
    3rd IFAC Symp. on Computer-Aided Design in Control and Engineering Systems, Kopenhagen.

6. Lauber, R., and Lempp, P., 1983, 'Integrated development and project managament support system',
    Proc. 7th COMPSAC 1983. IEEE Comp. Soc. Press., Los Angeles, CA.

7. Lempp, P., 1986, 'A Possibility to make Project Progress Visible - The Progress Diagram within the EPOS-System', (to be published in) ACM SEN, Spring 1986.

8. Lempp, P, and Zeh, A., 1985, 'Report on the ASSET Feasibility Study - Highlighting Automatic Transformation from EPOS to Ada',
    Commission of the European Communities, Preprints of the ESPRIT Technical Week 1985, Brussels.

9. Snowdon, R.A., Munro, N.C., Davis, N.W., and Jackson, M.I., 1985, 'Advanced support environments; an industrial viewpoint',
    Peter Peregrinus Ltd, 'Integrated Project Support Environments', London, 189 - 202.

10. Talbot, D.E., 1983, 'Alvey Software Engineering - a strategy overview', DTI Publishers.

Chapter 3

Developing an environment manager for an IPSE

M. Higgs and P. Stevens

1. DEVELOPING AN IPSE

Whereas 'APSE','IPSE' and 'PSE' were once rather esoteric acronyms the publicity generated by Alvey and projects such as ESPRIT has now ensured that the term 'IPSE' has acquired a significant number of misconceptions. This is perhaps because most of the attention of IPSE developers is focused on the technical problems of IPSE development although it is obviously equally important to ensure that the user benefits of IPSE technology are widely known.

1.1 What Do Users Want From An IPSE?

One objective of the Alvey project was for commercially viable IPSE's to emerge before the end of this decade, if this is to be the case then these IPSE's must be widely accepted by industrial 'users' outside Alvey. These 'users' have a wide range of technical requirements - often not directly concerned with the technical advantages or strengths of the IPSE concept itself. The variety of the products developed by potential IPSE 'users' and the different organisational requirements introduce other non-technical requirements. An interesting point is that many users' perception of their needs are still defined by focusing on specific problems and tools required to address these problems - rather than considering environments or complete IPSE's. Some of these requirements are listed below:

- Evolution not Revolution.
- Specific functionality.
- Portability.
- Performance.
- Adaptability.
- Manageability.
- Integrability.
- Existing systems.
- Configurability.
- Security.
- Distribution.

IPSE developers face the crucial problem of convincing industrial 'users' that their product provides the solutions which they need and addresses the requirements above. This is important given the significant investment by industry likely to be required to obtain the full benefits of IPSE technology in terms of better, cheaper and more predictable software development projects.

1.2 What Constraints Does This Place On The IPSE Developer?

The IPSE developer must:

- Allow *flexibility*. So that different customers or different projects can have essentially different IPSE's to suit their own particular requirements.
- Develop an *open systems* environment, not in conflict with existing or de-facto standards.
- Provide a *framework* which will allow the use of existing tools in conjunction with IPSE tools - without complex redevelopment or intervention by the IPSE developer always being required.
- Enable IPSE's to address *specific problems* or areas of development and grow incrementally. This makes technology transfer to IPSE based technology easier by providing an incremental investment path over project lifetimes.
- Make at least basic IPSE technology available on *existing* systems, and define an evolutionary path towards future generations of IPSE's based on more advanced systems.

These constraints reflect the fact that the many of potential IPSE 'users' can be observed to be using development environments less sophisticated than a first generation IPSE [1]. These potential IPSE 'users' would benefit substantially from even limited access to 1st/2nd generation IPSE technology supported largely by *existing* systems and by limited investments in further hardware. This would begin the process of technology transfer which should eventually see these users investing in more advanced IPSE technology.

1.3 How Does The GEC Software IPSE Fulfill Those Requirements?

A clear conclusion from the requirements of section 1.2 is that a a real IPSE is in fact many different IPSE's, to reflect different user requirements for different organisations and projects. Thus rather than attempting to provide a *total IPSE "for all seasons"*. IPSE development should be directed at providing an *IPSE Framework*. Using this approach it is the *environment* created by the IPSE Framework within which tools are used which becomes special - rather than the tools themselves.

GEC Software has viewed the development of the IPSE framework as spanning three generations which reflect changing user requirements for "integration". These three generations broadly correspond to evolution between first and second generation IPSE's as conceived by the Alvey Project [1].

- User interface integration.
- Data interface integration.
- Tool interface integration.

The design of the GEC Software IPSE Framework utilises existing systems and technologies as far as possible, and emphasises evolution based on 1st generation IPSE facilities [1] rather than revolution. At the same time the functionality and facilities of the GEC Software IPSE Framework are designed to be reproduced compatibly using 2nd generation database IPSE technology [1] in the future

This approach allows the GEC Software ISPE Framework to be:

- *Flexible*: different project models can be supported.
- *Standard*: the ˙Framework uses utilises industry standard operating systems and distributed systems standards wherever possible.
- *Adaptable*: the Framework allows the use of existing tools through the standard interfaces.
- *Configurable:* to the requirements of different users and projects.
- *Evolutionary*: the IPSE Framework can be used on existing systems and hardware, and will evolve towards a second generation IPSE.

In this way the development of the GEC Software IPSE Framework will parallel the growth in maturity of potential IPSE customers.

2.   GEC SOFTWARE IPSE FRAMEWORK: FACILITIES AND FUNCTIONALITY

An IPSE based on the GEC Software IPSE Framework is composed of *datasets* (or *filesets*) and *toolsets*. The information in the *datasets* is transformed by the *toolsets* subject to *semantic constraints* regulated by the IPSE Framework. All user interaction with the IPSE is through the *Common User Interface (CUI)*, interaction with *datasets* is always via a *Common Data Interface (CDI)*, and interaction with *toolsets* is always via a *Common Tool Interface (CTI)*.

2.1   Common User Interface

A pre-requisite for an IPSE Framework for an evolutionary IPSE is that the Common User Interface employed must be compatible with existing widely used display technologies such as de-facto industry standard terminals. The *CUI* must also be compatible with existing and future bit-mapped display technologies such as those employed in high performance workstations. Finally the *CUI* must support a corresponding range of operational idioms so that the IPSE Framework can exploit the full capabilities of the relevant technology.

These objectives have been achieved at GEC Software by selecting a user interface product called TEN/PLUS*, developed by INTERACTIVE Systems [2], as the basis of the *CUI* for the IPSE Framework. All interaction between the user and IPSE tools is performed through the IPSE Framework via the *CUI*. Several *styles* of user interaction are supported:

- Menu-driven using a small subset of the function keys available, for new TEN/PLUS users or for unfamiliar applications. The

  minimal subset of function keys is considered by INTERACTIVE Systems to be ten - hence the name TEN/PLUS.

- A comprehensive and powerful set of function keys for different functions for the experienced TEN/PLUS user and frequently used applications.
- Access to the operating system command language; either via execution of short command sequences in pop-up boxes without leaving the visual interface or by escaping to an operating system "shell" to perform a sequence of operating system commands.

As with a number of other IPSE interfaces all user interaction with the IPSE is via a single full screen editor. This editor is based on the INed* full screen editor already available as standard on a number of systems, including versions of UNIX sold by IBM for IBM machines. The basic operational idiom of the *CUI* provided by TEN/PLUS is the visual selection of a data object by cursor positioning (or a mouse when appropriate). In the *CUI* the user always views the environment through *forms* - the form to be used is defined by the users's *context*. A context is an extension of the users's UNIX* environment and is defined by the current data object type together with a number of configurable TEN/PLUS search paths which are used to locate TEN/PLUS components.

2.1.1 *TEN/PLUS operation* Because the idiom of TEN/PLUS operation is the selection of data objects rather than the invocation of commands, the user invokes TEN/PLUS applications as a side effect of selecting an application data object, although 'generic' applications *can* be invoked directly on any object. On UNIX TEN/PLUS application data objects are typed using extensions to a filename, for example ".c" for a C program, ".prj" for GECOMO data and ".frm" for a TEN/PLUS form. A TEN/PLUS application is called a TEN/PLUS *helper* and is identified by the same naming convention as forms, thus selecting a GECOMO data object will cause the system to locate and invoke the TEN/PLUS application helper "prj.help" on that data object.

The features of TEN/PLUS will be described briefly by reference to the TEN/PLUS UNIX filesystem interface - since many readers will be familiar with the basic UNIX filesystem interface. There is no space available here for an complete description and the interested reader is referred to the extensive documentation available [3].

---

* TEN/PLUS is a trademark of INTERACTIVE Systems Corp.
* INed is a trademark of INTERACTIVE Systems Corp.
* UNIX is a trademark of AT&T Bell Labs, Inc.

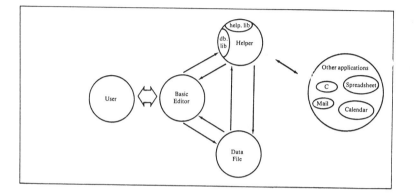

Figure 1. "Structure of the TEN/PLUS system"

Figure 1 shows the basic architecture of the TEN/PLUS system - including the essential processes.

In all applications the user navigates the hierarchical TEN/PLUS environment by means of ZOOM-IN and ZOOM-OUT commands, although the experienced TEN/PLUS user can "jump around" quicker than this. An example of this is navigating the hierachical UNIX filesystem by using ZOOM-IN and ZOOM-OUT commands rather than sequences of the UNIX commands "cd <dirname>", "ls", "cd ..". The notion of hierarchy is smoothly extended into TEN/PLUS data or "*structured*" files, so that to examine the contents of any file the user selects the directory entry for that file in the usual manner and presses the ZOOM-IN key. A TEN/PLUS data file may have an arbitrarily complex internal hierarchy which is navigated using the same commands, thus the user retains the same interface within TEN/PLUS applications as in navigating the UNIX filesystem.

Access to system and application specific functions is provided via the MENU and LOCAL-MENU function keys. The menu presented by the MENU function key is user tailorable and remains the same whatever context the user is in, the menu presented by the LOCAL-MENU function key is application dependent and is actually provided by the TEN/PLUS helper which is running in the user's context.

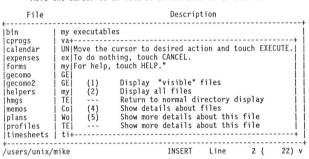

```
                        INTERACTIVE TEN/PLUS SYSTEM
                 Move the cursor to an item below and ZOOM-IN to see it.

          File                              Description
     +---------------------------------------------------------------------+
     |bin       | my executables                                           |
     |cprogs    | va+----------------------------------------------------+ |
     |calendar  | UN|Move the cursor to desired action and touch EXECUTE.| |
     |expenses  | ex|To do nothing, touch CANCEL.                        | |
     |forms     | my|For help, touch HELP."                              | |
     |gecomo    | GE|                                                    | |
     |gecomo2   | GE|  (1)    Display "visible" files                    | |
     |helpers   | my|  (2)    Display all files                          | |
     |hmgs      | TE|  ---    Return to normal directory display         | |
     |memos     | Co|  (4)    Show details about files                   | |
     |plans     | Wo|  (5)    Show more details about this file          | |
     |profiles  | TE|  ---    Show more details about this file          | |
     |timesheets| ti+----------------------------------------------------+ |
     +---------------------------------------------------------------------+
     /users/unix/mike                      INSERT    Line    2 (    22) v
```

Figure 2. "TEN/PLUS directory view and LOCAL-MENU"

Figure 2 shows the view of a standard UNIX directory seen by a user who has selected that directory using TEN/PLUS and then pressed the LOCAL-MENU function key. A real TEN/PLUS directory normally displays 22 entries. The TEN/PLUS "directory" helper combines with the TEN/PLUS editor to produce a visual interface which subsumes the standard UNIX commands for manipulating the filesystem. Every operation which would have been possible using standard UNIX commands can be performed using TEN/PLUS editor commands, although these UNIX commands can still be accessed directly if required.

To delete the directory entry "expenses" the user 'selects' "expenses" using the cursor keys to position the cursor anywhere on the line containing "expenses" and presses the DELETE function key (the type of the directory entry does not matter). To create a file the user presses the INSERT function key (or positions the cursor on an empty line) and types the name of the new entry. When this new entry is selected as a working context TEN/PLUS will ask the user to specify the type of directory entry that is required, UNIX ASCII file, TEN/PLUS structured file or UNIX directory. To rename an existing entry such as "expenses" the user simply positions the cursor over the first character of the entry "expenses" and overwrites the old name with the new name.

By selecting the appropriate option from the TEN/PLUS directory helper LOCAL-MENU the user can access or modify the information normally displayed by the various options of the UNIX command "ls". During all these operations the user is still using the same keystrokes to modify the UNIX directory as he would use to modify a text file. If the user attempts an operation which is illegal for some reason then the TEN/PLUS directory helper will prevent the operation and will display an appropriate error message.

```
                    INTERACTIVE TEN/PLUS SYSTEM
       To see detailed file status information, select an item and ZOOM-IN.

       File Name T Owner    Size    Modification Date    Permissions
       +----------------------------------------------------------------+
       |bin       |d|mike    | 3023 | Nov 21 1985 14:41:49 | rwx r-x ---|
       |cprogs    | -------------------------------------------------+x|
       |calendar  || Move the cursor to desired action and touch EXECUTE.|x|
       |expenses  || To do nothing, touch CANCEL.                        |x|
       |forms     || For help, touch HELP.                               |x|
       |gecomo    ||    (1)     Display "visible" files               |x|
       |gecomo2   ||    (2)     Display all files                     |-|
       |helpers   ||    (3)     Return to normal directory display    |-|
       |hmgs      ||    ---     Show details about files              |x|
       |memos     ||    (5)     Show more details about this file     |x|
       |plans     || (ZOOMIN)   Show more details about this file     |x|
       |profiles  |+-------------------------------------------------+x|
       |timesheets|d|mike    |  512 | Mar 17 1986 07:04:00 | rwx rwx r-x|
       +----------------------------------------------------------------+
       /users/unix/mike                     INSERT   Line    2 (   22) v
```

Figure 3. "TEN/PLUS detailed directory listing and LOCAL-MENU"

In Figure 3 the same directory shown in Figure 2 is shown after LOCAL-MENU option (4) has been invoked to obtained detailed information for the directory entries, and the LOCAL-MENU function key has again been pressed. The differences from the LOCAL-MENU in Figure 2 illustrate how the LOCAL-MENU presented may be sensibly context driven by a TEN/PLUS application helper.

Now the TEN/PLUS user can edit detailed file information directly. For example the permissions on a UNIX directory entry may be changed by visually editing the entry, so for the directory entry "timesheets", group write permission can be removed by overwriting the existing "rwx" entry with "r-x". Note that this will only be possible if the user is allowed by the UNIX operating system to do this - so the user must still have the appropriate UNIX permissions. Also, not all fields in the listing in Figure 3 may be modified by the user; fields such as "Size" are reserved for use by the operating system and the TEN/PLUS directory helper will block any attempts to edit the entries in such fields.

Finally (in this short description), within any TEN/PLUS application data objects can be "cut and pasted" using generic PICK-UP, PUT-DOWN, PICK-COPY and PUT-COPY function keys. For example, within a UNIX directory a copy of a directory entry may be made by selecting that entry and pressing the PICK-COPY function key. That entry can then be moved into another UNIX directory by selecting a suitable position in the new directory and pressing the PUT-COPY or PUT-DOWN function keys. Note that exactly the same function key sequences are used whether the original directory entry was a UNIX file or a UNIX directory. In general, data objects of the same type may be moved between different TEN/PLUS applications using the function key sequences described above.

2.1.2 *Integration using the TEN/PLUS system* TEN/PLUS itself allows the operation of certain standard UNIX tools, particularly filters, to be integrated within the visual interface. For example, tools which generate textual output (ie. most UNIX tools) may be invoked from within a text field of a TEN/PLUS data file using the DO function key, and the output from the tool will be inserted into the file at the position selected by the cursor. In addition, areas of text may be "marked" and specific filters run over those areas using the DO function key to perform functions such as justification of text, substitutions, spelling checking etc.

In addition TEN/PLUS can include a "Programmers Tool Kit" [3] which facilitates the development of TEN/PLUS applications helpers. This includes a forms building tool and a set of program libraries. External tools are integrated by a process of:

- Designing a suitable screen based representation(s) of application data (not always as obvious as it might seem).
- Writing the application helper(s). The functionality can be developed from scratch in the helper or can be that of existing tools whose input/output is trapped and transformed into the appropriate TEN/PLUS representations.

As can be seen from this short description some of the features of TEN/PLUS are similar to those of an object oriented environment [4], although this has been achieved by hardwiring data types and operations into the TEN/PLUS applications and data files rather than by an underlying object manager. An advantage of basing the GEC Software IPSE Framework on the existing UNIX filesystem based implementation of TEN/PLUS is that distributed filesystem technology such as NFS [5] can be used as the basis of a first generation distributed IPSE. By porting TEN/PLUS onto a 2nd generation IPSE distributed database such as that used in PCTE [6], existing TEN/PLUS tools will immediately become available within a 2nd generation distributed IPSE and TEN/PLUS itself can potentially be extended and enhanced by the distributed object management capabilities of the 2nd generation IPSE. In the shorter term many tools for 1st generation IPSE's would benefit from access to the features of current relational databases and the development of an interface between standard relational database management systems and TEN/PLUS is planned.

2.2 *Common Data Interface*

The data object orientation of TEN/PLUS means that it forms a natural basis for a Common Data Interface. GEC Software have developed the *CDI* for the IPSE Framework by extending the TEN/PLUS UNIX directory_ helper to provide the basic interaction with the "IPSE database" and the IPSE user. Each IPSE user is given a view of the IPSE database by the GEC Software IPSE Framework *CDI* and is restricted to this view; ie. to the user the IPSE appears *only* to consist of the view they have been given. This section considers how appropriate views are generated for each IPSE user in the *CDI*. Section 2.3 shows how the GEC Software IPSE Framework can control the operations of tools on data visible through the *CDI*.

At "*Structured Login*" to the GECSW IPSE Framework, before being allowed to access IPSE data or tools the user is presented with a menu of different "views" of the IPSE database. Each entry on the list corresponds to a particular role of the user called a *project instance* which has been created in a *Project Description File (PDF)* using the GEC

Software IPSE Framework Manager Toolset (see section 3 for a description of a *PDF*).

When the user chooses the project instance with which he intends to work the GEC Software IPSE Framework prototype will either generate the actual view of (in this case) the UNIX filesystem from the files and directories specified in the appropriate *PDF* or use an existing view which the user has been using previously.

```
GECSW ENVIRONMENT MANAGER    Environment is currently:
          V0.0
                    +-------------------------------------+
        File        |GECSW-IPSE V0.0 Structured Login     |
  +-----------------|                             |----------+
  |                 ||You are registered to the following|    |
  |                 ||projects. Use the arrow keys to put|    |
  |                 ||the cursor on the one you wish to   |    |
  |                 ||use and touch EXECUTE to continue.  |    |
  |                 ||                             |    |
  |                 ||Use CANCEL if you wish to abort     |    |
  |                 ||this Structured Login.              |    |
  |                 ||                             |    |
  |                 ||  ipse:development            |    |
  |                 ||  ipse:demo                   |    |
  |                 ||  ipse:proj_management        |    |
  |                 ||  gecomo:user                 |    |
  +-----------------|  a combination of above      |    |
  +-----------------+-------------------------------------+----------+
  /mike                               INSERT   Line    2 (   22) v
```

Figure 4. "IPSE Framework - initial screen and menu"

Figure 4 shows an initial screen and menu presented by the GEC Software IPSE Framework when a user logs in. This is done by the *Common Data Interface Manager* (*CDIM*) which replaces the standard TEN/PLUS directory helper in the GEC Software IPSE Framework. In this case the user selects the entry for "gecomo:user" (an ordinary user of the gecomo project) and the IPSE Framework will create the actual view of the filesystem for this project instance, as shown in Figure 5.

In the IPSE Framework prototype the actual view of the UNIX filesystem which is generated is called a *Virtual File System* (*VFS*). As far as the user is concerned he is viewing a UNIX filesystem through the *CUI* and using TEN/PLUS operations to navigate the directory hierachy or examine files in "gecomo:user", but the *CDIM* will not allow the user to "escape" from the view specified in the *PDF* used to generate the *VFS*.

In the GEC Software IPSE Framework prototype a *VFS* is automatically generated using UNIX *links*. Familiar problems such as name collisions and circularity can occur and are detected during the creation of the *VFS*. In the prototype the user is prompted interactively by the *CDIM* to resolve these problems.

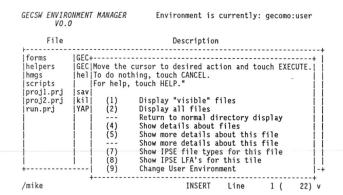

```
GECSW ENVIRONMENT MANAGER        Environment is currently: gecomo:user
        V0.0

        File                             Description
+------------------------------------------------------------------------+
|forms       |GEC+------------------------------------------------------+ |
|helpers     |GEC|Move the cursor to desired action and touch EXECUTE.| |
|hmgs        |hel|To do nothing, touch CANCEL.                    _   | |
|scripts     |   |For help, touch HELP."                              | |
|proj1.prj   |sav|                                                    | |
|proj2.prj   |kil|   (1)    Display "visible" files                   | |
|run.prj     |YAP|   (2)    Display all files                         | |
|            |   |   ---    Return to normal directory display        | |
|            |   |   (4)    Show details about files                  | |
|            |   |   (5)    Show more details about this file         | |
|            |   |   ---    Show more details about this file         | |
|            |   |   (7)    Show IPSE file types for this file         | |
|            |   |   (8)    Show IPSE LFA's for this tile              | |
+------------|   |   (9)    Change User Environment                   |-+
             +------------------------------------------------------+
/mike                                  INSERT   Line     1 (    22) v
```

Figure 5. "GEC Software IPSE Framework directory view and LOCAL-MENU"

Figure 5 shows the directory created by selecting "gecomo:user" from the initial menu, after the LOCAL-MENU key has been pressed. The *CDIM* runs as a TEN/PLUS helper and provides additional functions concerned with the IPSE Framework which are not present in the standard TEN/PLUS directory helper - these appear as LOCAL-MENU functions (7), (8) and (9).

If the user now selects LOCAL-MENU option (9) to change environment he will again be presented with the menu of different views in Figure 4. If he then selects the entry "ipse:development" the *CDIM* will construct the *VFS* shown in Figure 6.

```
GECSW ENVIRONMENT MANAGER     Environment is currently: ipse:development
         V0.0

     File                    Description
    +---------------------------------------------------------------------+
    |bin        | Binary executables                                      |
    |common     |                                                         |
    |cpiofiles  | transferred files from 750                              |
    |demo       | material for demonstration                              |
    |demonstrator|                                                        |
    |example.pdf | example PDF file                                       |
    |examples   |                                                         |
    |gecomo.pdf | PDF file for 'project GECOMO'                           |
    |logfile    | error logging file                                      |
    |login      |                                                         |
    |profiles   | TEN/PLUS profiles directory                             |
    |scratch    | scratch directory for Framework                         |
    |sundemo    | files to transfer to SUN                                |
    +---------------------------------------------------------------------+
     /mike                          INSERT   Line     6 (    22) v
```

Figure 6. "GEC Software IPSE Framework directory view and LOCAL-MENU"

Thus, the Common Data Interface described controls all user interaction with IPSE data, provides completely flexible support for project models (see section 3.1), is reconfigurable automatically, enhances the security of IPSE data and organises IPSE data in a manner which reflects the "real" organisation of the project and the "real" role of the particular IPSE user.

2.3 *Common Tool Interface*

This section continues on from 2.2, by showing how the behaviour of IPSE tools can be controlled by the Common Tool Interface component of the IPSE Framework. Within the *CTI* all tools are invoked using the *CUI* exactly as described in section 2.1.

When the user selects a project instance as described in section 2.2 he is also allocated a corresponding set of IPSE tools. These tools are also defined in the Project Description File when the project instance is created. When the *CDI* generates the appropriate *VFS* it also starts up the *User Environment Manager (UEM)* process. This process executes a binary image which is automatically generated by the IPSE Framework from a set of "tool descriptions" corresponding to the entries in the *PDF*.

Each tool description specifies the transformations which the tool will perform on the IPSE database, in terms of input, output and side-effects. This tool description is currently stored in a complex hierarchical TEN/PLUS structured file called a *"TCDF"* file - TEN/PLUS allows the complex syntactical structure of the information to be hidden by a series of "forms".

When a command sequence is invoked by the user, either directly by accessing the operating system command language or indirectly by a TEN/PLUS helper operation, the sequence is translated into a TEN/PLUS data object. This data object is then passed to the *UEM* which the IPSE

Framework has initiated for the user. The *UEM* then "parses" this data object against the tool definitions which have been compiled into it. One immediate effect of this is that any errors in the command sequence passed to the *UEM* can be detected before the command sequence is executed and the *UEM* can provide appropriate error and help messages. In this way the *UEM* can actually control the command sequences which can be executed by a user, perhaps eliminating certain optional or alternative behaviour according to the user's role on a project. In addition the *UEM* can at least potentially provide substantially superior error and help messages than those provided by the underlying operating system.

The structure of the *TCDF* allows the "tool integrator" to include a detailed description of tool behaviour in terms of its effect on the IPSE database (filesystem) and also to specify semantic *actions*. When a user invoked *command sequence* is passed to the *UEM* process and is parsed against the "tool description" in the *TCDF*, the semantic actions which have been included in the tool description will be executed at the appropriate points in the parsing process.

The IPSE Framework extends the TEN/PLUS notion of typing data objects, by filename extensions on UNIX, to allow data objects to have many types and many attributes by introducing a "layered" implementation of *Local File Attributes (LFA)*. When *actions* are executed during the parsing process they can interrogate or modify any of the *LFA*'s maintained by the IPSE Framework and it is for this purpose that *LFA*'s were introduced into the IPSE Framework. The *UEM* process can modify or block the intended user *command sequence* before it is executed by the underlying operating system. This allows the IPSE Framework to impose semantic constraints on the actions of tools; for example, certain types of files can only be modified by certain tools. The action of the *UEM* also provides a basis for allowing the IPSE Framework to perform tool composition operations. Simple UNIX tool composition operations are defined as individual tools and have corresponding *TCDF* entries but in the more complex cases integration between different tools can be achieved by the *UEM* performing suitable transformations on the output of a tool to match it to the input required by the next tool in the command sequence.

Thus, the Common Tool Interface described controls all user interaction with IPSE tools, provides completely flexible support for project models (see section 3.1), is reconfigurable automatically, can be used to assist the user, can be used to monitor the usage of resources by particular tools, forms a basis for automatic integration of non-trivial tools, enhances the security of IPSE data by controlling the operation and accessibility of IPSE tools and organises IPSE tools in a manner which reflects the "real" organisation of the project and the "real" role of the particular IPSE user.

3.   *CONFIGURING AN IPSE FOR A PROJECT*

To use the IPSE Framework successfully a number of data files must be created and maintained, either by one nominated individual manager or by a number of individuals. The complexity of the IPSE Framework and the files required to utilise it mean that suitable tools must be provided to ensure that the relevant data files may be created quickly and easily and are always consistent with each other, together with the necessary tools for generating and installing the components of the IPSE Framework from the data files. Thus the IPSE Framework has its own toolset, developed using TEN/PLUS for the *CUI*, and integrated into the IPSE Framework.

- A tool for creating and editing *TCDF* entries and aggregating tool descriptions into particular IPSE *Toolset Description Files (TDF)*.
- A tool for creating and editing the Project Description Files which define the various user views available within the IPSE.
- A tool which creates and edits the *User Description Files (UDF)* which defines the users of IPSE projects and the various project instances available to particular IPSE users.
- A tool to automatically generate components of the IPSE Framework from the *TDF*, *PDF*, and *UDF* data files.
- A tool to automatically integrate the components of the IPSE Framework with the *CUI* presented to all IPSE users.

3.1 *Installing a Project*

The *PDF* used by the IPSE Framework is a TEN/PLUS based implementation of a simple project description language. Projects are defined in terms of "core" toolsets and files common to all project instances, and the toolsets and files which are specifically provided for each project instance. The project description language will support virtually any project model and in the future a TEN/PLUS tool will be provided to control the definition of the project according to the model chosen.

The top-level of a *PDF* file is shown in Figure 7. To create or edit a project description the user selects the appropriate entry and presses the ZOOM-IN key. Further levels of hierarchy are used to extend the detail of the project description and to reflect the structure of the project model being used.

```
                        Project Description

                  Generic Project Name
                  +----------------------------+
                  |ipse                        |
                  +----------------------------+
                                              +-+
                  Core File System            | |
                                              +-+
                                              +-+
                  Core Tools/Toolsets         | |
                                              +-+
                                              +-+
                  Total Resources             | |
                                              +-+
                                              +-+
                  Project Instances           | |
                                              +-+
```

Figure 7. "IPSE Framework Project Description File"

The users of an IPSE project as defined in a *PDF* must also be defined. This is currently achieved by a simple TEN/PLUS data file containing the

structure shown in Figure 8. The information in the *UDF* is fairly self-
explanatory: the syntax for specifiying a project instance is
"<project-name>:<instance-name>" as shown in Figure 8.

```
                            User Description

Login name    Full Name                           Telephone
+---------+   +-----------------------------+     +-------+
|mike     |   |Mike Higgs                   |     |223    |
+---------+   +-----------------------------+     +-------+

              Projects
              +-----------------------------+
              |ipse:development             |
              |ipse:demo                    |
              |ipse:proj_manager            |
              |gecomo:user                  |
              |                             |
              |                             |
              |                             |
              +-----------------------------+
```

Figure 8. "IPSE Framework User Description File"

3.2 *Installing a Tool*

To install a tool in the IPSE Framework the user must create a valid
tool description in a *TCDF*; as with the other IPSE Framework data files
this is stored as a TEN/PLUS structured file. The top level of the *TCDF*
file for the UNIX C compiler is shown in Figure 9. The remainder of the
entry may be edited or examined using the ZOOM-IN and ZOOM-OUT function
keys to navigate the hierarchy of the data file.

```
                         Tool Description

Toolset name                        Tool name
+---------------------------+       +---------------------------+
|C_toolset                  |       |cc                         |
+---------------------------+       +---------------------------+

                            +-+                               +-+
Input Package               | |     Output Package            | |
                            +-+                               +-+

                            +-+                               +-+
Options Package             | |     Side Effects Package      | |
                            +-+                               +-+

                            +-+
Cost Of Tool Package        | |
                            +-+
```

Figure 9. Top level display for a *TCDF* entry

The structure of the *TCDF* in the IPSE Framework prototype has, if anything, proved overcomplex and as a result a simplified design is being developed.

4. GEC SOFTWARE IPSE FRAMEWORK ARCHITECTURE

The overall architecture of the GEC Software IPSE Framework reflects the use of TEN/PLUS as a basis for the *CUI* (cf. section 2.1 and Figure 1) and also the fact that the prototype was developed on UNIX. Figure 10 shows a "notional" view of the architecture of the IPSE Framework in which all activity is process based. The "actual" architecture of the IPSE Framework will be tailored to reflect the biases of the target system and for the UNIX prototype corresponds to the architecture in Figure 10. The communication between the User Environment Manager process and the TEN/PLUS applications helpers is implemented using "sockets", whereas the communication between helpers and the TEN/PLUS editor is based on UNIX "pipes". If necessary, this communication can be avoided by combining the various TEN/PLUS processes into a single image.

Using this type of architecture for the IPSE Framework reflects the increasing local availability of processor power in software development workstations in the future. However, it does not preclude the use of the IPSE Framework on existing timeshared systems although some re-engineering is likely to be necessary to avoid performance degradation. In all cases implementation and system differences will normally be hidden from the user by the standard idioms used in the *CUI*.

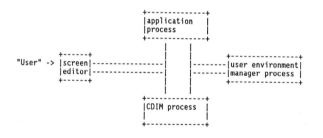

Figure 10. "Architecture of GEC Software IPSE Framework"

The *CDIM* process shown in Figure 10 is the IPSE Framework helper which replaces the standard TEN/PLUS directory helper. It is invoked to perform the process of "Structured Login" described in section 2.2. In addition, this process is responsible for the initiation and termination of the specified *VFS* and the *UEM* process generated at "Structured Login". As far as possible the work of creating and controlling the user environment has been implemented in the initial process of "Structured login" to minimise runtime overheads of the IPSE Framework.

Clearly the efficiency of the implementation of the IPSE Framework depends on the extent to which the support of the *CDI* and *CTI* must be layered over existing operating system facilities. In the future it will be possible to take advantage of 2nd generation IPSE workstations, such as PCTE workstations, on which this layering is reduced to a minimum.

5. GEC SOFTWARE IPSE FRAMEWORK: CURRENT STATUS

5.1 Experiences with the Current Framework Prototype

The prototype IPSE Framework has been used to support the definition of IPSE toolsets and IPSE users. The prototype then performs the automatic generation and integration of the various components of the IPSE Framework. In order to implement the *CDI* and *CTI* the support of Local File Attributes has been added to the basic TEN/PLUS directory helper and data files. The *CDI* contains the code to initiate and terminate User Environment Manager processes. Thus the prototype demonstrates the three generations of "integration" considered in section 1.3, although only the *CUI* has so far been incorporated into a product.

The integration of tools into the Framework involves the creation of "tool descriptions" as described in section 3.2. Based on the tool descriptions we have developed so far for various UNIX based tools we have been able to integrate a number of IPSE toolsets successfully into the prototype IPSE Framework using three different approaches:

- ⊕ "Tight" integration of toolsets developed to utilise a TEN/PLUS user interface, where the source of the toolset has been recompiled and modified to utilise the IPSE Framework libraries.
- ⊕ "Loose" integration of externally developed or standard operating system toolsets which use a standard UNIX command language based user interface, by writing "tool descriptions" using the Tool Description Language and performing "controlled" execution of these toolsets from within the IPSE Framework.
- ⊕ "Effective" integration of externally developed or standard operating system toolsets with UNIX command language user interfaces interfaces, by using the Common User Interface to develop a visual TEN/PLUS based interface for the toolsets, without any modification of the toolsets themselves. It is difficult for non-expert users to distinguish these toolsets from tightly integrated toolsets developed internally at GEC Software.

GEC Software now employs a range of TEN/PLUS based tools very successfully over a range of systems, including VAX/4.2BSD, SUN/4.2BSD, VAX/VMS* and GEC63/System V. Some of these tools have been developed internally (sometimes by adding TEN/PLUS interfaces to existing tools) and some tools have been developed elsewhere. These include TEN/PLUS helpers for electronic mail, for C programming, for Ada programming using VADS*, for a commercially available configuration management tool,

---

* VAX and VMS are trademarks of Digital Equipment Corp.
* The Verdix Ada Development System, VADS is a trademark of Verdix Corp.

for cross referencing, for our in-house software problem reporting system, for in-house project recording and monitoring and for generating standard company documentation. All these tools will be integrated into the next prototype of the IPSE Framework.

5.2 *Further Development of the Current Prototype*

Although the IPSE Framework prototype has been developed on 4.2BSD UNIX in C the Common User Interface is already available on a wide variety of systems including VAX/VMS. Further development of the IPSE Framework prototype will include porting the next prototype onto a range of internetworked in-house systems and workstations using both UNIX and VMS. This will allow GEC Software to enhance the IPSE Framework prototype to satisfy the requirements of a mixed hardware and operating systems environment. It will also enable us to investigate the use of the prototype as the basis for a multi-machine heterogenous IPSE Framework based on an existing distributed filesystem.

We have already begun to use the IPSE Framework and the toolsets which have been integrated for its own development and further toolsets will need to be integrated to continue this process. In addition, we are investigating the correspondence between monitoring the usage of resources by the IPSE Framework and the descriptions of projects in *PDF* files used to generate environments, in order to automate parts of the data collection necessary for project management tools. The performance of the prototype suggests that the IPSE Framework can be expanded considerably in this area without serious degradation.

References

1. "INTEGRATED PROJECT SUPPORT ENVIRONMENTS". A State of the Art Report. (Draft). P. Mair, National Computing Centre Ltd. March 1986.

2. "Giving Magic to the UNIX System". P. Marvit, UNIX System Encyclopedia. Yates Ventures 1984.

3. "TEN/PLUS Progammer's Tool Kit Guide." INTERACTIVE Systems Corp, April 1985.

4. "Project Support in the Smalltalk-80 integrated environment" L. Peter. Deutsch. In - "Integrated Project Support Environments", Peter Peregrinus, 1985.

5. "Distributed File System Strategies". G.R.Sager & R.B. Lyon, UNIX Review, May 1985.

6. ESPRIT: "A Portable Common Tools Environment", 3rd Edition, 1985.

Chapter 4

PCTE proposal for a public common tool interface

Ian Campbell

The PCTE Proposal for a Public Common Tool Interface is
the result of a number of studies and prototypes carried out
in Europe. Much of this article has already appeared in one
form or another in the proceedings of the Esprit Technical
Week 1985, where the authors are the members of the PCTE
project team (from Bull, ICL, Siemens, GEC, Nixdorf and
Olivetti).

This article presents the background and general characteristics of the proposed Public Common Tool Interface. It
covers mainly the PCTE project, a PCTE implementation called
Emeraude and some European actions based on the PCTE tool
interface. It tries to clarify answers to questions like
who ? why ? when ? what ?

1. OVERVIEW OF OBJECTIVES

1.1 Background

The area of Software Technology is one of the five
areas of the ESPRIT European collaborative R and D programme which are recognised as prioritary in order to preserve
and improve the competitiveness of the European Information
Technology Industry. Projects undertaken in the S.T. as
well as in the other ESPRIT areas will require software to
be developed and exchanged by various teams all over the
Community. This aspect has led to the notion of a common
environment, to be used by the different research teams
involved in ESPRIT, and facilitating not only the development, but also the exchange of software between the teams.
Such an environment should provide a suitable basis for the
various projects, and be available on different categories
of machines, so as to cover the needs of the various teams.

A suitable Software Engineering Environment (SEE) should
offer specific facilities that are generally not found in
conventional systems. The natural conclusion is therefore
to use a dedicated system for development activities, distinct from the machines for which the software is developed.
This host/target development paradigm is generally admitted
in the context of embedded systems, but appears more and
more necessary also in the context of general data-process-
ing systems, in which the specific requirements of development activities are often seen as nuisances.

Software development is accomplished more and more with the new generation of personal workstations linked together by fast Local Area Networks. These workstations are personal computers with pointing devices and high resolution raster displays capable of supporting several character sets and graphics ; the LAN facilities can provide each workstation with several services, such as file and data base services, print services, software development services, and communic- ation services, both store-and-forward (e.g. electronic mail) and dialogue (conversational). The main advantage of these kinds of environments is that they put the power of a time-sharing system in an immediate and direct fashion into the hands of one user, allowing the user to carry on several different or related activities as they best suit his needs and preferences.

PCTE takes into account the current evolution towards advanced workstations and the use of local area networks, and defines basic concepts for Software Engineering Environ- ments which can be adapted for both conventional and distri- buted systems. Thus, the distribution of functionalities is an important factor, and the human interfaces are oriented towards the best use of modern technology. However, because PCTE should be usable in realworld contexts, where conven- tional hardware (main frames and CRTs) will remain installed the environment should also operate in such contexts. Of course, information will be available in a less comfortable fashion on conventional systems.

1.2 Guidelines

Most software engineering tools that are presently available result from individual efforts and tend to cons- titute a collection of vaguely related products, each filling a particular function, but without much considera- tion for the software development process as a whole. On the other hand, research in software technology will lead to the implementation of a variety of integrated tool sets to support theories, methods, and production of software. These tools will most likely be developed in the context of different projects. It is therefore important that PCTE offers a structure based on state-of-the-art technology that can :

- reduce the development costs of software tools,
  contributing to their widespread use, and therefore,
  to an improvement of software productivity,
- facilitate the exchange of software (tools and products based on the PCTE Public Common Tool Interface)
  throughout the European software community,
- allow for and encourage the integration of tools in
  comprehensive, uniform and homogeneous Software
  Engineering Environments,
- speed up the dissemination of ideas and techniques
  throughout the industrial and the research communities
  by providing a common frame of reference,
- support the smooth transition from existing practices
  by allowing the easy migration into PCTE of existing
  tools.

1.3 Goals

The above considerations naturally lead to the concept of a unifying framework that could be used for the development and integration of a variety of tools in order to constitute a family of complete environments, each one with its own specific characteristics in terms of methods, application area, etc.
PCTE is aimed at the definition of a common framework, within which various software tools can be developed, integrated and exchanged so as to provide complete environments for software engineering. Different trends in software technology are focused in PCTE :
- the openness of an environment, encouraging people to develop their own tools as epitomised by *UNIX,
- the need to conceive an environment around powerful mechanisms, especially in the area of object management, corresponding to the Stoneman philosophy,
- the improvement of programmers' productivity by means of powerful user interfaces, an avenue explored especially in the Interlisp, Mesa, Smalltalk, and Cedar environments developed at Xerox PARC.
As a definition of a Public Common Tool Interface for advanced software engineering environments, PCTE can have a significant impact on the European Software Technology industry ; however, the objectives of the PCTE initiative can only be achieved if PCTE will become available sufficiently early to be used effectively within ESPRIT projects and the industrial community at large, to demonstrate its suitability as a de facto standard.
Thus, the main objective is to provide a powerful, state-of-the-art system that offers high-level mechanisms for the development and integration of a variety of software tools. However, the success of the PCTE initiative also relies on the achievement of two main strategic goals :
- Portability : the interface should be provided quickly on a wide scale without incurring large costs,
- Compatibility : the new environment framework must allow for a smooth transition from existing software development practices.

1.4 "Preferred" Architecture

A state-of-the-art developemnt environment has to provide above all a great comfort of use. Such comfort can be characterised by :
- the raw power available to the user in terms of instant computing power and large storage capacity,
- the quality of the dialogues with the machine : one of the key elements there is the so-called bandwidth of the flow of information, whereby for a given effort from the user, one can increase the amount of information entered or displayed,
- the overall ease-of-use of the system,
- the general availability of the facility.

*UNIX is a trademark of AT & T.

These considerations quickly led to the conclusion that, although the system should be available on a large variety of machines and architectures, there was an optimal choice on which efforts should be concentrated.

The preferred architecture would consist of powerful, single-user workstations offering a reasonable amount of local computing power (1 Mips) and main storage (at least 2 Mbytes). These workstations should be equipped with a high-resolution display, capable of the textual and graphic representation of large quantities of information (corresponding to several A4 pages), and some pointing device.

However, it is important to realise that the development of a large or complex piece of software results above all from the work of a team. This should be reflected in the environment, which should be an environment for a project, and not only for individuals. The various workstations must therefore be connected physically so that a user working on one workstation can access information located on, or communicate with, other workstations. They must also be connected logically so as to treat a user as an actor in a larger context, rather than as an individual who interacts with other individuals.

The architectural support can thus be seen as consisting of a net of workstations connected through a high-bandwidth local-area network and sharing common physical and logical resources ("servers") such as printers, disks, communication channels or specialised processors.

The software architecture should however preserve the visibility of a unique set of resources accessible to everyone. In other words, we should have a single system, whose resources are distributed in a transparent manner among the various physical components, and not a number of individual systems that have to communicate explicitly. The insistence on the transparency of the distribution is seen as fundamental if we want to preserve the portability of the system towards different kinds of hosts.

1.5 Design Objectives

Detailed below are the principal individual objectives strived for during the design of PCTE facilities, and how these can be interpreted in the context of the resulting functionalities.

1.5.1 Generality. The hosting structure should be capable of providing the basis for a number of environments, differing in such aspects as the application domains, the development methods, the project organisations, or the programming languages used.

The basic environment, on the other hand, provides powerful mechanisms upon which these specialised environments can be built and operated. The mechanisms should therefore cater to a variety of needs, offering the maximum relief to the tool developer, while avoiding any interference with his design decisions.

Of particular importance in this respect is the need to separate the mechanisms from the policies that can govern

their use. The basic environment should offer ways to control the use of the various primitives, but should not
impose any control of its own.

1.5.2 Flexibility. A consequence of the approach described
above is that the structure must be adapted to a variety of
needs. This tailoring can be achieved effectively if the
basic primitives offered are themselves fairly simple, but
represent a complete set of functionalities. Thus, it is
always possible to build more complex functions on top of
the basic ones, thereby tailoring the upper layer that will
be made visible to the end user.

It is important not to be preemptive in this respect,
and to recognise the existence of three categories of actors
dealing with the environment :
- the tool developers construct tools and software
  layers as to tailor the environment to specific needs,
- the SEE architect constructs an integrated project
  support environment with the PCTE and the appropriately chosen tools,
- the end users merely use an environment together with
  its tools in the context of their daily work.

The design has to cater for the needs of tool developers, SEE architect and end users ; the three categories
represent the "users" (in a general sense) of the system.

1.5.3 Homogeneity. One of the most salient demands placed
on an environment from the user's point of view is the homogeneity among a given set of tools, as well as of the environment as a whole. Homogeneity appears at three different
levels :
- a logical level which corresponds to the functions
  performed by the various tools : each tool should
  have a precise function that complements exactly
  those of other tools, without overlapping with them.
  Within the context of a particular development approach, each tool has its place, and the whole set of
  tools should provide complete support throughout
  development and operational use,
- an internal level corresponding to the objects and
  operations accessed by the tool. These are governed
  by the facilities offered by the basic system, but
  also by design choices regarding the various tools,
  such as the internal representations of the manipulated information which must be consistent between the
  various tools,
- an external level which defines the interface between
  the end user and the tool. It is important that the
  man-machine interfaces for the various tools be uniform and consistent.

The logical level is mainly dependent on the choice of
a particular development approach and of the associated
tools. The internal level is also largely dependent on
implementation choices. However, the basic environment can
indeed foster the homogeneity of operations and the integration among the various tools by offering an adequate
set of functionalities, well adapted to the particular needs

of tool development. The notion of Software Engineering
Database is clearly central to this issue ; therefore, the
Object Management System is considered as a central feature
of PCTE.
   At the external level, much can be done to promote
homogeneity as perceived by the end-user : the forms of
dialogue, the style of command languages, the provisions for
on-line assistance, can be defined at the level of an entire
environment, and supported by mechanisms and meta-tools that
can facilitate their adaptation to a particular, given tool.

1.5.4 Portability. Two main aspects are identified for the
implementation of PCTE basic mechanisms :
   - one is centred around portability of tools (which
     stresses compatibility with UNIX as the means to
     exploit and reuse the large pool of existing UNIX
     tools),
   - the other is centred around a portable architecture to
     obtain the highest degree of portability of PCTE basic
     mechanisms.

1.5.5 UNIX compatibility. The support for migration path
from UNIX based environments to those offering the PCTE
interface is a principal short term goal. This is a vital
factor which will determine the future role of PCTE. In this
connection PCTE has, first of all, to gain acceptance as a
readily available, easy to adopt alternative to existing
practices ; it must be possible for tools, data and people
(project teams or individual users) to migrate towards the
new environments with a minimum of effort. The key issue in
this respect is the ability to reuse directly existing
tools, thus the absolute requirement for a complete compatibility of PCTE interface facilities with the corresponding
UNIX ones.
   One   goal   of the PCTE interface is to support directly the immediate reusability of tools developed to run on
System V (and thus of all UNIX tools which do not rely on
some facility specific to a given, non System V version of
UNIX). Thus the existing tools, as for data items, can be
installed in the OMS base and can be executed in a PCTE
framework. Given the number of tools one can expect to find
on a given UNIX installation, the only suitable avenue
(from the user point of view) is an installation procedure
which does not require to modify the tools. The best solution is the installation of tools by just copying the tool
executable representation into the OMS base.
   In general, UNIX based tool sets will not exhibit the
properties one expects for proper Software Engineering
Environments, especially in terms of integration, of management of complex information bases and of friendliness of
the tool <=> user interfaces : new tools, designed and
developed to take advantage of the advanced PCTE facilities
will gradually become available to be integrated into cons-
istentSEEs. However, the ability to reuse existing tools
will play a paramount role in the initial, critical phases
in which transition to PCTE based SEEs has to take place.

2.   THE PROJECTS

2.1 The PCTE project in the Esprit software technology subprogramme

The project "A Basis for a Portable Common Tool Environment (PCTE)" is carried out by a consortium led by Bull (France) and including GEC and ICL (United Kingdom), Nixdorf and Siemens (Federal Republic of Germany) and Olivetti (Italy).
The actual functionalities of PCTE are described in the PCTE Functional Specification report (the third edition of which is publicly available inside ESPRIT), which gives the detailed definition of the PCTE functionalities in a form which can directly be used in the design of tools and programs which will eventually be integrated into a PCTE hosting framework.

2.2 The French National Software Engineering Project

The French national software engineering project set as its main goal the promotion of the development of a host framework to act as the cornerstone for the implementation of software engineering environments.
Three companies Bull, Eurosoft and Syseca decided to share their experience and knowhow in a united effort to develop and sell their joint product Emeraude which is an implementation of the PCTE defined hosting structure and offers the PCTE proposed Public Common Tool Interface.

2.3 Other European Projects

Tools resulting from projects in the software technology area of the Esprit programme will have, as one of their goals, to be able to be integrated into environments offering the PCTE defined interfaces. The same kind of requirement exists in France with respect to tools developed under the aegis of the national software engineering project, which must also be able to be integrated to run in Emeraude based environments.
Some specific projects exist which use PCTE as the basis for the construction of software engineering environments : the PACT project in Esprit will build general purpose common tools integrated into an environment using the PCTE facilities. Other projects are in the process of being agreed : one of these has as a goal to provide Emeraude, offering the PCTE interfaces, on a range of different machines ; another, in the context of Eureka, proposes the integration of new and future state-of-the-art tools in order to create a range of integrated project support environments based on the Emeraude implementation of the PCTE interfaces. Collaboration is in progress with some projects in the UK Alvey programme, in order to harmonise the use of the same Public Common Tool Interface.

2.4 Timescale

The PCTE project has published its proposal for a Public
Common Tool Interface in its Functional Specifications
report. The Emeraude project will be able to supply a PCTE
implementation before the end of this year (field tests are
planned from this spring). The PACT project will publish a
general presentation this summer and an initial tool set
enabling a limited use of the PCTE implementation is planned
for the beginning of next year (the full results of PACT
providing a minimum method-independent environment basis
will be available early in 1989, but most of these results
should be available progressively throughout 1988). Trans-
ports of the Emeraude framework are scheduled to take place
this year and next, with the first machines being available
early next year. Most of the other ongoing or soon to be
started projects plan to have their results in three years ;
the Eureka East project is planned in two stages : the first
in three years, the second in six.

3.   OVERVIEW OF THE BASIC PCTE FACILITIES

A PCTE implementation is a hosting structure designed to
be the basis for the construction of modern Software Engineering Environments (SEE). Each PCTE based SEE is regarded
as an integrated collection of tools and services specific
to a particular project life cicle model and/or application
domain.
In the model architecture implied by the PCTE approach
there is a clear separation between the tools and the underlying structure that hosts them. Indeed, some seemingly
central aspects of the environment, such as a command
processor, are relegated to the tool level.
The Public Common Tool Interface to the PCTE services
is defined by a set of program-callable primitives which
support the execution of programs in terms of a virtual,
machine independent level of comprehensive facilities. The
following sections present the principal aspects of PCTE
namely :
 - the Basic Mechanisms : these correspond to the functionalities required to manipulate the various entities that can exist in a development context. These
   entities are essentially programs that can be executed
   (typically tools, or programs under test), and various
   objects manipulated by the programs (data objects,
   such as various representations of the programs being
   developed, the documentation, input and output data ;
   and also physical objects such as terminals and device
   drivers),
 - the User Interface : above the basic mechanisms, which
   deal with the internals of tools, PCTE provides a
   number of facilities to assist in the construction of
   various aspects of the tools that will be directly
   visible to the end user. These aspects concern the
   forms of dialogue and of interactions (exchange of
   information) between users and tools, and the graphic
   facilities,

- distribution : although not a direct concern to the user, the implementation of the environment on a network of workstations requires the definition of mechanisms and protocols to support the transparency of the distribution.

3.1 Basic Mechanisms

The PCTE Basic Mechanisms are subdivided into five categories : Execution, Communication, Inter Process Communication, Object Management System and Activities.

3.1.1 Execution mechanisms. The execution primitives deal with the notion of a program in execution. They define how an execution can be started or terminated, how it can be controlled, how parameters can be passed to the program, and more generally define the relations between a running program and the environment within which it executes. Facilities are provided for running a program (process), for defining and controlling the interactions between a program and its surrounding context.

3.1.2 Communication mechanisms. The communication primitives deal with the way a program can access the file type unstructured data (contents of objects) which are kept in the Object Management System database. They correspond to conventional input-output facilities and are closely modelled on those of UNIX.

3.1.3 Inter Process Communication. Special mechanisms are provided to allow different processes to exchange information. Although these could be viewed as part of the communication facilities, or of the execution facilities, they are treated specially because they play an important role in the implementation of the rest of the system.

In addition to traditional UNIX pipes and signals, PCTE provides a message-passing facility, and the possibility to share memory segments between users. These mechanisms are upward compatible with the ones found in UNIX system V, although they offer some additional functionalities.

3.1.4. The Object Management System. A key aspect of an environment, and one that has a major impact on the complexity of a tool-writing process, is the set of functions that are provided to manipulate the various objects in the system.

The various "agents" in the environment (users and programs) "operate" on a number of entities that are known to the system and can be designated in it, and that are globally referred to as "objects". These may be files in the traditional sense, peripherals, pipes, or the description of the static contexts of a program, but also objects representing information items such as project milestones, tasks, project management and progression records.

In many projects, a huge number of objects are created which may have complex relationships. Among the numerous

examples, one could mention :
- the documentation and the source code of a program
  (the latter may itself contain several modules) ;
- the history and the derivation trails for a given
  version of a given object (representing, a program,
  a program fragment, a document or other items to
  which Configuration Management can be applied) ;
- the test set for exercising a particular version of a
  mòdule with the set of sample results that are suppo-
  sed to be produced by these tests.

A uniform treatment of the various classes of objects,
and powerful mechanisms to store and designate these objects, are two important requirements on a software engineering environment. The natural solution is a system that
allows the user to associate a number of attributes, whose
values represent specific properties, to objects, and to
represent the various relationships which can exist between
objects.

The basic OMS model is derived from the Entity Relationship data model (ER) and defines Objects and Relationships
as being the basic items of the environment information
base.

Objects are entities (in the ER sense) which can be
designated, and can optionally be characterised by :
- a "contents" i.e. a repository of unstructured data
  implementing the traditional UNIX "file" concept ;
- a set of attributes that are primitive values which
  can be named individually ;
- a set of relationships in which the object partici-
  pates.

Relationships allow the representation of logical
associations/dependencies between objects as well as structured information. In particular, one might need to introduce new compound objects, composed of several objects (a
notion that supercedes the traditional directory), or to
establish explicitly a reference from one object to another.
Relationships also may have attributes, which can be used
to describe specific properties associated with the relationship, and which allow the designation of a specific
relationship (among the   possibly many in which a given
object may participate) by the values of its (key) attributes.

Designation of relationships is the basis for the designation of objects : the principal means for accessing
objects in most OMS operations is to navigate the OMS object
space by "traversing" a sequence of relationships designated
by a string value type pathname. The syntax induced by the
OMS on such strings is (of course) compatible with the
syntax of UNIX pathnames.

Objects and relationships have a type which defines
their basic properties. Object, attribute and relationship
type definitions are contained in special objects of the
predefined type Schema Definition Set (SDS). SDSs can be
specific to individual users and/or tools or be common to a
community (of users or tools).

At any time, a process operates with a set of visible
definitions, that constitute its working schema. The working

schema is established for a process as the well-formed composition of a set of SDSs and can be dynamically re-establi-
shed so as to change the working context of a process. A
working schema corresponds to a description of certain constraints on the properties of a collection of objects and
relationships which are operated by a given process. A
working schema can thus reflect the specificities of a given
tool when applied to the objects and relationships specific
to a given user.

Thus, different users and tools may operate with different working schemas, though accessing the same object,
resulting in the facility to particularise the way in which
an object is "seen".

These mechanisms resemble in many ways a full-fledged
DBMS, with some significant differences :
- the goal of the system is not to make complex computations with the values of the attributes that are associated with an object : the major part of the computation will be performed on the object contents, whose
  details are administered by the tools ;
- the user must have the possibility to use the system
  for his own needs, and to modufy its working context
  by the definition of new object and relationship
  types, without having to go to a higher authority.

3.1.5 Activities. The lack of data access synchronisation
and recovery mechanisms is one of the recognised deficiencies of UNIX like environments. It is overcome in PCTE by
adapting the well known notion of transaction to the context
of Software Engineering Environments.In a general sense, a
transaction can be regarded as a work-frame in which individual operations take place. A transaction can be defined
to have certain properties, namely
- it is atomic, the effect on data of operations performed on behalf of a transaction is either applied as a
  whole or is not applied ;
- it is serialisable, the effects of executing several
  transactions to operate on the same data domain at
  the "same" time are expected to be the same as if the
  same transactions were executed in mutual exclusion.

In PCTE, the concept of transaction is generalised to
the concept of "Activity".

One important and distinguising aspect which is dealt
with by PCTE Acitivities is the concept of "granularity" of
tools, which means regarding each tool (either program,
script or program fragment) as a modular component, performing a well defined (hopefully atomic) function. More
powerful tools can be assembled out of simpler ones ; the
new tool can become itself a new grain participating in the
construction of other tools.

Each tool can be regarded as a primitive ; functional
layers can in this way be built out of tool sets. The failure of one of the tools may or may not be interpreted as a
complete failure depending on the context in which it was
invoked. The natural solution is to allow for nesting of
Activities, in a way similar to the dynamic first-in-last-
out management of the local context of blocks and procedures

in modern programming languages. Thus, PCTE Activities can
be nested ; the basic PCTE facilities support a complete and
consistent model featuring implicit as well as explicit recovery and synchronisation mechanisms (locks) which fully
support the atomicity and serialisability requirements.
Furthermore, Activity types and object level operations are
supported which allow the tool writer to tune the mechanisms
to the desired level of data consistency and concurrency
control, ranging from the UNIX like "unprotected" behaviour
to proper, fully protected atomic and serialisable "transactions".
   Activities are meant to support in a systematic and
standard way the construction of robust tools.

3.2 Distribution

   The host framework is built on a number of work stations
over which all the OMS objects are distributed. Since these
stations communicate with each other by means of a local
area network, the distribution consists in offering to a
station user transparent access to the functionalities and
objects of the other stations.
   The distribution has three major aspects :
   - process distribution,
   - OMS distribution,
   - the network.
   The advantages brought by the distribution include :
   - resource sharing between all the work stations,
   - non-dedicated stations although some may be assigned
     to specific tasks such as : archiving, execution,
     compiling...
   Therefore, PCTE does not impose an architecture on the
software engineering environment, but rather authorises all
configurations, that in addition do not depend on the simultaneous correct operation of all the stations.

3.2.1 Process distribution. Every process is created within
the framework or another process (the first process being
started at initialisation time).
   Process distribution thus means that when a parent
process creates a child process by means of call or start
primitives, the latter may be run :
   - on the same station (local execution),
   - on another station (remote execution).
   The user can impose the station on which the process
will be run. By default, it is the system which selects the
station depending on the execution class. This execution
class is one of the elements in the static context of the
program to be run, and it indicates the characteristics
which the selected station must have.
   It is thus possible, by manipulating the system so that
a specific station corresponds to a program's execution
class, to ensure that this program will always be run on
the same station, which thus becomes an execution server.

3.2.2 OMS Distribution. The OMS distribution goes along with
process distribution and the repartition of objects over the

various stations. It provides for transparent access to the
objects managed by the OMS.
Within the system, an object is known by :
- the volume on which it is created,
- an identification number on this volume.
The OMS database is partitioned into volumes which are
seen as collections of objects.
OMS distribution requires the evaluation of access paths
to remote objects. For this purpose, every station is aware
at every moment of all the volumes mounted.

3.2.3 Distribution of Activities.
The concurrency and inte-
grity control facility of PCTE (Activities) also operates in
a distributed context. System wide identification of activity contexts, management of volume level logging as well as
the distributed termination of activities (two phase commit/
roll-back protocol) are supported by the distribution mechanism.

3.2.4 Inter Process Communication.
As a process structure
becomes distributed so may its means of Inter Process Communication (IPC). All forms of IPC supported by PCTE basic
mechanisms may be distributed, that is named and unnamed
pipes, named and unnamed message queues.
Named pipes and named message queues are special OMS
objects and consequently are managed as such. Unnamed pipes
and message queues become distributed by the creation of a
distributed process structure. A user need not be aware, by
use, that IPC is distributed.

3.2.5 Network management.
Each workstation is represented by
an object in the database, and is also identified in a globally unique way by the identification number (host_id). This
number is assigned when the work station is initially created. All PCTE primitives that circumvent the transparency of
the distributed system make explicit use of the host_id.
The distribution mechanism has to manage the static
topology of workstations as well as the connection and dis-
connection of workstations from the system.
The distribution mechanism itself requires configuration
and management, in order that it may act as efficiently as
possible in particular installations, and that it may hide
the installation's physical topology and provide an invisi-
ble service. This information has to be maintained in a
replicated form on all workstations as each station is to be
permitted to function autonomously.
In addition to the Remote Procedure Call and broadcast
communication protocols, the distribution requires the
presence on each station, in the form of objects with identical contents, of a set of data including :
- the users and the groups of users,
- the existing volumes and the volumes mounted,
- the existing stations and the stations connected,
- the SDS of the system and the OMS root,
- the date.
The information is maintained so as to be consistent on
all the stations.

Finally, every station takes an active part in the management of the network through monitoring functions to detect
network and station errors.

3.3. User Interface

The User Interface comprises all the means employed to
let users start applications/tools, control and dialogue
with them.
The challenge is clear : how to provide the user with
ways of communicating with tools that are agreeable to use
without at the same time imposing serious constraints on the
programming of the tools themselves. There is a growing
amount of agreement about the ingredients of user friendly
communication. They include the use of windows that can be
made bigger and smaller and moved about on the screen, the
use of menus, of icons and graphics, of pointing instead of
typing and so on. However there is much less agreement on
how the ingredients should be put together to form a coherent and versatile system.
The following general ideas are followed where possible:
- existing tools should be reuseable without modification,
- a tool should be able to do whatever the user can do,
- preconceived rules laying down what a user or a tool
  might want to do are to be avoided. Thus while it
  might appear reasonable not to allow one tool to move
  windows created by another tool, this is precisely
  what a tool to optimise the use of the display area
  would want to do,
- the user should not be aware of getting in and out of
  modes. For example the user should not have to do
  something like typing in an escape character to get
  out of input mode,
- the interactions should accomodate both the expert and
  the novice user. The expert should not be forced into
  expressing his commands in a lengthy exchange ; on the
  other hand the novice should not be expected to remem-
  ber quantities of cryptic commands,
- displays should reflect the actual state of data held
  by a tool,
- menus should not propose choices which are not available,
- tools should not have to manage all the intermediate
  interactions with the user which go into composing a
  command,
- different tools should be able to share the screen and
  input devices,
- the use of alphanumeric interactions as well as mixed
  text and diagrams should be supported where possible.

3.3.1 General principles. All the services offered by the
user interface are based on multi-windowing, which makes it
possible to display simultaneously several sources of information.
A system of menus provides for a simple choice of commands by means of the pointing device. Basic editing allows

the selection of zones on the screen, their reproduction, relocation, or deletion, by means of the pointing device. The combination of these mechanisms helps in the construction of project support environments in which the tool activation mode will be consistent and uniform.

The user interface has also been designed so as to provide tool developers with easy access to all of the PCTE functionalities, and to offer them mechanisms facilitating tool developement (editing assistance and menu management, for example).

Use is of course made of the dimensions and the high resolution of the workstation screen by providing, in addition to the textual display of large volumes of information, for the representation and manipulation of data in graphic formats.

3.3.2 Mechanisms. The User Interface offers functionalities which adapt themselves to the degree of complexity of the tools whilst ensuring the consistency and uniformity of the dialogue between user and tool. Its mechanisms tend towards separating the applications and the actual display of the screen. For this reason, the applications are provided with frames which they use according to their needs in their display operations.

The user can view all or part of what is present in these frames in windows that he manipulates on his screen. Several windows can be simultaneously opened for different applications. These windows can be copied, moved, extended, or reduced ; they can also be changed to symbolic drawings, called "icons", which remind the user of their existence without occupying too much space on the screen.

In order to make possible this separate management of the screen and the applications, the user interface is organised in two layers :
- the user agent is the central part of the user interface. It receives the events originating from the keyboard and pointing device, manages windows, and coordinates basic editing ;
- the application agents manage the applications input/ output by means of virtual terminals. They also reply to user agent requests with respect to display formatting or user input processing. Of course an application can act as its own "application agent".

In order to simplify the development of tools, the EMERAUDE implementation of PCTE offers a Standard Virtual Terminal which can operate in various modes, including :
- a mode compatible with the input/output that a tool can perform on an alphanumeric terminal,
- a mode providing for the display of data entry forms, designed to permit an easy interaction between the user and tools, and the display of graphic or multi-font text zones.

3.3.3 Command Language. The menu, and selection-based command mode is the preferred command mode. However, it is not sufficient. It is also necessary to have a command language. For the compatibility and portability already mentioned, the

command language is the standard UNIX SHELL, to which some
functionalities have been added to provide for :
- the respect of the syntax of the access paths leading
  to OMS objects,
- the specific PCTE interface function calls.
The objects formed by the user interface are windows,
icons, characters, strings, graphical elements, etc. The
basic interaction mode is represented by first selecting an
object and second performing an operation on the selected
object. For instance, the user may select any object currently visible in any window on the screen, specify the
destination (which does not have to be the same window) and
issue the generic copy-command. The User Interface generates
information about the type of the selection and hence it is
able to determine which specific actions are required to
perform the generic copy.

4   CONCLUSION

   In the industrial information technology community there
is a need for standardisation in the underlying framework of
software engineering or project support environments. The
Esprit PCTE project proposes a set of interfaces to make the
basis for a Public Common Tool Interface. This interface is
being implemented, and one implementation called Emeraude
will be available at the end of this year.
   The interfaces defined by PCTE include basic mechanisms
that revolve around an Object Management System and UNIX
System V compatible execution and communication mechanisms,
with transparent distribution facilities over LAN providing
distributed processing using a Remote Procedure Call protocol and supporting a distributed object base, and a tool-
user interface based on modern multi-windowing text and
graphics facilities.
   Other projects are already in progress, or scheduled to
start soon to construct particular software engineering
environments and integrated project support environments
based on the proposed PCTE Public Common Tool Interface,
and to provide the Emeraude PCTE implementation on a set of
different machines.
   The tool results of European research and development
programmes will be integrated on the basis of the PCTE
interfaces : this is already true of the Esprit programme,
the French national programme and certain results of the
Alvey programme. Analysis of the opportunity to use PCTE as
a basis from which to start in the construction of a Common
APSE Interface Set is in progress.
   The PCTE proposal, for the above mentioned reasons, is
a valuable basis for the definition of a Public Common Tool
Interface for Software Engineering Environments.

   (Much of this paper has already appeared in the proceedings of the 1985 Esprit Technical Week where the authors
were the PCTE project team.)

Chapter 5

An object-based file system for large scale applications

S. Crawley

Abstract.

This paper describes the **entity system**: a model for an object oriented file system. The main aim of the entity system is to extend abstract data typing to the level of the filing system. A key feature of the model is support for the independent evolution of data objects and the programs that use them. The entity system achieves this by separating the abstract type of an object from its implementation, and by providing a dynamic type coercion mechanism. The ultimate result will be a base system which supports the initial development and continued evolution of large software systems with complex persistent data requirements.

1. Introduction.

An important problem area in computer applications with complex data requirements is the trade-off between short and long-term data storage. Conventional programming languages typically support only the simplest of long-term data types. If something more complex is needed, the application is expected to translate data between strongly typed short-term and typeless long-term forms. Hand written translation code is conceptually unsafe, as well as being tedious and messy to implement. Standard access methods provided as runtime libraries can help to remove some of the tedium. Unfortunately, access methods are not usually type-safe either. Another problem is that as an application evolves, it often becomes necessary to change the layout of the stored data. In general, the only option available is a costly and time consuming data conversion process. At the same time all related application programs need to be updated.

Database systems and related languages guarantee the long term type-safety of stored data and allow the application program to access such data safely and efficiently. Many database systems address the problem of data evolution using schema and sub-schema (CODASYL (1)) or similar mechanisms (Date (2)). However, the data models supported by database systems are generally too limited for handling complex data structures such as a program parse tree.

Implementations of languages such as Smalltalk-80 (Goldberg (3)) have mechanisms for checkpointing and restoring a program's state, effectively making all data items long-term. Despite its conceptual simplicity, check-pointing is unsuitable as a general storage mechanism for many reasons. It is often difficult to avoid checkpointing temporary data objects along with data that really needs to be saved. Small updates can incur an overhead out of all proportion to the size of the change. Finally checkpointing is unsuitable when the data will not fit into a program's address space, when concurrent access is required, or when the data is used by more than one program.

Persistent programming techniques seem to offer the best prospects for solving the problems of long-term management of complex data. Persistence support can be added to existing programming languages either as a runtime library (Herlihy and Liskov (4) and Smith (5)) or as a generalisation of the language's type system (Atkinson et al (6)). Typically a persistence manager uses runtime type information to traverse the application's data structures in primary memory and convert them into a location independent form that can be saved on disc.

Existing examples of persistent programming tend to have problems with reliability and concurrent access. Changes in data layout are not usually catered for. A reason for these problems is that the persistence and atomicity mechanisms provided are global in scope and do not provide the programmer with the fine grained control. Another reason is that the relevent persistent type systems take an explicitly or implicitly representational view of data types rather than an abstract or object-oriented view.

The entity system model provides a different approach to persistent programming. Rather than providing representational persistence for an existing type system, the model provides a method for defining abstract data types outside of application programs. The implementation of an abstract type has full control over the persistence, atomicity and concurrency properties of data objects. An application program does not depend in any way on how the abstractions are represented. A dynamic type coercion mechanism helps to overcome problems arising from changes to abstract types. It also gives the entity type system a degree of polymorphism. Taken together, the features of the entity system model provide a solution the data evolution problem.

2. Active and Passive Entities.

An **entity** is an abstract data object in the entity system. An **entity** is characterized by three components; the class, implementation and representation. Every entity has an existence that is independent of the programs that use it. Entities are usually long-term objects though this is not always the case.

The **class** of an entity is the entity's abstract data type. Thus an entity may be thought of as an instance of a particular class. An entity's class defines the set of **operations** that could be applied to an entity by a client program. A class defines the operations applicable to all entities of that class in terms of the names and types of its formal arguments and results. Ideally, the definition will include a formal (though not necessarily complete) specification of the semantics of an entity and the operations it supports. The specification might well include the entity's concurrency properties, timing characteristics and behaviour in the event of a hardware failure. In practice, the semantic specification of a class is necessarily limited to an informal description.

An **implementation** is the type manager for one or more entities. Each implementation provides a set of **operation procedures** which carry out the operations defined by the class. The implementation encapsulates both the layout of the data that represents an entity and the algorithms that are used to perform the operations. There may be any number of implementations for a given class, using different data layouts and different algorithms for managing the data and having different properties within the scope of the class definition. However, the entity system ensures that a client does not need to be aware that a given pair of entities of the same class may have different implementations. This means that the programmer can write a new implementation for a class and introduce it without changing or even recompiling any client programs.

The **representation** of an entity is the collection of data items which make up the entity's state. The representation is managed by the implementation, and is only accessible by means of the operation procedures. An entity's representation normally consists of a transient part known as an **entity activation** which only lasts while a client is actively using the entity, and a persistent part which is held in long-term storage. The persistent part of the representation will be omitted when the entity is defined to be inherently transient.

The persistent part of an entity's representation is typically stored using a storage object. A **storage object** is simply an entity whose purpose is to store the representation of data. Different classes of storage objects can be defined to satisfy a variety of needs. Some will be analogous to conventional access methods. Others will provide more conventional persistence or database management. The programmer can select the class of storage object most appropriate to the needs of the entity implementation being written, taking into account the trade-offs between ease of programming, efficiency and reliability. An implementation could well use one storage object to store the representations of a number of entities.

Entities can exist in two possible states: active and passive. An entity in the **passive** form resides entirely on long-term storage. It is known to clients by a long-term, essentially typeless **entity identifier**. All identifiers for an entity are bound to a **triple** giving the identifiers for the entity's class, implementation and persistent representation. The only operation that a client can invoke on a passive entity is the **Open** operation which **activates** the entity.

An **active** entity, which has both transient and persistent parts to its representation, allows a client to invoke entity operations. It is known to clients by a short-term typed **handle** which can be considered as a capability to apply operations to the corresponding entity. In addition, a handle can carry additional state such as the current position pointer for a file. Each class defines its own entity handle type, and defines the entity operations in terms of this type. When a client has finished, it calls the entity's **Close** operation to destroy the handle and possibly **passivate** the entity.

The concepts outlined above can be illustrated by a simple example. In figure 1 we see the identifiers and triples for three passive entities **X**, **Y** and **Z** of class **C**. Entities **X** and **Y** have the same implementation **I**, while **Z** has a different implementation **J**. The implementation **I** uses a storage object of class **S-C** to hold the persistent representation of each entity. Thus the representation id slots of **X** and **Y**'s triples contain identifiers for storage objects **S1** and **S2**. In contrast, implementation **J** uses some other method of holding the **Z** entity's representation, and puts a private tag value in the representation id slot.

In figure 2 we see two clients **A** and **B** using entities **X**, **Y** and **Z**. Client **A** can invoke operations on entities **X** and **Y** using handles 1 and 2 respectively. Likewise, client **B** is refers to entities **Y** and **Z** using handles 3 and 4. Note that there are two handles (2 and 3) for the entity **Y**. If clients **A** and **B** are separate processes, they both apply operations to the entity simultaneously. The class **C** may well prevent handles with read and write access from existing simultaneously. At any rate, the implementation is responsible for the synchronisation

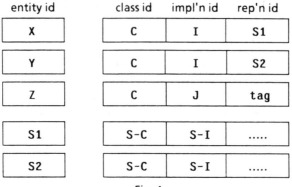

Fig. 1

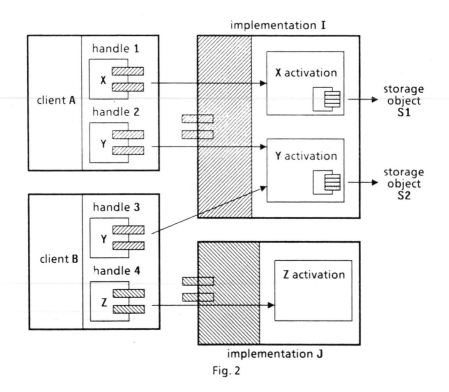

implementation J

Fig. 2

of concurrent operations.   To simplify matters for the implementation, the entity system ensures that there is never more than one activation for any entity.

Ideally, all class definition, implementations and entity clients would be written in a purpose designed object-based programming language.   In practice, the effort invested in existing programming languages makes it unlikely that such a system would gain acceptance.

Therefore, the entity system model takes a more pragmatic approach. Client programs and entity implementations are written in an existing **target** programming language. While classes can be defined in the target language, this makes class definition both tedious and prone to error. It is better to write class definitions in a concise **Class Definition Language** (CDL). CDL definitions can then be translated into source modules or macros for the target language then compiled in the normal way. If the associated problems of cross-language type compatibility can be solved, clients and implementations could well be written in a variety of target languages.

3. Entity Operations.

A client interacts with an active entity by invoking operations on a handle. The class associated with an entity handle defines the set of operations that can be applied. The operations defined by a class fall into two groups. **Class specific** operations have semantics which are meaningful only for entities of that class. Most entity operations fall into this category. In addition, a class defines 2 or 3 **generic** operations.

Let us assume that the CDL definition for class C includes the following declaration for a class specific entity operation:

```
C.op:  OPERATION [arg₁: atype₁, ... argₘ: atypeₘ]
       RETURNS [res₁: rtype₁, ... resₙ: rtypeₙ];
```

If the target language is object-oriented such as CLU (Liskov et al (7)), this definition can be translated into a declaration of an object type **C**. An invocation of the **op** operation might then look like:

```
handle: C
...
r₁, ... rₙ := handle$op(a₁, ... aₘ)
```

If the target language is not object-oriented, the class definition would be translated into an explicit declaration for a handle type and a series of operation procedures. In Mesa (Xerox (8)) for example, the class definition would be translated as a **DEFINITIONS** module **C** exporting the type **Handle-Type** and a set of operation procedures. An invocation of **op** would look something like:

```
handle: C.HandleType;
...
[r₁, ... rₙ] ← C.Op[handle, a₁, ... aₘ];
```

In Modula-2 (Wirth (9)) a procedure can only return one result, so the invocation would need to be expressed in the form:

```
handle: C.HandleType;
...
r₁ := C.Op(handle, a₁, ... aₘ, r₂, ... rₙ);
```

where r_2 through r_n are **VAR** arguments. In all cases, the target language compiler can statically check the types of the handle, the arguments and the results of the invocation.

The real work of an invocation is performed by an operation procedure provided by the implementation. Part of each entity handle is a class specific record structure known as an **operations table**. For each operation defined by the class, a field in the operations table holds a reference for the appropriate implementation procedure. When an operation is invoked, the implementation procedure is taken from the handle's operations table and is called with the client's arguments. The level of indirection provided by the operations table insulates the client from needing to know about the implementation. The translation of class C into Mesa would include the following declarations for the handle type and the stub procedure for op:

```
HandleType: TYPE = LONG POINTER TO RECORD [
    ...
    opProc:   PROCEDURE [handle: HandleType,
                         arg₁: atype₁, ...
                         argₘ: atypeₘ]
              RETURNS [res₁: rtype₁, ...
                         resₙ: rtypeₙ],
    ...
    ];

...
Op: PROCEDURE [handle: HandleType,
              arg₁: atype₁, ... argₘ: atypeₘ]
    RETURNS [res₁: rtype₁, ... resₙ: rtypeₙ] =
    BEGIN
    RETURN [handle↑.opProc[handle,
                         arg₁, ... argₘ]];
    END;
```

At first sight, operations on more than one entity appear to present a problem. In object-based languages like CLU and Simula-67, all abstract objects of a given type have similar concrete representations making it easy to implement non-monadic operations. In the entity system, each of the operands of a non-monadic operation may have a different implementation. The answer is to implement such operations using other monadic operations in one of two ways. The operation can be expressed asymmetrically. For example, **handle DyOp handle2** can be expressed as follows:

```
C.DyOp: OPERATION [handle2: HandleType,
                  arg₁: atype₁, ... argₘ: atypeₘ]
        RETURNS [res₁: rtype₁, ... resₙ: rtypeₙ];
```

This can be implemented as an operation on **handle** which invokes operations on **handle2** in the normal way. The alternative to define the operation symmetrically and arrange that it can be implemented entirely in terms of lower level operations on the handle arguments. Such an operation would be independent of the representation of the entity operands, and would only need to be implemented once.

The three generic operations defined by a typical class are **Open, Close** and **Create**. Though these operations have the same function for all classes, they take arguments whose types are class specific. Create and Open are unlike other entity operations in that they are not applied to entity handles. Unlike class specific operations, the generic operations all require the assistance of the **kernel** of entity system.

A **Create** operation allocates and initialises a new entity. The entity system kernel selects the implementation for the entity, and if necessary dynamically loads and initialises the implementation code. Then the kernel calls the implementation passing the class specific create arguments. The implementation typically allocates storage objects and initialises the persistent representation according to the class specific arguments. Finally a triple is assembled and bound to a new entity identifier and the identifier is returned to the client. A client program written in Mesa might invoke class **C**'s create operation with a procedure call of the form:

```
entityId: Id;
...
entityId ← C.Create[implSelection, arg₁, ... argₘ];
```

ImplSelection is a data structure which gives either an explicit implementation id or a search expression which the kernel uses in selecting the appropriate entity implementation.

An **Open** operation activates an entity and assembles a handle for it. The client invokes an open operation passing an entity identifier and some class specific arguments. The latter specify such things as the access that the client requires, and the way that the client wants to use the entity. The kernel type-checks the entity by comparing the class identifier in the triple against the class id implied by the open operation. Next it finds the implementation using the implementation id in the triple, and if necessary loads and initialises it. The kernel then searches for an activation for the entity. If it cannot find one the implementation is called to activate the entity. Finally the implementation is called with the class specific open arguments. It will check the client's access, reserve any necessary resources and build the handle for the client. A program written in Mesa might invoke class **C**'s open operation with a procedure call of the following form:

```
handle: C.HandleType;
...
handle ← C.Open[entityId, arg₁, ... argₘ];
```

A **Close** operation frees an entity handle and passivates the entity if appropriate. The client invokes the close operation with arguments specific to the class. First the implementation is called to dismantle the handle and complete any outstanding work on behalf of the client. The close arguments may well tell the implementation what to do with half completed transactions. The kernel then checks to see if there are any other handles for the entity. If not, the implementation is called to passivate the entity. A client program written in Mesa might invoke class **C**'s close operation with a procedure call of the following form:

```
handle: C.HandleType;
...
C.Close[handle, arg₁, ... argₘ];
```

The stub procedures for the generic operations in a particular target language depend too much on the host environment to be described in detail here. The same also applies for the interface between an implementation and the kernel that is used, for example, to initiate the activation and passivation of entities. Unlike the class specific operations, the stub procedures for generic operations require the use of loopholes in the target language's type system. However, assuming that the translation of definitions from CDL to target language is done automatically, the use of loopholes is conceptually type-safe.

In the entity system model, entities are generally removed by garbage collection rather than by explicit deletion.   At some time after an entity becomes inaccessible (ie when there are no handles for the entity and no copies of the entity's identifiers can be reached by potential clients), the garbage collector calls the entity's implementation to delete the object.   The implementation releases the entity's representation and removes any links with the rest of the file system and finally destroys the entity triple.   A client can hasten deletion by calling the kernel to explicitly invalidate an entity identifier. If all of its identifiers have been invalidated and no handles for it exist, an entity can be deleted without garbage collection.

4. Projection.

Many problems arise when a type system is extended beyond the execution of a single program.   By using abstract data typing and arranging that an entity and its clients are decoupled, the basic entity system model avoids some of these problems.   Unfortunately the model as described above has a couple of important short-comings.

While the basic entity system model allows the programmer to introduce a replacement implementation without trouble, changing a class is more difficult.   If a class definition is altered in a way that is incompatible with any existing entity implementation or client, this must be done by creating a new class with a new class identifier.   No existing entities will be type compatible with clients which use the new class and vice versa.

A second short-coming of the basic model is that it makes no provision for utilities which manipulate entities of a number of different classes.   Each class needs its own suite of utilities, or general purpose utilities must deal with each class as a separate case.   What this demonstrates is that the entity system's type system needs support for type polymorphism.

In fact, the entity system model also provides a scheme known as **projection** for getting around type incompatibility.   When the client opens an entity, it is making the statement that it wishes to view the entity as having a particular class.   This class (ie. the class which provides the open operation) we will call the client's **perspective class**. The entity itself has a class (corresponding to the class identifier in the triple) which we will call the **actual class**.   If the perspective and actual classes differ, an attempt is made to **resolve** the entity in terms of the perspective class.   If **projection resolution** succeeds, the client is given an entity handle of the perspective type which allows it to invoke operations on the entity in terms of the perspective class.

Projection resolution is carried out by **resolution functions** called from the kernel.   A resolution function is called, passing the entity id and the client's open arguments.   If the function succeeds in building a viable handle for the entity, this handle is returned to the client.   Otherwise the kernel proceeds to call the next possible resolution function.   The number of possible resolution functions is finite and hopefully small.   If the kernel tries them all without success, the client is informed that the open operation has failed.   This form of open failure is conceptually equivalent to a runtime type error.

The aim of a resolution function is to build a handle of the type defined by the perspective class which will map perspective operations onto operations on the real entity.   In order to do this a function will usually start by opening the entity to obtain a handle.   Then it can use a combination of the following techniques to build the perspective handle for the client.

• Insertion of operation procedures provided by the implementation into the operation table of the handle being constructed. This technique can be used when the only difference between a pair of operations in the perspective and actual classes is in their names.

• Interpretation of the (perspective) open arguments provided the client. For example, if a resolution function is only capable of producing a handle allowing read-only access to the actual entity, it will check that the open arguments do not specify read-write access.

• Invocation of entity operations to extract information or initialise handle state during the resolution process.

• Insertion of local procedures defined by the resolution function into the operation table being constructed. This technique gives projection its real power and flexibility. A simple procedure can be used to make a minor transformation to the arguments or results of a perspective operation. More complex procedures can simulate an operation that is missing from the actual class or perform a major transformation of the actual entity.

• Use of a **projection activation** for storing transient information. A projection activation serves a purpose similar to that of a normal entity activation. For example, it can hold the handle for the actual entity that is used by a substituted local operation procedure.

• Multi-stage resolution. When a resolution opens the underlying entity, it can itself use a perspective that is different from the entity's actual class. This would result in the resolution process being applied recursively.

A number of experiments have been performed using an early version of the entity system in order to explore possible uses for projection. For example, projection has been used as the basis of a perspective for displaying arbitrary entities in a textual form. Projection has also been used to navigate a path to an object held in a directory system. These experiments lead the author to believe that projection is considerably more than just a type coercion scheme.

There are two serious difficulties with the projection scheme. The first is that, while automatic generation is feasible in simple cases, it is generally necessary to hand code large parts of each resolution function. A single resolution function is normally capable of resolving projections for just one combination of perspective and actual classes. If there are N classes, order N2 different resolution functions might be needed in theory. In practice the majority of combinations of perspective and actual class will be nonsensical. Multi-stage projection resolution can also help to keep the number of resolution functions manageable.

The second difficulty is that projection gives the entity type system some rather undesirable properties. For a start, the compatibility of a given client / entity combination will vary as new resolution functions are registered and old ones deleted from the system. What is worse is that there can be situations where there is more than one way of resolving a projection with each way giving an entity handle with different semantics. Given the strategy of trying resolution functions until one succeeds, the semantics of the handle given to the client can depend on the order in which functions are tried. This is not really acceptable. One way of improving the situation is to allow the client to alter the order in which the functions are tried. Another way is provide an extra argument for every open operation so that the client can tell the resolution functions which alternative to choose.

5. Data Security and Access Control.

If the entity system model is to be used for valuable or sensitive data, the issues of data security and access control become important. In the entity system (as with most other systems) a high degree of security and protection against unauthorised access is only possible if each client and implementation's address space is protected against unwanted access by others. The ideal architecture for a secure entity system would be based on hardware supported fine-grained capabilities.

In practice, the security firewalls are likely to be based on conventional memory mapping and protection hardware, or on running clients and implementations on separate machines in a distributed system. Such firewalls add to the problems of implementing an entity system. The model assumes that it is cheap for a client to call an implementation procedure. These forms of firewalls add the overheads of address space switching or network communication, and of copying arguments and results back and forth. It becomes difficult to pass procedure variables and pointers as operation arguments and results. Distribution adds the problems of recovery from network errors or host failure, and of keeping track of things like entity activations. All in all, it is better if we can allow implementations and clients to occupy the same address space.

There is more to data security than guarding against random overwriting. A robust entity implementation needs to make sure that a machine crash leaves open entities in a tidy, well defined state. This requirement may well affect the programmer's choice of storage object class. An implementation also needs to be able to recover when a client leaves entity handles open. To prevent problems with entities being locked indefinitely, the kernel must keep track of all active handles. Then, when a client crashes or exits without closing its handles, the kernel can call the appropriate implementations telling them to **Abort** the handles.

Some sort of access control is highly desirable even in a system where all the users are honest. Access control schemes in most conventional operating systems work in the following way. The directory manager checks the client's requirements against its entitlement to access a file. If the directory manager is satisfied, it issues a handle for the object with the appropriate rights. This on the directory manager being trustworthy and to a lesser extent on the handles it issues being short-term and non-transferable.

Schemes of this nature are awkward from the point of view of the entity system model. A client cannot be given an identifier as this would allow it to open the entity with whatever access it wanted. Instead, any entity analogous to a directory would have to invoke the appropriate entity open operation on behalf of its clients. Every class of entity that might be held in a directory has its own **open** operation taking different open arguments. In most target languages, the only option is to have each class provide a special version of the open operation that can be invoked by a directory entity without needing to know about the class specific arguments.

Given the nature of the entity system model, an access control scheme based on **capabilities** is the most natural. An entity identifier can be thought of as a long-term capability allowing a client to open the entity. (An entity handle may similarly be thought of as a short-term capability to invoke operations.) The representation of an identifier includes a long random component making it practically impossible to guess.

Bound to each entity identifier is a set of bits which determines the access that a client can ask for when opening the entity. The entity system kernel provides services for **sealing** an identifier for a new entity, and for **refining** an existing identifier to give a new identifier with a subset of the rights. Thus a client can be given an entity identifier without giving away all rights. Finally the holder of an identifier may **invalidate** it at any time, stopping other clients from using it or its refinements.

If an entity system is to be secure, it is also necessary to consider the problem of **trojan horses**. Unlike a conventional operating system, there is nothing to stop a malicious user from writing a bogus implementation or resolution function for a class that is responsible managing priviledged information and using it to steal information. To prevent this from being a security problem, the entity system needs to make sure that the registers of implementations and resolution functions are well protected, at least as far as the critical classes are concerned. It also needs to provide a service for checking that the implementation associated with a given handle can be trusted.

6. Implementations of the Entity System Model.

To date there have been two implementations of the entity system. An experimental version was written in Modula-2 and ran within a single UNIX process. This system was used to try out various versions of the model, and later on, to experiment with the projection mechanism. By the time development stopped a simple command environment had been built with a user file system and a number of utilities. We were even able to dynamically load and run a modified version of the Modula-2 compiler that used the entity system as a file system.

A new version of the entity system which runs in the Xerox Development Environment on a Xerox 8010 workstation is currently under active development. This version implements the model described in this paper including a capability-based access control system. A variety of storage object classes have been implemented, along with a number of classes for representing such things as implementations and resolution functions and their associated mapping tables. The immediate goal is to implement a simple CDL and the tools needed to generate Mesa source code stubs. The system is also being used for some small scale programming environment projects by the author's colleagues.

In the longer term, there are plans to use the XDE entity system as the basis of a program editing and compilation system. The idea is to have all of the tools including the editor operate on programs stored as decorated parse trees rather source text. Projection would be used for mapping the parse trees for editing, and possibly for code generation. This approach could have considerable benefits both in terms of compiler efficiency and the functionality of the system. It could also simplify the development of other tools such as source level debuggers, configuration managers and revision control systems.

References.

1.   CODASYL DBTG, 1971, 'CODASYL Data Base Task Group', Conference on Data Systems and Languages Proceedings, ACM.

2.   Date, C. J., 1984, 'A Guide to DB2', Addison-Wesley, Reading, MA., USA.

3.   Goldberg, A., 1984, 'Smalltalk-80: The Interactive Programming Environment', Addison-Wesley, Reading, MA., USA.

4.   Herlihy, M. and Liskov, B. 1981, 'A Value Transmission Method for Abstract Data Types', Laboratory of Computer Science, MIT., MA., USA.

5.   Smith, L.D., 1984, 'The Management of Persistent Data in Modula-2', VLSIC Design Aids Group, Acorn Computers UK Ltd, Cambridge, UK.

6.   Atkinson, M.P, 1984, 'PS-algol Reference Manual', Report PPR-4-83, University of Edinburgh, UK.

7.   Liskov, B., et al, 1981, 'CLU Reference Manual', Springer-Verlag, Berlin, Germany.

8.   Xerox, 1981, 'Mesa Language Manual', XDE3.0-3001, Office Systems Division, Xerox Corporation, Palo Alto, CA., USA.

9.   Wirth, N., 1980, 'Modula-2', Intitut für Informatik, Eidgenössische Technische Hochschule, Zurich, Switzerland.

Chapter 6

Total system design in Ipses

G.S. Blair, R. Lea, J.A. Mariani, J.R. Nicol and C. Wylie

1. INTRODUCTION

Recent years have seen increasing interest in the area of Program Support Environments (PSEs). The work was perhaps given its impetus (or at least crystallised) by the appearance of the STONEMAN document (Stoneman (1)) which listed the requirements for an Ada PSE (APSE). It is commendable that the Ada group identified the critical need for such a system. The British Alvey computing research initiative in the area of Software Engineering also includes the production of a major Integrated Project Support Environment (IPSE).

It seems certain to us that such Integrated Project Support Environments (IPSE's) will be increasingly based on distributed computer systems. It is now more cost effective to design a system with a configuration of a number of workstations interconnected by a local area network (Hutchison (2)).

The bulk of IPSE development to date has been targeted towards higher-level issues within the IPSE application itself. There has been little emphasis placed on the supporting sub-structure for an IPSE. We believe it is of the utmost importance that attention be given to the support required for an IPSE. This is especially important if the IPSE is to operate in a distributed environment.

In this paper, we are interested in sub-structures for a distributed IPSE. In particular, we consider the requirements for an operating system kernel to support a distributed IPSE.

2. OPERATING SYSTEM SUPPORT FOR DISTRIBUTED IPSE'S

Some design experience has accumulated from early attempts to build distributed systems and IPSE's. Most frequently, existing operating systems have functionality added by introducing new layers of software. These systems, despite having enjoyed some degree of success, have yielded an important lesson: contemporary operating systems do not provide an appropriate platform on which to base the design of either distributed systems or IPSE's. The reasons for this are presented in the next two sub-sections.

2.1.   Operating Systems and Distribution

Because most contemporary operating systems were developed prior to the advent of distributed computing, they provide little or no support for local area networking. The first distributed system designs commonly featured the implementation of a distributed layer on top of a contemporary operating system. This approach proves unsatisfactory for a number of reasons:

*   the autonomy of the local operating systems conflicts with the need to manage resources on a global basis,

*   the overhead due to excessive layering, and the implementation of new functionality at the wrong level of the system, leads to poor performance, and

*   functionality is constrained by the respective structures of the host operating systems.

It is our contention that to exploit fully the potential benefits offered by LANs, distributed operating systems must be designed from first principles. An important part of their design will be to incorporate the LAN as an integral part of the system - not as an additional service.

We have had some experience of trying to extend an existing operating system (UNIX) to a distributed environment (Blair (3), Blair (4)). This work confirmed in practice the problems outlined above and provided the initial stimulus to look at operating system support for distribution.

2.2.   Operating Systems and IPSE's

Recent attempts to implement IPSE functions, e.g. Aspect (Hitchcock et al (5)) and Eclipse (Alderson et al (6)) have also tended to layer functionality on top of existing operating systems. We argue that this approach is ultimately unsatisfactory for a number of reasons, e.g. operating system filestores do not lend themselves to supporting the sophisticated functionality expected of an IPSE, performance is unlikely to be satisfactory, and problems could be caused if users are able to circumvent the facilities.

As an illustration, consider the UNIX operating system (Ritchie and Thompson (7)). UNIX was designed and implemented before the interest in IPSE's. It is therefore a perfect example of a system which requires further layers to implement an IPSE. It is instructive to reflect on the problems that have been encountered in this task. A good example of adding an IPSE function to UNIX is the version control scheme offered in many releases of the system.

SCCS (Source Code Control System) provides a project with control over files in two ways. First, the differences between the versions of all files under SCCS control are stored as 'deltas'; new versions of an file can be obtained by applying desired deltas to the original version of the file. Second, SCCS provides a primitive locking facility to ensure that only one writable version of an file exists at any given time - this overcomes the serious omission of file locking in UNIX.

Despite these benefits, SCCS must still be controlled manually: programmers are responsible for deciding which files to place under SCCS control, deciding when to make deltas, and for keeping track of which versions are which etc. In short, because the SCCS tool has been added on to UNIX to provide a mechanism for file control, the responsibility for using the tool correctly and efficiently lies with human programmers, and not the system.

In summary, SCCS functions well when all users conform to its protocols, but there is no way of enforcing this; if one user breaks ranks then chaos can result.

Similar comments could be made about the limited configuration control scheme in UNIX (Feldman (8)).

A more general IPSE, providing a full set of IPSE functions through an integrated set of tools, would pose even greater problems. Most proposals for more general IPSE's require that a database be layered on top of the existing operating system. The inclusion of a central database was one of the major requirements listed in the STONEMAN document. The rationale for a central database (Buxton and Druffel (9)) can be summarised as follows:-

*   it acts as a repository for information gathered and generated by the use of the system, and

*   it provides means of co-ordination and communication between tools.

It is now well recognised, however, that most operating systems provide very poor support for implementing a database (Stonebraker (10)). This often leads to databases which are very inefficient and lacking in functionality.

3. TOTAL SYSTEM DESIGN

We believe that a common solution to both aspects of operating system design, lies in the concept of total system design. By total system design we mean that all levels of the system are designed specifically for a target environment and not merely to provide general, higher level abstract machines. By employing a total system design approach, we are essentially adopting a more top-down design strategy.

We are particularly interested in the application of
the total system design approach at the kernel level of the
operating system.

With respect to distribution, total system design
implies that the kernel should be <u>tailored</u> to operate in a
local area networking environment. The lowest levels in the
system are then aware that the system is distributed. We
believe that the kernel should be responsible for handling
distribution and that above this level the distribution
should be completely transparent.

With respect to IPSE's, total system design led us to
the decision to include a database in the kernel of the
operating system.

We believe that attempts to provide IPSE database
facilities through normal filing systems will lead to major
problems and that the only way to improve performance and
functionality of an IPSE is to provide a database as a fundamental component in the system.

Applying these notions, we have developed a kernel
model, derived from the object model, which provides a <u>uni-
fied</u> solution to many of the problems found in both distributed computing and programming environments. This model is
fundamental to our work and is explained in some detail in
the next section.

4.   THE COSMOS MODEL

The Cosmos model is greatly influenced by the object
model as described by Jones (11). More specifically, our
model provides a single abstraction called an object†.

An object is generally defined by:-

*   its type

*   the operations permitted on it - this is determined by
     the type of the object

*   the access rights and/or restrictions associated with
     the object

*   its attributes

*   the underlying object itself.

_____

† We do not intend to implement the object model in its
most general form. New objects cannot be layered hierarchi-
cally above the kernel; the object model is merely being
used as a structuring technique within the kernel.

The attributes of an object effectively provide additional semantic information pertaining to that object. Consequently, we can regard the object model as providing a
simple database of objects.

4.1. A Semantic Network of Objects

The object model records semantic information about
objects but no information pertaining to the relationships
between objects. We have therefore extended the basic
object model to provide a more sophisticated database. The
attributes of an object can include inter-relationships
between objects; this makes our database very similar to a
semantic network (Winston (12)).

Each node in our semantic network contains all the
information pertaining to a particular object. The structure
of this information is defined by a frame. Different frame
templates exist for each distinct object type. When a new
object is created, a node is added to the network, the new
node being an instantiation of the appropriate frame.

4.2. Immutability of Objects

An important property of objects in our system is that
the contents of an object cannot be changed, i.e. objects
are immutable. Instead of updating objects, new objects are
created from old objects by a series of operations (a
transformation); the old objects remain as before. Transformations are guaranteed to be atomic: either all the operations in a transformation are performed or none of them are.
Immutability has several major benefits and has been adopted
in recent projects (Tanenbaum and Mullender (13), Lampson
(14)).

4.3. Types of Objects

In Cosmos, it is assumed that a small and fairly stable
set of types will be defined. These can vary from one
implementation to the next. As an illustration, the types
provided in the pilot implementation are briefly described.

Files provide the basic mechanism for permanent information storage in the system. Files can contain text, segments of program, semi-compiled code, etc.

The basis for a naming policy is provided by catalogues. Catalogues maintain a mapping from arbitrary textual
names to internal names for objects.

Manipulation of objects is performed by objects of type
tool. Basically, a tool is an executable program. Tools,
however, remain passive until they are invoked.

A tool invocation requires another object of type virtual processor. A virtual processor is an abstraction of a
physical processor, many virtual processors being mapped on

to a single physical processor. A tool invocation is then
the execution of a tool on a virtual processor.

A further object of type byte stream provides a mechanism for two tools to communicate. A byte stream is a one-
way, buffered communication path between tools.

Other objects in the pilot implementation will include
various devices, e.g. printers and terminals.

5. ASSESSMENT OF MODEL

The model is particularly well-suited to our project as
it provides excellent support for an IPSE and it is ideal
for a distributed environment. This is not an accident: it
is a direct result of our total system design philosophy.
In the following sections, we describe briefly why the model
is so well-suited for distribution and for supporting an
IPSE.

5.1. Support for Distribution

The Cosmos model handles networking gracefully. There
are several reasons for this; these are listed below:

*   Techniques for extending the object model to work in a
     distributed environment are well understood. Remote
     procedure calls (Nelson (15)) provide a simple mechan-
     ism for performing remote operations on objects.
     Furthermore, there is some evidence that this technique
     can be made very efficient (Spector (16)).

*   Using remote procedure calls, operations on all objects
     (whether local or remote) can be made to look like
     ordinary procedure calls. Hence, distribution can be
     made transparent at a very low level in the system.

*   Nodes with widely different characteristics can readily
     be accommodated by describing a node as the set of
     objects (and attributes) it makes available to the net-
     work. For example, a terminal concentrator would be a
     node providing only objects of type terminal, a per-
     sonal workstation may not make any objects available to
     the network but could use the various services pro-
     vided, another node could provide a large range of ser-
     vices such as processing, file storage and printing.

*   Immutability of objects has important repercussions for
     distributed computing. We have investigated the pro-
     perties of immutable objects and have discovered that
     problems of consistency and concurrency control in a
     distributed system are greatly simplified (Blair et al
     (17)). One major problem in distributed computing is
     maintaining consistency of replicated copies of an
     object (mutual consistency). It is important to sup-
     port replication in a distributed system in order that
     important objects can survive node failure. Algorithms

for mutable environments tend to be very complex and in many cases incomplete. We have devised an algorithm for maintaining mutual consistency of replicated, immutable objects which is considerably simpler than the mutable counterparts (Nicol et al (18)).

5.2. Support for IPSE's

The use of the Cosmos database, which contains semantic information about individual objects and their inter-relationships, will offer support for several key functions of an IPSE. Furthermore, because the database will be built into the kernel as an integral component of the system, attempts to access objects illegally by circumventing the database will be impossible.

The support that the Cosmos model provides for IPSE functions is best illustrated by example. The following sections demonstrate how the model supports important IPSE functions such as semantic checking, version control and configuration control.

5.2.1. Semantic checking.
Using the Cosmos database, it is possible to check the semantics of all operations performed in the system. We concentrate on one particular example of semantic checking: typing.

The subject of typing has received much attention in relation to programming languages. In contrast, however, there has been little work carried out on typing in operating systems. Essentially, typing is a means of checking the validity of operations in a particular context. It provides a form of protection against actions which make little sense.

The basic object model provides a limited form of type checking in an operating system. Only certain operations are defined for a particular class of object. For example, read and write are defined for text files, whereas it would be illegal to attempt to read a printer. We are interested in using the database to extend this primitive form of type checking.

A tool, Ti, can generally be thought of as taking m inputs, I1 to Im, performing some processing, and producing n outputs, O1 to On. It is intended to provide a level of checking on the validity of input objects I1 to Im. The basis of the solution is to maintain typing information in the database for objects of type tool. The frame for a tool would then contain at least the following information:-

```
TOOL                    ::    INPUT SPEC, OUTPUT SPEC
INPUT SPEC              ::    I1 -> TYPE DESC1
                             I2 -> TYPE DESC2

                             .
                             .
                             Im -> TYPE DESCm
OUTPUT SPEC            ::    O1 -> TYPE DESC1
                             O2 -> TYPE DESC2

                             .
                             .
                             On -> TYPE DESCn
```

The frames for other types of object would also have to record extra typing information, e.g. objects of type file would have further information defining the contents of the file (whether it is a source file, a document, etc.).

Using this information, it is possible to check the validity of the given input objects in an invocation. In addition, it is possible to automatically generate the type information for the output objects.

There is one major problem to be overcome with this approach.

If the level of type checking is too strong, it will be difficult to incorporate essentially generic tools such as editors. Specialised tools would have to be provided for each type. This would be too rigid a discipline for many computer users.

If, however, the level of type checking is too weak, unreasonable operations will be permitted, e.g. editing an object file. The prime example of this kind of operating system is UNIX. In UNIX, all objects are mapped on to the single abstraction of an unstructured byte stream. This approach provides a very high degree of freedom; this could be a particular problem for the naive user.

We propose a flexible strategy to overcome this (c.f. polymorphic or generic types in programming languages). The key to the solution is a hierarchy of types. A typical hierarchy is shown in Fig.1.

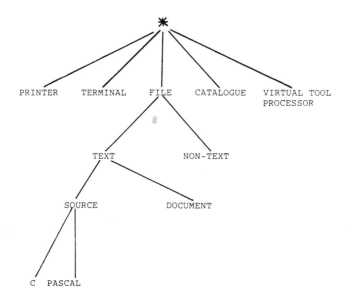

Fig.1 Type hierarchy

Generic tools can then be catered for by selecting a type at a high level in the hierarchy, e.g. an editor could take any file (i.e. object of type file) with attribute text. Other tools can be more specific, e.g. a C compiler should only be allowed to operate on a file with attributes text:source:C.

A benefit of this type checking is that more intelligence can be provided in the man-machine interface. For example, it would be relatively easy to generate error messages of the form:-

Editing a non-textual file is not permitted.

We see this insurance of sensible actions from the operating system as a practical aid to programmer support. It is this kind of feature, brought about by the active use of the database, which will allow operating systems of the future to become more intelligent programming environments.

5.2.2. Version control. Version control in a PSE is required to retain and manage different versions of an object throughout the entire history of a project. The Cosmos approach to version handling relies on a fundamental property of our database model, i.e. that objects are immutable. Once an object has been created, it can never be altered and indeed can never be destroyed. Versions are therefore already maintained by the kernel. We do however require a means of managing versions and presenting a meaningful interface to the user.

The Cosmos model provides direct support for version control management. A set of 'transformed into' and 'transformed from' relationships can be used to maintain the version history. A number of version attributes can then be associated with each object. The most important attribute is the version selector (a textual string identifying that particular version). Further attributes can be added, e.g. the reason for creating that version and the date of creation.

The following example illustrates the use of a semantic network to manage version histories. The figure shows a number of versions of an object called program.

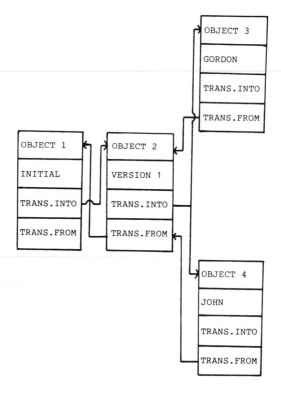

Fig.2 Version control in Cosmos

Particular versions of an object are named by the following syntax:-

<object name> [<selector>]

Fig.2 then shows program[initial] being transformed into
program[version1]; program[version1] is then transformed
into program[gordon] and program[john].

A particular version can be tagged by the user as the
default: if no selector is specified, then this default is
provided. Again, this tag is an attribute of the object.

Transformation of a particular version results in a new
node being linked into the semantic network. The selector
field is set up to some user specified string; the default
is a system generated string.

This is a very general version naming scheme. More
specific naming disciplines, e.g. the nested version number-
ing of RCS (Tichy (19)), can easily be super-imposed. We
feel very strongly that this generality is required in a
PSE. Any less general version naming schemes that we considered can be shown to be too restrictive in certain circumstances.

5.2.3. Configuration control. Configuration control is a
vast topic relating to the inter-relationships between
objects in a system.

A good configuration control system should be able to
provide information about such inter-relationships. For
example, it should be able to provide answers to questions
like:-

*   what objects did we use to create certain other
    objects?

*   what are the global consequences of changing a particu-
    lar object?

In addition, a configuration control system should be able
to automatically maintain related objects.

In the Cosmos project, at present we choose to concentrate on this latter aspect of configuration control. Other
aspects of configuration control will be considered in the
future.

Our configuration control scheme is again fully supported by the semantic network.

We introduce the notion of related objects. A related
object is an object which is intimately associated with
another object in the system. For example, a binary is a
related object to the source from which it was produced.
Similarly, documentation is a related object to its source.

Related objects then simply map on to inter-relationships in the semantic network.

Consider the previous example as shown in Fig.2. 'program' could have two relations associated with it: 'binary of' and 'documentation of'. We could then refer to:

binary of program[gordon]

documentation of program

etc.

In many operating systems, related objects have to be explicitly named and a convention used to indicate relationships. Consider, for example, a C source file in UNIX called 'sort.c'. It is likely that the binary and documentation would be called something like 'sort.o' and 'sort.doc' respectively. In Cosmos, there is no need to explicitly name related objects: a single name refers to the main object and relations used to access associated objects.

5.2.4.   Rule base. A mechanism is provided for automatically creating related objects. This depends on a rule base which contains rules of the following format:

<relation name> <mapping> <action>

where 'relation name' is a name of an inter-relationship from the configuration control scheme, 'action' defines the tool to be invoked to produce the related object from the original object and 'mapping' defines the valid types for the domain and range of the action. The exact means of storage of this rule base is not discussed until Section 5.2.6.

The following is then a valid rule in our rule base:

'binary of' : source->binary : compile

i.e. the relation 'binary of' is a mapping from source to binary; this is derived by invoking the tool 'compile'.

The selection procedure for rules allows duplicate entries for a particular relation name provided that the mapping is different. The mapping information is then used to resolve the ambiguity. This allows for generic naming of relations as the following example illustrates:

'binary of' : c->binary : cc

'binary of' : fortran->binary : fortran

Returning to the earlier example, if binary of program[john] is requested and it is known that program is a C source, then the related object can automatically be created by invoking the C compiler (cc). A relationship can then be added to the database to indicate that the related object now exists.

5.2.5. Coercions. The configuration control mechanisms described above can, however, be rather cumbersome in certain circumstances. For example, if the user has to type:

binary of program

whenever he/she wishes to execute the program. It is often implicit in the context that a related object rather than the original object is required. If the user simply types:

program

then the context demands an object of type binary rather than an object of type source.

We provide another type based feature called coercions, to handle this situation. Coercions are similar to the notion of projections as discussed in (Crawley (20)).

Again, the rule base provides the necessary information to implement coercions. In a given situation, should the context require an object of type1 and the user specifies an object of type2, the rule base is searched by mapping for a relation which will map type2 into type1. If the search reveals no ambiguity, then the related object can be substituted for the original object (it can of course be created if necessary). If however the search reveals ambiguity, then the user must resolve the conflict.

5.2.6. Tailored environments. Many of the features described in this section are very potent and may not appeal to all users. We have therefore been experimenting with the notion that the user should be free to tailor his/her programming environment to their own particular needs and tastes.

Each user has a personal profile, a file containing information related to their programming environment. This contains standard information such as search paths and authentication information, but also contains the information required for type checking, configuration control and coercions. It is this personal profile then which contains the rule base referred to in the previous section. The configuration control mechanisms can therefore be by-passed. Similarly, the environment can be extended to include types and rules for a particular application domain, e.g. word processing.

An interpretive language is provided to allow the user to edit this profile. This language has a straightforward syntax and can therefore be illustrated by example.

A possible environment description for a user is as follows:

```
type file, text, binary
type source, document
type c, pascal, fortran
type unformated, formated
text, binary ms file
source, document ms text
c, pascal, fortran ms source
unformated, formated ms document
rule 'binary of' : c->binary : cc
rule 'binary of' : pascal->binary: pascal
rule 'binary of' : fortran->binary: fortran
rule 'formated of' : unformated->formated: nroff
```

Three types of command are introduced in this example:

the type command -- this allows the user to create   new types,

the member of set (ms) command -- this allows the   user to set up an arbitrary type hierarchy, and

the rule command -- this allows the   user   to   add   new rules to the rule base.

There are a further three   commands   to   remove   types, member of set information and rules respectively.   These are subject to certain semantic checks, e.g. it is not valid   to remove a type if it is referred to in a rule.

A standard profile is provided to all   new   users.   This will   include   various   system   types   and useful rules. The standard profile can be freely altered to suit a   particular user's requirements.

6.   STATUS OF PROJECT

The model described above has been used in   the   design of   a distributed operating system called Cosmos. The archi- tecture of Cosmos is as shown in Fig.3.

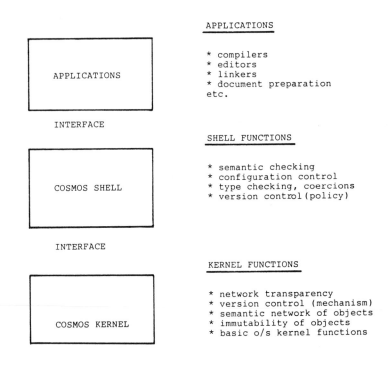

APPLICATIONS

APPLICATIONS

* compilers
* editors
* linkers
* document preparation
etc.

INTERFACE

SHELL FUNCTIONS

COSMOS SHELL

* semantic checking
* configuration control
* type checking, coercions
* version control(policy)

INTERFACE

KERNEL FUNCTIONS

COSMOS KERNEL

* network transparency
* version control (mechanism)
* semantic network of objects
* immutability of objects
* basic o/s kernel functions

Fig.3 Cosmos architecture

The Cosmos kernel is a direct implementation of the model; the Cosmos shell contains the various IPSE functions. Because the kernel directly supports the various IPSE functions, there is no need for an intermediate layer.

Having completed the initial design of Cosmos, we decided to develop a simulation of the kernel. This is now practically finished with kernel support for semantic checking, version control, configuration control, coercions and tailored environments fully implemented. The simulation is written in C and runs under UNIX. It was initially written for a Vax 11/750 but since has been ported to a SUN workstation.

Developing the simulation first has been an invaluable exercise. The development resolved the many problems and ambiguities in the design. More importantly, however, we are now in a position to develop a prototype IPSE and the kernel in parallel. The kernel is being developed for a number of M68000 systems interconnected by Ethernet; the design of the kernel is described in some detail in (Nicol et al (21)). The shell is initially being developed on top of the simulation but should be portable to the M68000 system. There is continual feedback between the two aspects of our work. As new facilities are required by the IPSE, so the structure of the kernel is altered.

There are many aspects of the project which require further investigation. Ongoing research will be considering the following problem areas:

* Properties of the model

    We are interested in gaining a deeper insight of the properties of the Cosmos model and in particular the repercussions of immutability of objects.

* Practical aspects of the model

    There are many practical issues to be resolved before the model can be successfully implemented. More specifically, overhead with respect to both space and time have to be minimised. Initial investigation has indicated that this should be possible (Blair et al (17)), but further work is required.

* Further IPSE support

    We are now searching for other features of IPSE's that can be supported by the Cosmos model. For example, typing and coercions are influenced by experiences with programming languages; other features of programming languages may usefully be extrapolated to IPSE's (Hall (22)). We are also interested in providing a sophisticated database query language and in working on the human-computer interface to Cosmos.

7. CONCLUSIONS

    The main motivation for this work was our observation that many proposals for Integrated Program Support Environments placed little emphasis on the supporting substructure. Instead, many IPSE proposals rely on existing operating systems. This inevitably leads to the inclusion of layers of software on top of the operating system to provide support for the IPSE. It is our premise that this will lead to problems because of the excessive layering and the poorly tailored base. We therefore set out to design an operating system which is specifically tailored for a IPSE. The major feature of this operating system is the inclusion of a database in the kernel.

    A simulation of the kernel has been developed. This has allowed us to investigate the degree of support that the kernel provides for IPSE functions. We are encouraged by our experiences to date. The kernel directly supports our solutions to the classic problems of version control and configuration control. Similarly, the association of typing attributes with objects has allowed us to implement a sophisticated and flexible level of type checking and a form of coercions.

We are now searching for other features of IPSE's that can be supported by the Cosmos kernel. In addition, we are working towards an implementation of the Cosmos kernel to investigate how well our ideas work in practice.

REFERENCES

1.   U. S. Department of Defense, 1980,
      "Requirements for an ADA Programming Support Environ-
      ment", STONEMAN.

2.   Hutchison, D., 1983,
      "Local Area Networks: An Introduction", Software and
      Microsystems, 2, 87-95.

3.   Blair, G. S., 1983,
      "Distributed Operating System Structures for Local Area
      Network Based Systems", Ph. D. Thesis, University of
      Strathclyde.

4.   Blair, G. S., Hutchison, D., and Shepherd, W. D.,
      1982, "Mimas - A Network Operating System for Strath-
      net", Proc. 3rd Int. Conf. on Distributed Computing
      Systems, 212-217.

5.   Hitchcock, P., Robinson, D. S., and Whittington, R. P.,
      1985, "Modelling-Primitives for a Software Engineering
      Database", Proc. 4th National Conf. on Databases, 131-
      146.

6.   Alderson, A., Bott, M. F., and Falla, M. E., 1985,
      "An Overview of the Eclipse Project", Proc. York
      IPSE Conf., 100-113.

7.   Ritchie, D. M. and Thompson, K., 1978,
      "The UNIX Time-Sharing System", Bell Sys. Technical
      Journal, 57, 1905-1929.

8.   Feldman, S. I., 1979,
      "Make - A Program for Maintaining Computer Programs",
      Software - Practice and Experience, 9, 255-265.

9.   Buxton, J. N. and Druffel, L. E., 1981,
      "Requirements for an Ada PSE: Rationale for STONEMAN",
      Software Engineering Environments (ed. Hunke H.), North
      Holland Publishing Company, 319-330.

10. Stonebraker, M., 1981,
     "Operating System Support for Database Management",
     CACM, 24, 412-418.

11. Jones, A. K., 1978,
     "The Object Model: A Conceptual Tool for Structuring
     Software", Operating Systems - An Advanced Course,
     Springer-Verlag, 7-16.

12. Winston, P. H., 1979,
     Artificial Intelligence, Addison Wesley, 181-183.

13. Tanenbaum, A. and Mullender, S., 1985,
     "A Distributed File Service Based on Optimistic Con-
     currency Control", Proc. ACM 10th SOSP, Washington,
     51-62.

14. Lampson, B. W. and Schmidt, E. E., 1983,
     "Organizing Software in a Distributed Environment",
     Proc. Symp. on Programming Languages, SIGPLAN 1983, 1-
     13.

15. Nelson, B. J., 1981,
     "Remote Procedure Call", in Internal Report CMU-CS-81-
     119, Dept. of Computer Science, Carnegie-Mellon
     Univ., Ph.D. dissertation.

16. Spector, A. Z., 1982,
     "Performing Remote Operations Efficiently on a Local
     Computer Network", CACM, 25, 246-260.

17. Blair, G. S., Nicol, J. R., and Yip, C. K., 1985,
     "A Functional Model of Distributed Computing", Inter-
     nal Report, Department of Computing, University of Lan-
     caster, Lancaster, England.

18. Nicol, J. R., Blair, G. S., and Shepherd, W. D., 1985,
     "A Functional Solution to the Multiple Copy Update
     Problem", Internal Report, Department of Computing,
     University of Lancaster, Lancaster, England.

19. Tichy, W. F., 1982,
     "Design, Implementation, and Evaluation of a Revision
     Control System", 6th Int. Conf. on Software Engineer-
     ing.

20. Crawley, S. C., 1983,
     "An Outline of the Entity System", Discussion Note,
     Computer Laboratory, Cambridge University.

21. Nicol, J. R., Blair, G. S., and Shepherd, W. D., 1985,
     "A Tailored Kernel Design for a Distributed Operating
     System", Internal Report, Department of Computing,
     University of Lancaster, Lancaster, England.

22.   Hall, J. A., 1984,
       "Database Issues in Program Support Environments",   ADA
       UK News, 5, 29-38.

Chapter 7

The analyst—a workstation for analysis and design

M. Stephens and K. Whitehead

This paper describes a system currently being developed called the "Analyst". The Analyst is a support system for analysis and design methods. The method support facilities are being implemented using expert system or knowledge based techniques. The user can add rules for additional analysis of the application facts. The explicit representation of rules and facts (i.e. the knowledge base) makes it relatively easy to add methods to cover different phases or aspects of the software life cycle.

1. INTRODUCTION

During the last nine months of 1983 we developed a prototype expert system [1] that supported part of the CORE method [2,3]. The hardware consisted of a high resolution graphics terminal connected to a VAX 11/750*. The objectives of the exercise were to investigate the feasibility of a knowledge based approach and experiment with different styles of user interface prior to developing a commercial product. The prototype demonstrated the value of a knowledge based approach, but led us to change our implementation stratgey. While the system was successful functionally, response times were unacceptably slow.

This was primarily due to the exclusive use of Prolog [4] as the implementation language. Prolog is well suited for knowledge based applications but compilers available for the VAX in 1983 generated relatively slow run-time code. To take advantage of the expressive power of Prolog and still achieve quick response times, we adopted a mixed language approach. PASCAL [5] is used for graphics and window manipulations; Prolog is used to express the method rules and to store and retrieve application information.

Choosing hardware for the Analyst was extremely difficult. The product is designed to be a personal workstation, replacing the need for a terminal. The cost had to be low enough so that an organisation could reasonably afford to buy a workstation for every programmer.

This eliminated several high cost/high performance
workstations such as the PERQ**, SUN***, and XEROX Star****.
Many low cost systems were eliminated because they lacked
adequate graphics resolution or performance. The Apple
Lisa/Macintosh TM***** range was selected as the best
compromise. In any case the Analyst is designed to be
portable to take advantage of future hardware offerings.
	Another major change between the prototype and the
current product is the incorporation of general document
preparation facilities. Many if not most of the products
of analysis and designs are documents which are not
direct results of the methods. Accordingly, a support
system for analysis and design should provide general word
processing and graphics facilities as well as facilities
for supporting methods.
	The last decision to be made was which methods to
install. Even though the Analyst was specifically designed
so that other methods could be installed relatively easily,
each method does require an investment of time and effort.
A detailed knowledge of the method is required prior to
specifying the syntax and semantics. Providing online
documentation and help is also very time consuming.
CORE and MASCOT [6] were selected as the requirements
analysis and design methods respectively. While the
surface syntax of these methods differ, the semantics
are very similar, enabling functional requirements to
be traced to a specific design.
	The next section describes the general facilities
available to the user. The model for supporting methods
is presented with an example of how a CORE action diagram
would be created and checked. The third section explains
the implementation of objects and rules, the storage and
retrieval of application information, and how a user
might extend the rules. The fourth section discusses
weaknesses in the system intelligence and identifies
future research areas.

2. USER INTERFACE

	The man machine interface philosophy is that of the
Apple Macintosh. The system has general facilities for
office automation. There are electronic equivalents for
many 'real world' objects in an office environment such
as filing cabinets, folders, documents, diagrams and trash
cans (rubbish bins). Each of these objects is represented
by a corresponding icon (see figure 1). The mouse is the
primary control device and is analogous to the user's hand.
Thus, to put a document in a folder, the user 'picks up' the
document (by moving the cursor to the document icon and
depressing the mouse button) and 'puts' it into the folder
(by dragging the document icon over to the filing cabinet
icon and releasing the button). Novice users have an
intuitive feel for how to operate the system since the
objects in the system look and behave like their real
world counterparts. Often first time users are able to
use the word processor, the graphics facilities and navigate

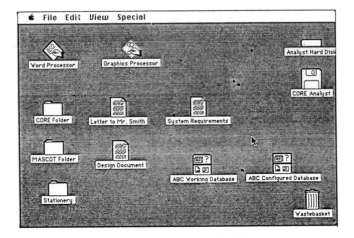

Figure 1

Figure 2

their way around the system with less than one hour of
familiarization.
   This style of interface is called object oriented
because most operations are performed by pointing at
an object and then specifying an operation. The window
is another concept central to the Analyst. For example, to
type a letter, the user must first open the word processing
icon by clicking twice rapidly with the mouse button. This
creates a window which is equivalent to a blank sheet of
paper. The word processing system provides 'rulers',
several fonts, styles and sizes which are selected by
pulling down the appropriate menu and selecting one of the
options (see figure 2). When the letter is finished and the
user has exited the word processor, a new icon is created
which may be given a name.
   The CORE and MASCOT methods are implemented within the
Analyst in a similar manner. Before we look at specific
examples though, it is useful to examine the concept of
'method'. Most popular methods consist of a set of
techniques for analysing and representing different aspects
of a system. Each technique (e.g. data structure, data
flow, entity-relation) consists of textual and graphical
symbols with rules for valid combinations. Normally the
method suggests or requires that these techniques be used
in a certain sequence with rules for relating information
between techniques. Often though, these techniques can be
used independently as well. Methods then can be viewed
as a set of related techniques which can be used in sequence
or independently. This method model is used within the
Analyst. For example, CORE consists seven stages or
techniques. Within the Analyst there is a folder which
contains seven icons representing these stages (figure 3).
The user may use the techniques in the sequence prescribed
by the method or independently. The system will give
warnings though if independent use of a technique causes
inconsistency with related information defined previously.
   The user interface to method techniques is best
illustrated by an example. Suppose the user wants to
create a CORE action diagram, check it for completeness
and consistency, and resolve any inconsistencies. The user
would begin by opening the 'isolated action diags' icon.
Figure 4a is an example of the resulting window. The user
is in the initial stages of creating a new diagram. Two
action boxes have been dragged from the template (on the
left side of the window) and positioned. The data flow
lines were drawn by clicking on the start point, dragging
out the line, and clicking for the bends. Then the user
selected the inner portion of the box and started to type
the name 'convert'.

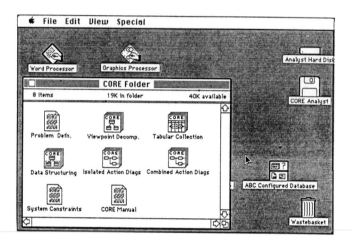

Figure 3

    Figure 4b is the same diagram after it has been
completed. The user now wishes to check it both locally
and against the project. The local checks are for self
consistency and completeness of the diagram. The
project checks compare this diagram with other diagrams
in the project data base file. One or more of the options
on the check menu can be selected. Although the user has
chosen in this case to perform the checks after the
diagram was created, validation options could have been
selected prior to creating the diagram. In that case the
checks would have been made where appropriate during the
creation process.
    Typical results of a validation check are shown in
figure 4c. Messages are categorized as guidance, warnings
or errors. Guidance are usually questions of style and
can be ignored with impunity. Warnings normally pertain
to incomplete specifications. Errors indicate
inconsistencies and in most cases should be fixed before
the diagram can be stored. In this example the first
message points out that the lower action box has no
indentification number. The second message is a project
warning stating that none of the diagrams in the project
data base contain an action which uses 'invalid request'.
Either a new (and possibly valid) data flow has been
identified or the name has been misspelled (maybe it
should be 'invalid command'). The third message is also
a project message.

Apparently the diagram 'management system' also derives 'reports'. This is classified as an error since data cannot be derived in two different places (according to the rules of CORE). Usually at this point the user will want to look at the offending diagram before deciding how to resolve the problem. This can be done simply by choosing the open option from the File/Print menu and clicking twice on the text 'management system' (see figure 4d). Diagrams are represented both by their icons and their textual names. It follows then that the same operation on the icon or the name should have the same effect. This interface model simplifies system navigation by reducing the number of operations a user must perform to achieve a desired result.

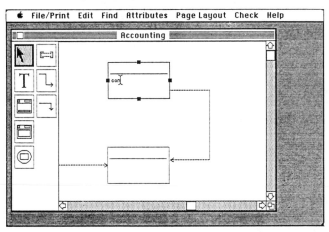

Figure 4a

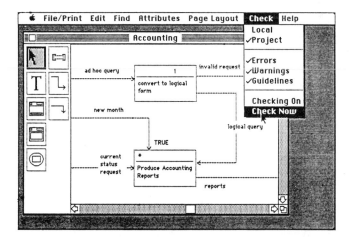

Figure 4b

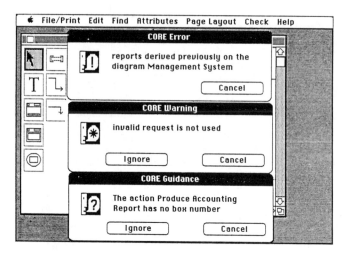

Figure 4c

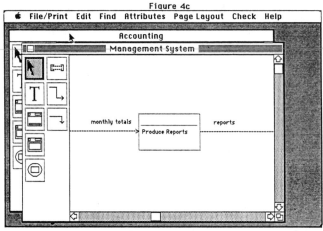

Figure 4d

3. SYSTEM ARCHITECTURE

Section 3.1 introduces three concepts which are important for understanding the implementation strategy. One is the model for implementing objects, the second is the model for implementing techniques of a method, and the third is the logic language used for method semantic rules, queries and user defined extensions. Section 3.2 explains how a CORE action diagram check is performed. Section 3.3 gives an example of a user extension.

3.1 IMPLEMENTATION CONCEPTS

The implementation of all objects (e.g. documents, folders, windows, etc.) is based on the same model. Every object has an associated software module. Any operation on an object (e.g. select, open, move, change shape) causes a message to be sent to the software module. The module contains segments of code for processing all message types.

These code segments define the behaviour of the object.
Frequently the processing of a message will result in a
response message being sent to another object in the
system. Objects, such as a window, may contain sub-objects.
Messages to a 'parent' object may cause it to send messages
to its sub-objects. Also associated with every object is
a local data area which defines the current state of the
object (e.g. position, shape, activate status, name).
The logic language is based on a subset of predicate
logic called Horn clauses (after Alfred Horn who first
investigated its properties). This logic language consists
of two forms of clauses:

1.1 a simple assertion or fact such as

    Mark is the child of Steve.

is represented as

    child_of(Mark Steve).

1.2 an implication or rule such as

        'F' is the father of 'C' if' 'C' is the child of
                    'F' and 'F' is male.

is represented as

    father_of(F C) if child_of(C F) & is_male(F).

Method techniques are implemented as objects (see figure 5).
Each technique consists of syntax rules (valid symbol shapes
and combinations) and semantic rules (the meaning associated
with a symbol or connection between symbols). These rules
form part of the software module associated with method
related objects. The semantic rules are implemented in a
logic based language and can be explicity displayed to the
user. The syntax rules are coded in PASCAL and cannot be
accessed. When a method technique is used to create a
diagram, both the physical and the associated semantics of
the diagram are stored in the object's local data area.
The physical information is stored as a series of graphics
primitives. The semantics are stored as 'facts' in a
database accessible by the logic language.
A good explanation of this logic language can be found
in [7]. We have adopted an additional notation to indicate
variable types. For example:

    father_of(human_male , human)

indicates the 'father_of' clause has two variables of the
type 'human_male' and 'human'.

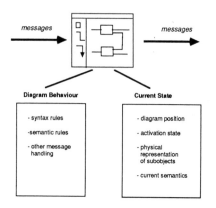

Method Technique "Object"

Figure 5

3.2 · IMPLEMENTATION OF A METHOD TECHNIQUE

First the user selects the Project and Errors options from the 'Check' menu. The system accesses the semantic information from the data base file and the current diagram. This forms a contiguous logical data base which consists of a set of 'facts' or assertions about the current diagram and other diagrams in the project data base. The system then transfers control to the Prolog system, passing it the Project and Errors, and the name of the current diagram. Project and Errors identifies a set of Prolog rules for checking inconsistencies between diagrams. The rules are 'executed' (by the Prolog inference mechanism) in sequence. When finished reviewing the error messages, the user closes the window.

In the previous example (see figure 4c) the project error message

"reports" derived previously on diagram "managment system"

was generated. This was a result of executing the following rules:

display_project_error(Current_Diagram) if

multi_derived (Current_Diagram,   Project_
Diagram, Data) and

write (Data, 'derived previously on diagram',
Project_Diagram).

It may be noted that this rule will only catch the first case of a multiply derived data item. This simplification was made in the interest of clarity.

3.3 USER EXTENSIONS

A major benefit of the explicit representation of rules and data (i.e. the knowledged based approach) is that the logic of the Analyst can be displayed and understood by the user. A second benefit is that the user can use this same knowledge representation language to extend the system rules. To illustrate this facility we have chosen an example analysis check that is frequently needed during the requirements analysis stage. During the last stages of system specification, changes are often made which potentially effect many other sections of the specification. It is generally extremely difficult to ensure that all possibly effected parts have been identified and checked. Let us assume that a data item was deleted and we wanted to identify all actions which either used this item directly or indirectly (e.g. used data derived by another action which used this item). This rule can be succinctly expressed as:

depends_on (Action , Data) <u>if</u>

    uses (Action , Data).

depends_on (Action , Data) <u>if</u>

    uses (Action , Other_Data) <u>and</u>

    derives (Another_Action , Other_Data) <u>and</u>

    depends_on(Another_Action , Data).

The user can easily add this rule to the Analyst.

4. FUTURE RESEARCH

The Analyst system should provide good support for the analysis and specification process, but when compared to <u>human</u> experts it is somewhat lacking. This point is best illustrated by two examples.
Consider figure 6a. The structure is perfectly valid according to the CORE method, but a CORE expert would question the analyst on the difference between 'Sensor data 1' and 'Sensor data 2'. How does the filter process decide? Are there meaningful names which would indicate the difference between the two outputs? The ensuring discussion might result in figure 6b.

multi_derived (Current_Diagram, Project_Diagram
Data If

derives (Current_Diagram, Action_1, Data) <u>and</u>

derives (Project_Diagram, Action 2, Data) <u>and</u>

not equal (Current_Diagram, Project_Diagram).

The merged logical data base of our example would contain the following facts about the 'derives' relation:

derives ('Accounting', 'convert to logical form', 'invalid request').

derives ('Accounting', 'Convert to logical form', 'logical query').
is
derives ('Accounting', 'Produce Accounting Reports', 'reports').

derives ('Management System', 'generate mgt reports', 'reports').

When the rule 'display_product_error' is called the variable Current_Diagram is instantiated to (i.e. given the value of) the name 'Accounting'. This parameter (or field in relational data base terminology) acts as a key to all facts associated with the current diagram. This rule has two subrules or subgoals, 'multi_derived' and 'write'. The objective of 'multi_derived' is to find a data item which has been derived on two different diagrams. 'Write' is an extra-logical rule which always succeeds and has the side effect of writing text to the currently active window. Since Prolog rules are executed in sequence, 'multi_derived' will be executed first. If it fails (i.e. no two actions derive the same data item) then the 'write' subgoal is never executed.

When 'multi_derived' is called, Current_Diagram is instantiated to 'Accounting'. The first 'derives' subgoal is satisfied by the first fact. The second 'derives' subgoal though is never satisfied since no other facts contain the data name 'invalid request'. This causes Prolog to backtrack or to try and resatisfy the first 'derives' subgoal. It is satisfied again by the second fact containing the data name 'logical query' but again the second 'derives' subgoal fails for the same reason.
Eventually the last two facts satisfy both 'derives' sub-goals and the rule 'multi_derived' succeeds with its last two arguments instantiated to 'Management System' and 'reports'. This in turn satisfies the rule 'display_project_error' with a corresponding message to the user.

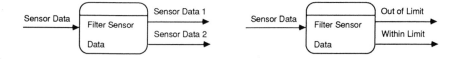

Figure 6

The second example concerns implicit human knowledge/
expectations (see figure 7).

Figure 7

Again this diagram is valid and reasonable in the
method but an expert would question why a process which
averages monthly totals would produce weekly averages.
    In the first example no particular knowledge of the
world is required. A general rule for this could be
informally described as "if the output data names are
sufficiently similiar then ask the user to create more
meaningful names". But in the second example the expert is
using knowledge about averaging and the relationship
between weeks and months. Thus a human analyst uses real
world knowledge as well as knowledge of the appliction. He
also uses different problem solving strategies to achieve
a meaningful system specification. In order for a computer
system to provide this level of intelligence it must have
"deep" knowledge both of the world and specific application
domains. To address this problem of deep knowledge, further
research is needed in the following areas:

1.1   Structures for Representing Knowledge

    This is needed both for specific application as well
as knowledge in general and relations between concepts (e.g.
the relationship between week and month).

1.2   General System Models for an Application Domain

These models could be used to recognise for example
an optimal design model which fits a certain specification.

1.3   Natural Language Processing

Natural language could be used for semantic
analysis of names as the input medium, or more ambitiously
for the intelligent appraisal of textual specifications.

1.4   Problem Solving Strategies

What questions does an expert analyst ask first?   How
does he recognize potential problems in an existing
specification?   How can these analysis strategies and
associated knowledge be encoded as a set of rules?

1.5   Machine Learning

If a human is given a set of related problems and
their solutions, he can begin to form generalisations or
common factors between the problems and their solutions.   A
computer syste s could do likewise if a method can be found
for storing and generalising from examples.
Given the current state of the art, we believe the
Analyst system provides a new level of sophistication or
"intelligence" for automated support of methods.   In terms
of true intelligence which approximates a human expert,
solutions to the above research issues must be found before
significant progress can be made.

5.   CONCLUSION

The object oriented user interface is a good model
because there are direct physical analogies.   Users have an
intuitive understanding of objects and operations which can
be performed on these objects.   This leads to a more user
friendly system with a minimal learning curve.   By extending
this model to incorporate software development objects and
methods, we can produce a workstation which provides an
integrated enviroment for office automation and software
life cycle support tools.   This will lead to greater
productivity, since many of the activities which were
either done manually or on separate systems (e.g. word
processing and diagram production) can now be performed
within one system.

The explicit representation of information and rules in a
logic based language also increases the user understanding
of the system since this representation is closer to the
real world format.   This also enables users to more easily
extend the system by using this same high level language.
The automatic tracing of requirements to design and
system implementation can be performed since all phases use
the same underlying representation.

A logic based language can be used as a common semantics model for various phases of the software life cycle. This would permit life cycle analysis tools.

FOOTNOTES

*	Trademark of Digital Equipment Corporation
**	Trademark of Three Rivers Computers, Inc.
***	Trademark of Sun Computer Systems, Inc.
****	Trademark of Xerox Corporation
*****	Trademark of Apple Computers, Inc.

REFERENCES

[1]   M. Stephens & K. Whitehead, "The Analyst - an Expert Systems approach to Requirements Analysis", Proc. of the Third Seminar on Application of Machine Intelligence to Defence Systems, June 1984.

[2]   G. Mullery, "CORE - A Method for Controlled Requirement Specification", IEEE 4th Int. Conference on Software Engineering.

[3]   "CORE - the Method", Systems Designers publication, November 1985.

[4]   W.F. Clocksin & C.S. Mellish, "Programming in Prolog", Springer Verlag 1981.

[5]   K. Jensen & N. Wirth, "PASCAL, User Manual and Report", Springer Verlag, 1974.

[6]   "The Official Handbook of MASCOT", MASCOT Suppliers Association, 1979.

[7]   R. Kowalski, "Logic as a Computer Language", Logic Programming, Academic Press, 1982, (pp 3-16).

Chapter 8

SSADM—how computing can help the practitioner

P. Eagling

1. INTRODUCTION

In recent years the use of structured methods for the analysis and design of commercial data processing systems has grown at such a pace that very few large organisations would now embark on a new computer project without at least considering one or more of these methods.

Although each method has its own peculiarities; the two things that they all have in common are the large amount of documentation that they produce (or rather, enforce the practitioner to produce!) and the extremely lengthy and tedious consistency checking that must take place between various parts of that documentation.

In the early days of structured methods, the production of documentation and the carrying out of consistency checking was a human based activity. In the last year or so, computer based tools have begun to emerge to relieve the practitioner from these long, tedious and therefore error prone tasks.

The Central Computer and Telecommunication Agency (UK Government's central computer advisory bureau) has been very active in both the research and development of one particular structured method - Structured Systems Analysis and Design Method (SSADM) and in the production of computer based tools to support users of that method.

2. SSADM - THE METHOD

The Structured Systems Analysis and Design Method (SSADM) is the standard method for systems analysis and design in Government batch and transaction processing projects. The method takes as its input an initial statement of requirements, and produces as output:-

- program specifications;

- user manuals;

- operating schedule;

- file design or database schema;

- plan for testing and quality assurance.

In SSADM, analysis and design are clearly seperated activities. Systems analysis is concerned with defining what has to be done, systems design with how it will be done. The complete process is carried out in six phases:-

SYSTEMS ANALYSIS

1. Analysis of current system

2. Specification of required system

3. User selection of sizing and timing options

SYSTEMS DESIGN

4. Detailed data design

5. Detailed procedure design

6. Physical design control

Each phase is broken down into steps and activities. There are clearly defined interfaces between steps in the form of working documents and criteria for review and project reporting.

3. SSADM - THE TECHNIQUES

There are three major, diagrammatic techniques involved in the development of an SSADM project, namely:-

- Logical Data Structures;

- Dataflow diagrams;

- Entity Life Histories.

Together these form an integrated, three-dimensional view of the data (and associated procedures) of the system, which can be checked, mechanistically, for consistency and completeness.
A brief description plus an example of each technique follows.

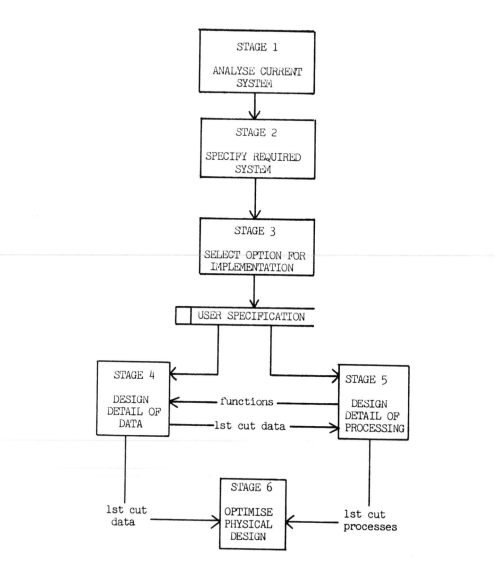

Fig.1 Block diagram of SSADM stages

3.1   Logical Data Structures.

The logical data structure is a user view of the
business, which is used as a basis for developing the system
to support the business. Logical data structures are
created at many different points in system development, from
initial trial attempts to describe the system in the early
stages of investigation, to a detailed synthesis of such a
model from third normal form data relations.
    When logical data structures are built, they are
validated by ensuring that the required functions can be
supported. If the structures cannot support the required
functions, then they are modified in order to do so.

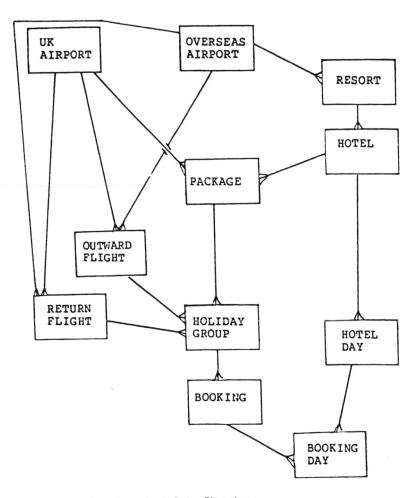

Fig.2   Example of Logical Data Structure

3.2   Dataflow diagrams.

The dataflow diagram is an operational picture of how
data moves around an information system, and moves between
the system and the outside world.   Whereas the logical data
structure is a user view of the business, the dataflow
diagram is the user view of the information system.

Dataflow diagrams are used to represent existing
physical systems, to abstract from these the information
flows which support user needs, and to define a logical
picture of the required system.   After physical design
control, the operations schedule is built around the
dataflow diagram.

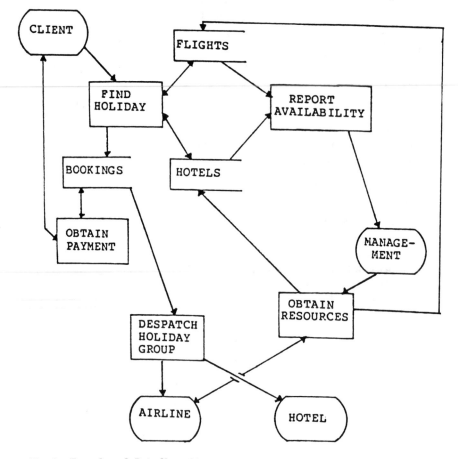

Fig.3   Example of Dataflow diagram

3.3 Entity Life Histories.

The life history diagram provides a third view of data
in order to show the effects of time on the system. For
each of the major entities which have to be represented in
the system, a chart is drawn showing all the events which
affect or update its data in the system.

When defining entity life histories the origin of each
transaction must be identified, and the processing of each
transaction defined. Further detail, such as error
recognition and processing and dealing with unexpected
events, is then added.

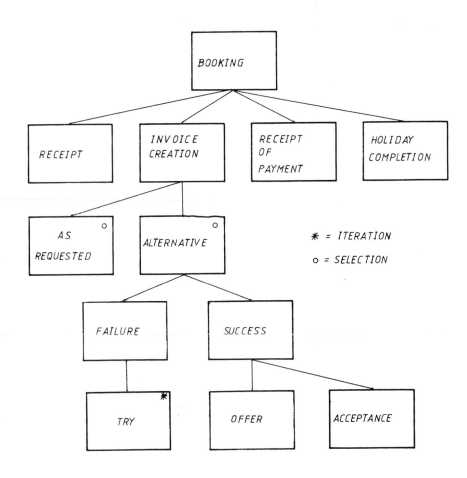

Fig.4 Example of Entity Life History

4. SSADM - HOW COMPUTERS CAN HELP THE PRACTITIONER

4.1 The early days of support tools.

CCTA began its work into the provision of computer support for the SSADM practitioner in 1982 with two distinct tools.

Firstly, a drawing package, based around a commercially available software tool called Autocad, which enabled the SSADM user to prepare and edit his diagrams on a computer and to be able to print them out for documentation purposes.

Secondly, a database package, using DBase II as the underlying repository for data, which recorded all LOGICAL information about the project under development and which provided the mechanism to carry out completeness and consistency checks.

Although the software was very useful and reinforced our belief in the general principle of computer support for structured system development, there were three main drawbacks that became immediately apparent:-

a. there was no automatic transfer of the logical information of a project, from the diagrams prepared on the graphics software, to the database. This resulted in the practitioners having to re-input that logical content directly into the database. This duplication of effort was obviously somewhat less than satisfactory;

b. there were severe limitations on both the size of diagrams and database that could be loaded onto the system;

c. the execution speed when dealing with a medium to large project was rather slow.

However, these two pieces of software were used with a good deal of success by around 24 projects throughout UK Government sites and in general were well received by those who were using them.

The search for a product which could be used as the basis for a package of software to provide automatic generation of database entries AND to improve the performance / sizing restrictions referred to above, was fairly short - there was nothing available on the commercial marketplace in Britain, Europe, or indeed the whole world and we therefore sought (succesfully) resources within CCTA to write such a suite of software in-house.

4.2 CCTA'S CURRENTLY AVAILABLE SUPPORT SOFTWARE

The software took 3 man-years to produce to the point
where it was in pilot use in 4 Government departments. This
development took place over 12 elapsed months and bears the
acronym 'MUST' standing for - Multi User SSADM Tools.
MUST is a set of tools from which the practitioner may
choose during most of the stages of SSADM. There is very
little in the way of advice or restrictions in when or how a
tool is used. The product runs on the IBM PC, the Apricot
and the Regne Centralen micro computers under Multi-user,
concurrent CPM.
MDBS III was chosen as the underlying database on which
all of the logical information pertaining to the project
under development is stored. This database package has
suitable, powerful primitives allowing rapid access for
multi-set searches (it was the lack of such facilities that
resulted in the slow running of the DBase II tools).
The graphics editors were written in 'C', the database
handling software in Pascal.
As the acronym implies, the system allows multi-user
working, essential for all but the smallest projects,
although there are some restrictions on multiple accesses.
The practitioner's use of the software commences with
the preparation of the three types of diagram referred to in
the earlier section on SSADM techniques. A medium size
project would contain approximately 40 diagrams (a mixture
of the three types) of A4 or A3 size.
The diagram editor contains many advanced graphic
handling features including automatic routing of dataflows
and other lines, optical and logical zooming and automatic
panning.
During the input or updating of these diagrams, all
logical information contained therein (not physical,
positioning information) is passed to the database, checked
for consistency (duplicate names etc) and will then cause
either an error report or an update to the database. This
all takes place interactively thus at all times the diagrams
and the database are kept in step.
At defined points in the method (SSADM), completeness
checks are run in batch mode against the database to ensure,
for instance, that there is an Entity Life History diagram
for each of the major entities defined on a Logical Data
Structure. Also run in batch mode are reports and cross
reference listings that are useful to the practitioner at
certain stages of the method.
Hard copies of diagrams, reports etc are available on
either dot matrix printers or graph plotters.
The software is now in use in a large number of
Government projects and is being enhanced as suggestions for
improved functionality are received from these users.

4.3 CCTA'S FUTURE PLANS FOR SSADM SUPPORT

MUST is a stable, supported product; we are now engaged
upon a new development, completely different in concepts,
which will result in a product on beta test in late 1986,
releasable in early 1987 which we believe will be an order
of magnitude in advance of the current (and other proposed
future) products in this area.

The acronym is already chosen (the most important
task!) and is 'CASE'. This stands for Computer Aided
Support Environment.

The key, innovative features of CASE are as follows.

4.3.1 Expert system. An expert system driven layer of
control completely surrounds all tools and it is with this
layer that the SSADM practitioner communicates. This expert
system has knowledge of all the stages and steps of the
method and how those components are applied in particular
circumstances.

Whereas with MUST the user of the tools can select
which tool to use at will, with CASE he is guided, advised
and protected as he proceeds with his work.

A convenient parallel exists which serves to illustrate
this idea. A carpenter works with a box of tools from which
he may choose at will during the course of his work. If he
so wishes he could select a hammer and knock in a screw with
it - not the right way to put in a screw, and not the
right use of a hammer. Again, he may choose to saw a piece
of wood, but because he is not holding the saw properly, the
wood gets cut at a strange angle. When using MUST or similar
toolsets, the SSADM practitioner is free to use a tool at an
inappropriate moment or, again like the carpenter, use the
correct tool, but in the wrong manner.

CASE will behave in a similar way to a carpentry
teacher, that is, to advise the beginner (or indeed,
experienced analyst / designer) on selecting the right tool
at the right moment and on the correct use of that tool.

Also included in this layer are project and
configuration control tools.

4.3.2 Two machine types. Separate machines / environments
are supplied for each practitioner (refered to as Personal
machines) AS WELL AS a machine solely employed to handle
project based information and functionality (the Project
machine). This separation is to provide computer power
where it is needed for different activities. Each
practitioner will have a large, high resolution screen plus
the processing power to manipulate it, ON HIS DESK; the
Project machine will be designed to store, and give rapid
access to, the large volumes of information about the
project. It is through this distribution of power that we
predict the massive improvements in analyst / designer
productivity.

4.3.3 Generic documents. A generic editor is a central component of CASE, used for creating and manipulating all documents whether they be diagrams, forms or plain text. This approach to document handling gives the SSADM practitioner a single learning curve, an important factor in a user's acceptance of a support environment.

All documents of whatever type are considered by tools within CASE to be the same and are treated in the same manner. The filing system stores all DOCUMENTS in a common fashion. The practitioner accesses and updates all DOCUMENTS with a common set of commands, tools etc.

In order to achieve this generality between what would at first appear to be significantly different classes of documents; the concept of a FIELD, within a document, was devised (this came about by seeking the highest common factors of all types of document).

Simply, a field is defined to be a rectangular shaped area within the total area of a document. For instance, within a dataflow diagram each process box would be defined as a field. In one of the many SSADM forms, each 'pre-printed' box, eg. date-of-completion, would be a field. In a document containing plain text, the whole document could be defined as one field.

All document manipulation primitives within CASE operate solely within the 'current' field.

All fields may be further defined as having sub-fields. This is recursive to an arbitary depth.

A field may be moved within the area of its parent field, but sibling fields must not overlap.

Fields may be linked to sibling fields. This is represented logically in the underlying database as well as physically on the display of the document. Dataflows, on dataflow diagrams and relationships, on logical data structures, are examples of linked sibling fields.

The advantage of generic document handling is the single learning curve and consistency of functionality that users deserve.

4.3.4 Database. As with MUST, CASE has a powerful, underlying database residing on the project machine from which all completeness and consistency checking is performed. This database is not based around a proprietary product but has been designed and implemented by first principles for reasons of access speed and economy of storage space. Again, as with MUST any amendments made to the diagrams are immediately validated against existing logical content and if all is well, the database is updated.

4.3.5 Portability. CASE is designed to be portable; this was achieved by defining very early on in the project, a set of primitives that were required to support all the higher level tools that manipulated SSADM entities (documents etc). If it is required to port the environment to a new hardware

/ operating system combination, all that it is necessary to
do is to rewrite the core of primitives. All SSADM tools
that are built in terms of these primitives are guaranteed
to work on any environment where the primitives have been
implemented. CCTA have already proved this approach by
porting all of the CASE software onto a different
environment (different that is to the development
environment) in a timescale of 2 elapsed weeks.

4.3.6 Implementation. At the moment, the development
environment is based around a network of 68000 processors
running Unix. We have ported the software (as described
above) to a CPM network that we had in-house, and we are
about to port to a large mini manufacturer's equipment.

5. OTHER TOOLS TO SUPPORT SSADM

CCTA have evaluated tools produced by other
organisations that are applicable to SSADM support albeit
not necessarily exclusively. These include Automate, (by
LBMS), a similar product to MUST but only single user, and
Excelerator, a product not specifically aimed at SSADM
support but nevertheless relevant to our studies. Reports
comparing these products with our own have been produced;
details available from the author to organisations that are
using SSADM.

6. SUMMARY

In summary, CCTA believe that:-

a. computer tools to support structured system
development methods should not just be considered as
an option but as an integral part of the method
itself;

b. with our current support tools (MUST),
improvements in analyst/designer productivity of
around 25% can be achieved (our measurements
currently average 26%);

c. using the latest hardware technology and with
software to be ready by 1987, improvements of around
60 - 70% are very confidently forecast.

All CCTA products are currently distributed at no charge to
Government Departments. Any organisations requiring further
information on the method, support tools and their
availability to non-government bodies, should contact, in
the first instance, the author, telephone 01 217 3134.

Chapter 9

SPADE—The Southampton program analysis and development environment

B. A. Carre, I.M. O'Neill, D.L. Clutterbuck and C.W. Debney

1. INTRODUCTION

With the ever-increasing use of software in applications where reliability is of paramount importance, software designers and end-users need more rigorous methods of program development and certification. SPADE - the Southampton Program Analysis and Development Environment - is an integrated set of software tools to aid in the efficient development, analysis and formal verification of programs written in a variety of programming languages - from high-level languages down to machine codes. The generality of the analysis tools results from the fact that they are not applied to programs directly, but to rigorous models of programs, defined in SPADE's Functional Description Language (FDL). An FDL model of a program can be constructed automatically, using a translator, or by hand. Automatic translation from a source text into FDL is currently available for Pascal, and an INTEL 8080 translator is nearing completion; a Modula-2 translator will also be constructed. Manual translation has proved acceptable in small projects where the cost of developing a special-purpose translator is not justified.

2. MODELLING PROGRAMS IN FDL

FDL is not a programming language; rather it is a language for describing a program in terms of its states, the conditions under which particular state transitions can occur, and the actions associated with each state transition. Intentionally, FDL has only primitive means of describing transfers of control, but it has a number of predefined data-types (essentially those of the languages Gypsy and Euclid) and it supports the use of abstract data types. FDL also has features to describe the interface between a model and its environment, allowing the modelling of hierarchies of sub-programs. Assertions can be placed in a text, for the generation of verification conditions, and the generation of "symbolic run-time checks" in the course of a symbolic execution.

3.   THE PORTABLE TOOL-SET

SPADE contains a suite of program "flow analysers" for performing control-flow, data-flow and information-flow analysis of an FDL text. Some of the functions performed by these tools are listed below. A unique feature of the SPADE flow analysers is the way in which they have been integrated, maximising their capabilities. It will be noted that in each case, as well as giving a detailed analysis of a program the tool performs a number of tests, to check that the program is "well-formed" in various respects. For ease of use, summaries of all three analyses and descriptions of any errors or anomalies found are collected in a "flow analysis report". In analysing a Pascal program in particular, SPADE can also insert information on errors which it detects at appropriate points within a listing of the program, in the same way as most compilers indicate syntax errors. SPADE also has semantic analysis tools, to assist in checking that a program performs its intended function; their roles are described in Sections 3.4 and 3.5.

3.1 Control-Flow Analyser

This "parses" the control-flow graph of the program (Hecht (1)) and describes it in (regular-algebraic) trace form, section-by-section; it also analyses the loop structure, indicating how loops are nested. The control-flow analyser reports on defects in control structure such as "dead" or unreachable code, statements from which a program exit cannot be reached, and multiple-entry loops.

3.2 Data-Flow Analyser

The data-flow analyser constructs tables of reaching-definitions (Kennedy (2), Carré (3)). This tool also signals conditional and unconditional data-flow errors (i.e. uses of undefined variables) and anomalies (unused definitions), and other undesirable program features such as invariant tests and loop-invariant assignments.

3.3 Information-Flow Analyser

Until recently, information-flow analysis has been used primarily to verify that information transmission between program variables cannot violate security requirements. However, it has recently been found possible to derive information-flow relations for a program that provide a very useful tool for software development and validation (Bergeretti and Carré (4)). The SPADE information-flow analyser computes these relations. Using them, it detects ineffective statements, ineffective parameters or global variables, use of undefined variables, and certain forms of non-termination of program loops. It also checks the consistency between the input-output relation which it derives from a text with a (mandatory) input-output relation provided in the text specification. From one of the computed information-flow relations, it is easy to extract automatically a "partial program", containing only those statements of a program (or subprogram) whose execution can affect the final value of a specified variable. This greatly simplifies program verification. This technique can be extended to yield a partial program containing only those statements which can affect the value of a variable at a particular point in a text (which is useful in error diagnosis) and, conversely, one can find all the statements and variables which can be affected by a modification at a particular point (which is important in program maintenance).

3.4 Verification-Condition Generator (VCG)

This constructs "path functions" describing the conditions under which particular paths through a program are executed, and the consequent transformations of program variables. If a specification is provided (in the form of pre- and post-conditions and loop-invariants), this tool can also generate the corresponding verification conditions, in a form acceptable to the SPADE theorem-checker which is described below. Given an assertion or a "check-statement" at any point in a text, the VCG can also give the corresponding weakest preconditions at other specified points. The VCG contains an algebraic simplifier.

3.5 Symbolic Interpreter

This tool performs a symbolic execution of a text, giving the path traversal conditions and variable transformations performed either along all execution paths, or along paths to specified points. The interpreter signals data-flow errors; also, each time an assertion or check-statement is reached in a text, the interpreter generates the corresponding "symbolic run-time check" (a theorem, in terms of initial values of the program variables, whose validity can be proved using the theorem-checker). Like the VCG, this tool contains an algebraic simplifier.

3.6 Theorem Checker

The SPADE theorem checker is an interactive proof checker, written in Prolog. It is user-driven, with tools for standardisation of arithmetic and logical expressions, application of replacement and inference rules via pattern matching with a database of rules and limited automatic deduction to fill in those details of a proof-step not provided directly by the user. Because the user guides the checker in a search for a proof, all tools may be selectively applied, so that only selected subexpressions need be modified, as the user requires.

Although the checker does not use any advanced automatic proof techniques, experience suggests it is adequate for use in attempting to find proofs of VCs. Helpful features include the ability for the user to use "wildcards" in subexpressions when specifying expressions and as rulenames when exploring possible next steps in a proof; "subgoaling", matching inference rules to goals to find possible subgoals to try to prove; house-keeping code to keep track of current proof-status and to monitor progress of various strategies (e.g. in a proof by cases or proof by contradiction); a type-checker, to ensure that the strong typing of expressions inherited from FDL is not violated in any proof-attempt; and an expandable rules database, making it easy for the user to define new proof functions and predicates and to add properties of them to the checker's knowledge base. Finally, because of the modularity of the checker, it is easy to add new tools or improve existing ones, allowing the power and effectiveness of the checker to be upgraded as experience dictates.

4.   SPADE "FRONT ENDS"

4.1 Pascal Translator

This translates programs or sub-programs written in SPADE-Pascal into FDL. SPADE-Pascal was derived from ISO-Pascal partly by excising from this language a number of features which give rise to ambiguities and uncertaintities (such as the use of procedures and functions as parameters, and variant records) and partly by adding to the language a number of "annotations", or formal comments. Some annotations are optional (such as pre- and post-condition specifications), but others are mandatory. As examples of the latter we have global-annotations and input-output dependency relations for procedures, which make explicit the interface between each sub-program and its environment. SPADE checks for consistency between these annotations - which are in effect forms of specification - and the program text. This enables the SPADE-Pascal translator to provide protection, for instance against aliasing through parameter-passing and "sneak-access" to global variables.

When complete specifications are provided (in the form of pre- and post-conditions and other assertions) the translator embeds corresponding assertions in its FDL translations. Then, by using the verification-condition generator, SPADE can furnish the verification conditions for the original Pascal program. Thus the Pascal translator, VC generator and theorem-checker together constitute a complete verification system.

The use of sub-program annotations, together with a feature allowing the temporary hiding of program blocks, also enables one to declare and specify a procedure, and analyse parts of the program which call it, before "refining" the procedure itself. In this way the SPADE-Pascal translator provides real support for top-down design and for the comparison of specifications with implementations.

The annotations in SPADE-Pascal are enclosed by

braces, of the same kind as are used to include comments in an ISO-Pascal test. Hence SPADE can be used in conjunction with any ISO-Pascal compiler.

4.2 INTEL 8080 Translator

Until "real" compilers can be verified, we cannot rely on the code which they produce, especially in safety-critical applications. Also, real-time constraints sometimes make it necessary to develop software directly in a low-level language. Either way, low-level code must ultimately be verified.

To this end, the language SPADE-8080 has been developed; this is a "safe subset" of the Intel 8080 assembly language supplemented with annotations (formal comments). Its definition excludes undesirable instructions such the indirect jump instruction (PCHL) and more clearly specifies the intended use of other instructions. For example, the legal address for the operand of a direct addressing jump mode instruction in the Intel 8080 is simply defined as an address. Whether this is an address of data or of a subroutine for instance is not evident from the assembly code. By assigning "types" to addresses in SPADE-8080 we are able to tighten the definition to say that only instruction label addresses are legal operands for the jump instruction. (There are other restrictions on this label relating to the use of the stack push and stack pop instructions and the execution of subroutines.) Other direct and indirect addressing mode instructions are defined similarly.

In common with SPADE-Pascal, SPADE-8080 has annotations for specifying dependency-relations, program assertions and for hiding subroutines. It also has annotations to define data structures; to specify the interpretation of integers as signed or unsigned; to describe the intended address of any indirect accesses to memory; to indicate the significance of arithmetic overflow on the correct execution of the arithmetic instructions, and to identify those variable definitions which are local to a subroutine. Using this information, the SPADE-8080 translator will detect such errors as unexpected side-effects of subroutines, array indices out of bounds and word accesses to byte variables. And, by generating assertions in the FDL model of the program, "shallow proof" of the absence of overflow and of the correct use of indirection can be performed.

The FDL model of a SPADE-8080 program includes information hidden in the source text such as status flag assignments and the interactions between registers and register-pairs. This enables the SPADE analysers to detect many errors resulting simply from the unexposed side-effects of executing an instruction.

SPADE-8080 instructions such as the arithmetic and logical instructions are modelled with FDL functions. These have been defined in a form compatible with the SPADE theorem checker and can be used to construct program proofs.

5. EXPERIENCES TO DATE, AND FUTURE DEVELOPMENTS

SPADE was originally developed primarily for research and pedagogical purposes: since 1982 the University of Southampton has been running extra-mural courses on program validation using SPADE, and now a hundred people from Government establishments and over thirty companies have attended these courses and had some "hands-on" experience of the system. Its success in these roles suggested that a refined version of the system should be developed for use in Industry; Program Validation Limited was formed for this purpose, and the system is now being used to produce and validate industrial software.

Although SPADE-Pascal imposes quite severe restrictions on the programmer, many of these simply enforce good programming practice, and the language has been found adequate for the development of safety-critical software. In analysing previously existing programs, SPADE tools have found errors which had remained undetected despite extensive program-testing and other forms of validation. The INTEL-8080 translator and the theorem checker are still in prototype form; these will be extended and refined in the near future. Work is also beginning (at the University of Southampton, under the sponsorship of the Royal Signals and Radar Establishment) on an environment to support validation and verification with the SPADE tools, using Flex (Currie, Edwards and Foster (5)).

ACKNOWLEDGEMENT

The prototypes of the SPADE tools described here were all originally developed in the Department of Electronics and Information Engineering of the University of Southampton. Much of this work was performed under research contracts, sponsored by the Royal Signals and Radar Establishment, Malvern.

REFERENCES

1. Hecht, M.S., 1977, <u>Flow Analysis of Computer Programs,</u> North-Holland, New York.

2. Kennedy, K., 1981, 'A survey of data flow analysis techniques'. In <u>Program Flow Analysis,</u> Muchnick, S.S. and Jones, N.D. (eds), Prentice-Hall, 5-54.

3. Carré,B.A., 1984, 'Validation techniques'. In <u>Software Engineering for Microprocessor Systems,</u> P.Depledge (ed), Peter Peregrinus, London, 173-197.

4. Bergeretti, J.F. and Carré,B.A., 1985, 'Information-flow and data-flow analysis of while- programs', <u>ACM Trans. on Prog. Lang. and Systems, 7,</u> 37-61.

5. Currie, J.F., Edwards, P.W. and Foster, J.M., 1981, 'Flex firmware', Royal Signals and Radar Establishment Report No. 81009.

Chapter 10

Using principles to design features of a small programming environment

A.J. Dix, M.D. Harrison and E.E. Miranda

User-centred design imposes constraints on the programmer-centred approach to program development. In this paper we describe a practical experiment using a three level design approach which incorporates at its top level an abstract model of interaction. The interaction model is used as the basis for proof that user-centred design principles hold for the system design. We also discuss refinement methods which achieve certain structural optimisations through the technique of "interface drift". A real system has been produced by these methods and is being used as a basis for test of alternative empirical evaluation techniques.

1.   INTRODUCTION

Formal specification provides designers with the possibility of reasoning about a design without being cluttered with unnecessary details of the implementation. Structural issues may be clarified. Design principles, conceived at the requirements stage, may be carried correctly through to implementation. This paper describes part of a practical design experiment in which features of an interactive "literate programming environment" (Knuth(1)) have been specified and implemented. The prototype system, implemented on a Whitechapel MG-1 under Unix, is providing information which will be used in the similar design of a fuller programming environment. Motivation for this Alvey supported research derives from the belief that interactive systems may be improved (in the sense that they are easier to learn or use) by means of precisely formulated laws of interface behaviour.

We report this research at an environments conference for two reasons. Firstly, the work represents part of an initial exploration of the design of an interactive literate programming environment (the other part has involved the development of a non-interactive system (Thimbleby(2)) for use with the C language). Secondly, the design method used involves some novelty in the sense

that two levels of formal specification are required and a
major intention of the development process is to assure
consistent incorporation of user engineering principles
(Harrison & Thimbleby(3)) in the different stages of the
design. We are currently considering requirements for
tools to support this design process.

2. THE PROTOTYPE FOR A SMALL PROGRAMMING ENVIRONMENT

The immediate purpose of this paper is to describe the
methods used in designing a prototype of the proposed
interactive literate programming environment that is
forming the exemplar for our research. In producing the
prototype the purposes were two: first, we needed a
manageable system that would permit paper and pencil
specification exercises without the necessity for automatic
tool support; second, we required a system which would
exhibit interesting components of the exemplar to provide
an early vehicle to assist the psychologists of our team in
their development of a suitable set of evaluation
experiments. The prototype is therefore constrained to
illustrate design of a small virtual display system and its
navigation properties. Each virtual display is associated
with a very simple editor and the display incorporates a
simple mechanism for fixing lines on the screen, in
contrast with an explicit folding mechanism.

The ultimate goal in the exemplar is to design a
display based interactive system for supporting entry of
documentation, program source and specification. Entry is
to be achieved by selecting the appropriate display. A
further display will give a collated view for use either in
deriving an overall picture of the system, or in navigating
around the system. Navigation in one display will cause
corresponding traversal in all the other displays. Cursor
movement in different displays will be tied together so
that each perspective of the same part of the system is
always available. Graphics will be used to differentiate
such information as indexes, cross references and folds.
(A fold is used to conceal unwanted information within
displays.)

3. THE DESIGN APPROACH

Design is based around three compatible models of a
system which give the same functionality though at
different levels of implementation bias. Each model is
constrained by the same set of principles that are proved
to be true at the top level. The first model abstracts the
interactive behaviour of the system to provide early
analysis of the design. User engineering principles are
initially expressed in terms of this abstract model,
thereby achieving a proof that one characterisation of the
design conforms to the principles, before being cluttered

with implementation detail. In our experiment we have used the PIE model developed at York (Dix & Runciman(4)) although other models might be used at this stage of the design, for example path algebras. (Alty(5)) The PIE model was however developed specifically with proofs of this kind in mind.

Once interactive behaviour is understood at the PIE level, the system specification is transformed into a second model (we happen to use equational specification techniques at this stage, but others would be equally appropriate). The mapping from PIE to "concrete specification" should preserve principles so that once they hold at the PIE level they may be readily proved to hold in the specification. Currently our approach is to produce a structural comparison of the three levels rather than a rigorous proof; we are considering the problems of providing interactive checking support.

The third model is the program itself. At this level we must understand how to achieve a refinement from specification to implementation. The technique used was similar to the two-tiered approach of Larch. (Guttag et al(6))

The motivation for our design approach is that:

(a) it provides a method which will encourage breadth-first design in which different designs may be discussed in the context of principles rather than as a completed design in the context of prejudices; we hope that the formal techniques will help in our understanding of the design process so that we can develop techniques that are appropriate outside the atmosphere of theoretical computer science;

(b) it allows design commitments (Runciman & Thimbleby(7)) to be delayed in the sense that, because design is layered, designers will handle the most abstract properties first and then when those properties are sorted out, push through to the implementation;

(c) it establishes refinement techniques which preserve the principles used in the design and assures that functional correctness is preserved as the design moves towards its implementation.

4. USER ENGINEERING PRINCIPLES AND THE PIE MODEL

There are two general principles that have been used as the basis of this design. These refer to the interactive behaviour of the system.

predictability: the ability to predict precisely what will happen next on the basis of displayed information, that is

for example the system will not be modified by side effects
that are hidden from the user - a notion like "the display
tells the user everything". Predictability is an abstract
form of WYSIWYG.

reachability: the ability to obtain any desired final
result regardless of the current state - "no matter what
sort of mess the user gets into there is a way out of it".

In many respects the two principles are too abstract.
We use them here to exemplify our method.

The interactive behaviour of a system may be
represented by an interpretation function I which maps
command sequences (P) to effects (E). P therefore
corresponds to sequences of keystrokes or mouse clicks and
E corresponds to displays, say the displayed window, as
well as the final result. Predictability and reachability
may be expressed simply within the PIE model(4) by first
introducing a notion of **equivalence** to describe when two
effects are equivalent.

We define **simple equivalence** of two command sequences:

$\forall$ p,q $\in$ P : p==q $\Leftrightarrow$ I(p) = I(q)

and **observation equivalence** of two command sequences:

$\forall$ p,q $\in$ P : p=*=q $\Leftrightarrow$ $\forall$ r $\in$ P, I(p::r) = I(q::r)

where $\forall$ p,r $\in$ P : p::r is the command sequence p followed
by the command sequence r.

<P,I,E> is **predictable** iff $\forall$ p,q $\in$ P : p == q $\Rightarrow$ p =*= q

In the PIE paper(4) refinements of these notions are
introduced to include the possibility of viewing more than
the current display in order to predict what is happening.

At the simplest level reachability is achieved when I
is surjective, that is for every effect there corresponds a
command sequence that will generate it. The notion used in
this paper is almost equally general:

<P,I,E> is **simple (observational) accessible** if

$\forall$ p,q $\in$ P $\exists$ r $\in$ P such that:

p::r == q (simple accessible) and

p::r =*= q (observation accessible).

that is for any state there corresponds a command sequence
which generates a state which is either simple equivalent
or observational equivalent to the required state generated
by another command sequence. We might further refine the

reachability notion by requiring that there are inverses
for each operation. Problems here relate to the size of
the set of inverses. Alternatively and more usefully we
might require a small set of functions which generate
inverses (e.g. undos and deletes).

5.   FUNCTIONAL DECOMPOSITION OF THE PROTOTYPE

Central to the design of the prototype is a process
manager which manages editing processes. The interactive
behaviour of each editing process is initially defined by
means of a predictable and observation accessible PIE. We
give an informal presentation of the components of the
prototype before embarking on a more rigorous analysis of
the components in later sections.

Each editing process provides a view which maps to a
frame within the display. Since the major purpose of the
prototype is not the provision of overall functionality, a
minimal display editor has been specified which supports
character insertion and deletion, mouse selection and
single row and column cursor movement. The characteristics
of the editing process's view mapping are important:

(a)   lines may be fixed so that they will always be
      displayed, even when intermediate lines must be
      concealed in order to achieve their display. This
      mechanism is in contrast to more typical syntactic
      folding mechanisms as for example provided by the
      Cornell Program Synthesiser; (Teitelbaum & Reps(8))

(b)   a formatting algorithm organises text for display as
      lines on the virtual display, and therefore there is
      an initial transformation between character strings
      and texts.

A group of editing processes is managed by a process
manager, this is a static window manager that handles a
fixed number of editing processes. The process manager
acts simply as a switch ensuring that input is associated
with the current editing process and also ensures that the
currently selected process is always displayed on the
screen.

Although the process manager handles a fixed number of
editing processes a mechanism is provided which has the
effect of "transforming" the process manager to provide
selection, growing, shrinking, closing, scrapping and
opening. In addition, this mechanism (the so-called shell)
supplies files to editing processes. A simplification
taken in designing the prototype is that each editing
process handles a distinct file; we discuss the problem of
interference between windows in a forthcoming paper. (Dix
& Harrison(9)) The effect of the higher order shell
mechanism is to transform the process manager so that it

deals with a new set of editing processes. The effect of the shell functions is as follows:

growing/shrinking: these functions reinstate the selected formatter (pretty-printer) so that the editing process operates within a new frame context.

close/scratch: these functions remove an editing process. close returns an updated file to the file manager and scratch returns the original unmodified file to the file manager.

open: this function introduces a new process into the system instanced by the appropriate frame and file.

6.   THE PROTOTYPE'S INTERACTION MODEL

Proof that the system is constrained by predictability and reachability is enabled by the definition of a suitable interaction model.

6.1. The editing process

Each editing process is modelled by a predictable and observation accessible PIE. In fact this PIE is itself defined by successively refining a simple stream editor: (Dix(10)) first into a text editor and then into a display editor. State information is associated with each atomic editing process consisting of:

(a)   the ***file*** which is supplied by the file manager via the shell;

(b)   the ***frame*** which dictates the depth and width of the displayed information;

(c)   the ***fixed*** lines;

(d)   a ***label*** for each window.

We give a diagram describing the different refinements:

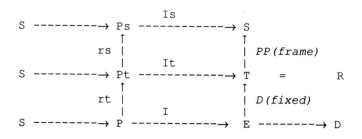

S: streams of characters

T: texts - consisting of sequences of lines, the length
      of the line being defined by the width of the frame.

E: effects - which have two components: the result space
      which is equivalent to T and the display space which
      is defined using the depth of the frame and those
      lines that are fixed.

Ps: The command sequences that manipulate streams.

Pt: The command sequences that manipulate texts. These
      commands are parametrised by text cursor pointers.

P: The command sequences that govern the operation of the
      full editing process.

All the PIE_i at this level are parametrised by a
string passed to them by the file manager when the shell
forms an appropriate process manager. The relations rs and
rt between command sequences must be temporal order
preserving.

Ps consists simply of sequences of *insert* and *delete*
commands and takes as extra argument the relevant position
in the string. <Ps,Is,S> can be proved to be predictable
and reachable quite easily.

The relationship between S and T is forged by a
pretty-printer which takes S and creates lines of text
appropriate to display within the frame. Pt is enriched by
including cursor movement commands and by transforming the
string pointer into a text cursor pointer. Predictability
and reachability of <Pt,It,T> is preserved if *PP(frame)* is
injective, and rs is surjective.

The relationship between T and E is more complicated.
This mapping relates T to an effect space which itself has
a result space: T itself, representing printed output and a
display space: incorporating a strategy for observing the
whole effect, and knowledge of the fixed lines. The proof
that the final <P,I,E> is predictable and reachable depends
on knowledge of pointer spaces and is given in a
forthcoming paper by (Dix(10)). P consists of all the
operations of Pt suitably transformed to incorporate
display pointers, cursor movement (*up* and *down*), mouse
selection and a means of fixing and unfixing lines.

6.2. The process manager

The process manager's interaction model is defined by
constructing a red PIE, see (Dix & Runciman(4)), from the
set of PIEs that describe the behaviour of the editing
processes. Since each editing process exhibits similar

properties (the main differences arise as a result of different display mappings, frame information and diplay identifiers) we can use a general construction to prove that the process manager is predictable and reachable. In the appendix we give details of the construction and give a framework that allows proof that the process manager is reachable and predictable if the component PIEs have these properties.

6.3. The Shell

As far as the interaction model is concerned, though this is not the whole story as will be seen when we consider the full implementation, the shell may be described as a set of "functors" transforming process managers. It is important therefore that the shell consists of predictability and reachability preserving functors. We consider these functors in turn:

grow and **shrink** modify the frames for specific editing processes, i.e. for each selected PIE_i a new frame, *frame* replace the old one and hence the formatting function PP_i (*frame'*) replaces PP_i (*frame*). So long as the resulting PP_i (*frame'*) is injective the required principles of predictability and reachability continue to hold.

close, scratch and **open** delete or insert editor processes from the process manager. In the case of open, a file is taken from the file manager pool to be used in constructing the new editing process. When a process is closed the updated file is returned to the file manager.

The process manager is constructed to inherit predictability and reachability; consequently all these functors preserve the required properties.

7.   THE PROTOTYPE'S CONCRETE SPECIFICATION

Once the interaction model has been specified it may be used to evaluate the effect of different interaction principles on the design of the system, a substantially easier job than that of considering the same set of principles in a fully detailed implementor's specification.

The next step, that of refining the interaction model to the concrete specification, may be carried out when the PIE model exhibits satisfactory interactive behaviour. It is important that there should be a structural relationship between the interaction model and the concrete specification so that the implementor is satisfied that he has achieved a faithful refinement of the higher level model. In this section we consider small components of the shell and process manager specifications to indicate informally the relationship between the two models. We

will notice that even at this stage transformations to the
concrete specification are made to provide a more intimate
connection between the different components of the
specification, for example: the execute button, invoked at
the shell level has two functions distinguishable by
context. The full specification has been produced as an
internal report. (Dix(11))

7.1. The Process Manager Specification

The process manager PIE model may be mapped directly
into a concrete specification. We give it in an equational
style akin to that of Larch (Guttag et al(6)) The
interface section of the specification describes the
minimum set of operations and axioms that must be satisfied
by an imported component, providing the possibility of
plugging alternative components, each satisfying equations,
into the specification. Here the specification is merely
sketched giving an impression of the structures and
mechanisms involved.

specification pm

      uses   screen, process, pname, command, frame

interface

      -- operations that are required from imported
      -- process components
          execute: process command $\rightarrow$ process
          pid: process $\rightarrow$ pname
          ... -- suitable equations defining
          -- predictability
          -- and reachability

          cursorin: screen frame $\rightarrow$ bool

passive operations

          sd: pm $\rightarrow$ process
          sc: pm $\rightarrow$ screen
          pi: pm process $\rightarrow$ bool

active operations

          select: pm pname $\rightarrow$ pm
          execute: pm command $\rightarrow$ pm

equations

```
--select
∀ win, win' ∈ pm, name ∈ pname
   ∃ p ∈ process s.t. pi(win,p) ∧ pid(p) = pname
                    ⇒ select(win, name) = win'
                    where sd(win') = p
   otherwise        ⇒ select(win,name) = win

--execute
∀ win ∈ pm, cmd ∈ command
  execute(win, cmd) = process.execute(sd(pm),cmd)
```

Hence select is used to change the currently selected process. The change takes place if there is a process which is named by the process identifier supplied as a parameter. The concrete operation select is therefore synonymous with the command s_r. It is common that transformations from PIEs to specifications will either translate commands into new operations or remain commands. The set of commands C therefore is translated by the refinement into an operation (select) and into a new set of commands called "command" which is used by the execute command within the editing process. The execute operation therefore takes the commands and pushes them into the specification of the editing process.

It should be noted that the interface definition requires that the operations connected with process be reachable and predictable. Any specification of an editing process, which has the required operations, and exhibits the required properties on the operations will be admissible.

7.2. The Shell Specification

The shell not only provides the set of transforming functions but also, in the process of building appropriate editing processes, will manage and supply state information to them. State information includes information about: the currently selected editing process, the currently constructed process manager, screen state (including text and mouse pointers) and the file store. A menu may be invoked providing access to the set of possible interactions: grow/shrink, open, close and scratch. A mouse controls a pointer which may be used either to select entries in the menu or to select processes. Buttons on the mouse are used to *select* a process or menu entry and to *execute* within the currently selected editing process. The select button has two possible useful effects and the specification needs must show that distinction: either it changes the currently selected process or it selects a menu entry and executes it.

specification shell

        uses   imenu: menu(interaction),
                        process, pm, screen, fileman

interface equations

        ... -- suitable operations and equations
            -- governing the operations

passive operations

        sm: shell $\rightarrow$ imenu
        st: shell $\rightarrow$ pm
        sp: shell $\rightarrow$ process
        sf: shell $\rightarrow$ fileman

active operations

        select: shell screen $\rightarrow$ shell
        enter : shell screen $\rightarrow$ shell

equations

    --select

$\forall$ s $\in$ screen, sh $\in$ shell, p $\in$ process
cursorin(s, context(sp(sh))) $\Rightarrow$ select(sh,s) = sh
cursorin(s, context(p)) $\Rightarrow$ select(sh,s) = sh'
                where sm(sh') = sm(sh)
                          st(sh') = st(sh)
                          sp(sh') = p
-- or the cursor is in the context of the menu
cursorin(s, mcontext(imenu))
                -- this equation will pick up the
                -- appropriate interaction and act.

otherwise $\Rightarrow$ select(sh,s) = sh

-- edit

$\forall$ sh, sh' $\in$ shell, cm $\in$ command
execute(sh, cmd) = sh'
  where sm(sh') = sm(sh)
     cmd = sr $\Rightarrow$ st(sh') = select(st(sh), pid(sr))
     otherwise $\Rightarrow$ st(sh') = pm.execute(st(sh),cmd)
     sp(sh') = sd(st(sh')) -- the select can
                      -- change the
                      -- selected process
     sf(sh') = sf(sh)

From the equations it can be seen that:

select:

    selects whichever process has a frame which currently
surrounds the mouse pointer or the appropriate menu entry.
If this process is either the currently selected process or
no frame or menu surrounds the mouse pointer no change to
the current process takes place.

execute:

    is an operation which corresponds to another mode of
operation - the keyboard as opposed to the cursor and
handles editing operations dealt with by the process
component.

8.   PROTOTYPE IMPLEMENTATION AND OPTIMISATION

8.1. Structural correspondence

    Many components of the specification are designed to
be generic in the sense that they may be parametrised by
families of specifications satisfying a specific set of
equations. These equations are given in an interface
specification and have semantics as may be found in (Ehrig
and Mahr(12)). For example the display mapping component
of our editing process specification is parametrised by a
text specification and a display frame specification. Any
text or frame specification that satisfies the specified
set of interface equations is suitable and therefore many
different actual specifications may be appropriate as
candidates. The major value of this genericity is that
changes may be made within the specification as long as the
modified specification satisfies the interface
specification.

    The flexibility provided by this genericity is
required in the implementation and so a simple pre-
processor is used to help in the production of compatible
specifications. Each unit in the specification corresponds
exactly to a module in the implementation, except in a few
minor cases where additional "system" procedures are
incorporated. All communication between modules is
achieved under properties of the relevant interface
specification.

    As well as preserving genericity this strong principle
of structural correspondence between specification and
implementation has two further advantages:-

(a)   In coding any module we have only a very small sphere
       of interest thus increasing our confidence in its
       correctness or, depending on how rigorous we want to
       be, simplifying its proof.

(b) Changes in the specification are likely to involve
     only a few units of specification. Structural
     correspondence implies commensurate effort for changes
     in the specification and changes in the
     implementation.

8.2. Refinement process - interface drift

The original concrete specification satisfies a simple
structural relationship with the interaction model.
Inevitably this structure is not always best suited to
efficient implementation although it may be used to provide
fast prototypes from specifications. (Henderson(13))

Although optimising transformations at the module
level are useful and are reasonably well understood, the
major cause of inefficiency in many implementations turns
out not to be the performance of individual modules but
rather interface bottlenecks. In the case of the prototype
this was particularly noticeable at the text/stream
interface where the character formatter and stream pointer
manipulation routines were called many times for each user
keystroke. Significant optimisations were achieved by
caching formatted structures thereby making maximum use of
information in the module interfaces.

However there is a limit to the amount of optimisation
that can be achieved at this level. Often structures that
are appropriate at the interaction model level are not
appropriate for effective implementation. Major structural
changes are required which involve changing interfaces,
thus risking potential chaos and the loss of principles and
value of the more abstract analysis. A clean way of
handling such transformations in the large is vital. Since
inefficiency often occurs at the boundary of a pair of
modules, we use the method of "interface drift". This
involves the called module performing tasks that were
previously in the calling module and involves
transformations which collapse nested function calls and
functions which deal with common data structures as used in
Feather's Zap system. (Feather(14)) Clearly, such tuning
will only be of value if a coupling between modules of this
kind may be achieved without prejudicing the called
module's relationship with other calling modules.

8.3. Mechanisms for interface drift

A general picture of interface drift is as follows.
Module A invokes B using an interface B-def. After
transformation there are two new modules A',B' with
interface B'-def.

In order to preserve correctness, the two composites
A-using-B and A'-using-B' must be proved equivalent. This
is difficult in general because of the scale and
separateness of A and B. In many cases the following easy
and clean alternative method may be used. The
transformation from B-def to B'-def may be carried out so
that B'-def is defined in terms of operations in B-def. In
this case a new transitional module C is defined, which
comprises exactly those definitions, and we get the
following situation.

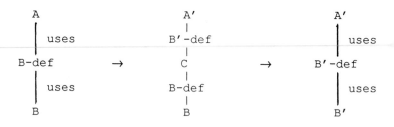

In the first stage we simply (since C is likely to be
small) prove the equivalence of A and A'-using-C. In the
second stage we satisfy ourselves that C-using-B is
equivalent to B'. Thus the proof effort is factorised. An
example of this is the adding of a line by line pretty-
print to the interface of stream. This operation is
defined to be precisely the result of repeated calls to the
character pretty-print.

As well as factoring proof effort this also gives us a
means of ensuring continuity in implementation. The
transitional module leads to a smooth implementation change
(whether or not formal methods are used), and if changes in
requirements lead to the specification of a new module D
satisfying B-def then this may be coded as D-coded where
C-coded-using-D-coded will interface properly to A'-coded.
Hence the technique may be used to produce a working
prototype with the new module, before defining a module D'
equivalent to C-using-D to bring the system back up to
speed.

This technique has been used several times in the
refinement process and is comparable at the system level to
program transformation techniques such as fold/unfold or
tail-recursion removal. We are also involved in a far more

extensive exercise in "interface drift" involving nearly all of the specification. This involves giving the file manager, which at the moment is very much a passive server, a more active role, and at the same time reducing the activity of the display and text maps. This will yield a specification more conducive to the efficient implementation of sharing between processes. Without using a highly structured method of transformation in the large, such an exercise would probably require a complete rewrite and a rather wistful hope that the new specification was equivalent to the original.

9.   CONCLUSION

We see this design approach as a fruitful method of designing systems without unnecessary premature implementation bias, a view confirmed by the practical design and implementation of a realistic system. These techniques are currently being used in the design and development of the full interactive literate programming environment.

Our current activities involve the development of tools to support the refinement process, including the management of interface drift and the development of alternative models to support interaction more appropriate to the support of principles such as those concerned with time and multiple modes.

10.   APPENDIX - The pm construction as an interaction model

Without loss of generality we assume that each component PIE_i has the property: each PIE_i is composed from a common set of commands C. All commands that are not valid generate errors in particular PIE_i and overloading of commands is not permitted. Each C_i is distinguished by including a special select command S_i.

The composite PIE_w formed from the individual PIE_i then has a *result*

$$R=R_1 \times R_2 \times \cdots \times R_n$$

and an effect space E defined as:

$$E=n \times E_1 \times E_2 \times \cdots \times E_n$$

where $n = \{1, \ldots, n\}$ defines the particular PIE_i that is currently selected.

Two maps are associated with the display:

$$\sigma : D \rightarrow n \text{ and } \tau:D \rightarrow \bigcup_{i=1}^{i=n} D_i$$

Guidelines for the Design of Interactive Systems´, People and Computers: Designing the Interface, Cambridge University Press, 161-171.

4.   Dix, A. and Runciman, C., 1985, ´Abstract Models of Interactive Systems´, People and Computers: Designing the interface, Cambridge University Press, 13-22.

5.   Alty, J.L., 1984, ´The Application of Path Algebras to Interactive Dialogue Design´, Behaviour and Information Technology, 3, 119-132.

6.   Guttag, J.V., Horning, J.J., and Wing, J.M., 1985, ´Larch in Five Easy Pieces´, DIGITAL Systems Research Center,

7.   Runciman, C and Thimbleby, H.W., 1985, Equal Opportunity Interactive Systems, YCS 80, University of York.

8.   Teitelbaum T. and Reps T., 1981, ´The Cornell Program Synthesizer: A Syntax-Directed Programming Environment´, Comm. ACM, 24, 563-573.

9.   Dix, A.J. and Harrison, M.D., 1986, Towards principles and interaction models for window managers, in preparation.

10. Dix, A.J., 1986, Formalising the design of a simple editor by means of an interaction model, in preparation.

11. Dix, A.J., 1986, The formal specification of a prototype multi-window editor, University of York Internal Report.

12. Ehrig, H. and Mahr, B., 1985, Fundamentals of Algebraic Specification 1, Springer Monograph on Theoretical Computer Science.

13. P Henderson, 1986, ´Functional Programming, Formal Specification, and Rapid Prototyping´, IEEE Transactions on Software Engineering, SE-12, 241-250.

14. Feather, M.S., 1982, ´A System for Assisting Program Transformation´, ACM Transactions on Programming Languages and Systems, 4, 1-20.

Chapter 11

The presenter—a formal design for an autonomous display manager

R. Took

ABSTRACT

Standard graphics and interface packages provide an abstraction for static display elements
like lines or boxes, but routines for dynamic
facilities like menus must still be bound in to
the application process. IPSEs place considerable
demands on the human interface, both to reconcile
the I/O requirements of ranges of devices, users,
tools, and tasks; and to consolidate their
representation on the screen. A *control* abstraction, in which screen objects inherit not only
appearance, but also behaviour, from an autonomous I/O manager with a consistent interaction
model, is considered essential for achieving this
integration. A formal design for such a manager -
ASPECT's PRESENTER - is specified in Z.

1. INTRODUCTION: INTERFACING AN IPSE

A defining goal of software engineering is enhanced programmer productivity. This may partly be achieved through a
more extensive set of tools, whose use and access to data
is integrated and coordinated by a centralised database.
But a major consideration in the design of an effective
software engineering environment must also be the suitability and power of its human interface. We may define two
perspectives on this interface. Externally, the 'user
interface' is that collection of symbols and mechanisms via
which the everyday user (the production programmer)
accesses and controls the facilities offered to him in the
environment. Equally important, though, particularly in an
environment configurable for particular purposes or extensible through the porting or creation of additional tools,
is the 'programmer interface', which provides the means for
constructing displayable representations of the interaction
state, and interpreting hard input. A programmer interface
that is inconsistent, incomplete, or simply at too low a
level can add enormously to the cost of installing a new
application or making global adjustments to the existing
user interface. This in turn impairs the responsiveness of

the environment to user needs, and jeopardises its effectiveness.

This paper emphasises the importance of design decisions at the programmer interface level to the development of both a cooperating and extensible set of applications, and a consistent user interface; suggests some principles towards this goal; and presents a particular design for an interface controller for the Alvey-sponsored ASPECT IPSE. This design is expressed in the formal specification language 'Z', developed by the Programming Research Group at Oxford. The full specification for this controller (called the 'Presenter') and its primitive operations, as well as an introduction to the Z language, is found in (1). For reasons of space, this paper assumes a knowledge of Z, and also presents only a subset of the complete design for the Presenter. Some functions are defined only informally, and must be taken on trust. A feature of Z, however, is the equal status given to explanatory text, and so innocence of the formal language is not a severe disadvantage.

Criteria for the success of a human interface relate not only to its users, but also to the system which it serves. A single-user, single-language system designed for exploratory or personal programming, such as Smalltalk (2), Interlisp (3), or Cedar (4), may have few built-in restrictions on the construction of the user interface, simply because the unity of the system ensures ultimate consistency. For this reason the programmer interface in such systems may also be ill-defined, in the sense of being freely extensible and merging inextricably with the underlying computational model. In such cases the interface may be judged largely on its external, user-oriented functionality.

A software engineering environment intended, on the other hand, for serious production operates under many more constraints. For reasons of cost or status, a variety of display and input devices might be expected to operate in parallel. Inevitably, numbers of programmers and other personnel are involved, possibly distributed geographically. A set of development tools will be available, ideally to be run concurrently with the program being developed. In short, an IPSE is likely to have to cope with ranges of devices, users, tools, and tasks. Success of the human interface under these conditions is related strongly to its ability to integrate this diversity, by providing a well-defined programmer interface to an independently configurable user interface.

1.1. Devices

At the extreme, display devices available in an IPSE may range from character mapped, 'glass-teletype' terminals like the vt100, to high-resolution, high-bandwidth bit-mapped displays. The goal of the programmer interface will be to exploit fully the power of the device, without on the one hand reducing interaction to a simple intersection of the capabilities of the available devices (text only, say), or, on the other, binding tools to particular devices by providing trapdoors through to device-specific code. This ideal of device independence is difficult to meet without providing the programmer interface with a comprehensive abstract screen representation which can be mapped, with more or less loss of information, to different display and input hardware.

1.2. Users

An IPSE must provide services for a variety of user roles, including programmers, designers, analysts, and managers, each with different needs; and to a variety of particular users, each with different levels of expertise and experience. Current software engineering environments adopt different interaction styles. CADES (5) and Perspective (6) use a purely textual interface, while DSEE (7) and JADE (8) use in addition windows and mouse-driven input by selection of icons or menus. However, the interface style provided is not configurable. The range of users and roles calls ideally for a range of interactive styles to be available within a single IPSE. As with the range of devices, this requires an abstract representation for interaction, which can be employed by applications at a level independent of style. The abstract interaction specification may then be interpreted by an interface manager which is modularised or parameterised to present the interaction in different styles at the request of the user. The precise mechanics of this is not dealt with here.

1.3. Tools

Tools may either be written specifically for a particular IPSE, or ported from another environment. In contrast to an exploratory environment, where lengthy tuning for response or performance can be tolerated, in a software engineering environment the premium is likely to be on rapid, reliable porting of existing tools, or fast prototyping of new tools. In either case, the ease of use and power of the programming interface will be critical to the costs involved. A consistent and intuitive model underlying the programming interface facilities is a major factor in its effectiveness.

1.4. Tasks

The emerging concept of an environment for software engineering is predicated on the ability to run several tools - compiler, debugger, run-time monitor, database, mail, clock etc. - concurrently. The prevalence now of window-managed personal environments reinforces the expectation for this multitasking. Not only should tasks run concurrently, but it is expected that their screen representation be persistent, visible, and updated dynamically. However, the conventional association between an application and a screen window is convenient, but purely arbitrary. The Presenter allows an application to present separate objects anywhere on the screen. The apparent anarchy is controlled because the Presenter arbitrates between the claims of competing applications, and the wishes of the user, for the allocation of screen space. The objects from one application, for example, may be obscured by another of higher priority, or the user may choose to corral the objects of an application without its intervention to a more convenient area of the screen. In order to handle multitasking of complex applications which may be ignorant of the screen requirements of their contemporaries, it is important that the user be given the ability to rearrange or reconfigure (change the size, priority, visibility of) application objects to fit the circumstances of the moment.

2. THE PRESENTER

The ability to handle ranges of devices, users, tools, and tasks, and to reconcile power and ease of use in the programmer interface as well as device independence and device exploitation at the user interface is no easy matter. A well-defined intermediate representation for the objects of interaction, and operations upon this representation, rather than upon device-specific constructs like bitmaps, is a pre-requisite. This enables mapping of application I/O to different devices, and facilitates porting of different applications into an environment using this representation. In decoupling tool computation from screen generation, such a representation in addition modularises user interface issues such as interaction style and the presentation of multitasking.

However, a standard interface package such as GKS (10), GEM (11), or any of a number of window manager graphics packages, implemented as a library of routines to be bound in to the application, is an abstraction solely of graphical representation - there is very little or no *control* abstraction. The application is still expected to handle minor screen events like redrawing, sometimes at a very low level. Even in more complex facilities like menu packages, control is simply handed over from the application to the code that drives the menu - no parallelism is involved. The exception is in some cases window interaction and cursor tracking which may be handled concurrently with applications.

The Presenter, as well as providing a powerful *display* abstraction, matches this with a corresponding *control* abstraction. Presenter objects are thus abstract data types in the sense not only of containing static information relating to their appearance (size, position etc.) but of responding consistently to dynamic operations (scaling, movement etc.), although these capabilities they inherit from the Presenter, in the manner of Smalltalk, via a set of attributes. The Presenter itself is an autonomous process running independently of applications, and to which they must communicate by message passing. In this scheme the user may be modelled equally as a process, communicating instructions to the Presenter. The difference is only that an application will be ignorant of its parallel processes and their objects, whereas the user will be aware of the whole domain. On the other hand, an application may prevent the user accessing or manipulating an object that it owns. Communication from the user to an application is via selection of a Presenter object belonging to that application. Presenter objects thus persist over display changes (automatic redrawing when uncovered) and even, through cutting and pasting, over changes in application ownership. In addition they have consistent, autonomous behaviour - they behave themselves.

2.1. Presenter Objects

Presenter objects are rectangular areas of the notional screen. The Z model calls these 'regions', and specifies their type as REG. They may have two types of basic content: a textual character, or a specification for a graphical image ('map'). At a fundamental level, then, the Presenter both provides for character-based textual interaction, and also puts no limits on the granularity of graphical interaction: an object may be as small or large as the screen is capable of displaying. However, if this were the only means of representation, the model would be a flat accumulation of discrete elements. Since we wish to construct complex objects which have associated behaviour (for example text strings which recognise editing operations), we also need a mechanism for recursive composition of objects into structures which can be manipulated by the basic operations. The Presenter models this structure as an ordered n-ary tree, with regions as its nodes:

REGIONSTRUCTURE_____

regiontree: COTREE [REG]
root: REG
allregions, leaves: $\mathbb{P}$ REG
parent: REG —|→ REG
children, ancestors, descendants, family, leavesof: REG ↔ REG
order: REG —|→ seq REG

_____

{root} ∪ leaves ⊆ allregions

_____

(For a full definition of COTREE, see (1)). All nodes on the regiontree, including the root and the leaves, are regions (objects), and the regiontree contains at least the root, which notionally represents the display screen. All regions are thus unique (an implementation would assign unique identifiers). The regiontree is a means of composing regions, determining the structure of this composition, and, through the 'order' function, defining the sequence of regions. ('order' maps a region to the sequence of its children). The sequencing will be important both in the display of text strings, and in the layering of screen elements. The tree is constructed via the 'parent' function, whilst the additional relations express the relationships between regions which their names suggest (the 'family' of a region are all its descendants plus the region itself).

The regiontree represents the logical structure of its

contents, as opposed to their physical structure as perceived in their sizes and positions on the screen. The
regiontree thus in a sense models the semantics of the
screen objects, in that object grouping and attribute
inheritance represented in the tree affect the extent and
character of the basic operations upon them. A similar
application for hierarchical structuring was proposed in
the work on Descartes (12).

The contents - text characters and graphical maps - may
only be linked in to the leaves of the regiontree. Text is
represented in the regiontree by a distinguished set of
regions ('textroots') the leaves of whose subtrees point to
characters (type CHAR) - that is, character id's abstracted
from any particular font. The relationship between individual characters and sequenced text strings is implicit in
the structure of the regiontree. A leaf may only point to
one character. All leaf regions can be traced back to a
textroot, but some leaves of textroots may be empty. Textroots cannot be nested:

TEXT_____ ⌐

  REGIONSTRUCTURE
  charlink: REG —|→ CHAR
  textroots: ℙ REG
  _____

  textroots ⊆ allregions
  dom charlink ⊆ leavesof (textroots)
  ∀ tr, tr1: textroots . tr ∉ descendants tr1
⌊_____⌋

In order to specify graphical images, we first define
sets of pairs of real numbers in the range 0-1, and sets of
these:

POINT ≙ ([0,1] × [0,1])

ALLPOINTS ≙ ([0,1] ↔ [0,1])

An object of type ALLPOINTS (a 'map') is thus a (possibly infinite) set of points, specified by real coordinates,
in a unit square of the plane, and may thus define any
image. Only leaves of the regiontree may point to such
maps, and each leaf may point only to one map:

MAPS_____ ⌐

  REGIONSTRUCTURE
  maplink: REG —|→ ALLPOINTS
  _____

  dom maplink ⊆ leaves
⌊_____⌋

The contents of the regiontree are therefore text (in characters), and maps. No leaf region can point both to a character and a map:

CONTENTS_____

    TEXT
    MAPS

    ———————————————————

    dom charlink ∩ dom maplink = { }

2.2. Display Control Information

In addition to the contents of the regiontree, other information must reflect the relation between the contents and their displayed appearance and behaviour. This control information can be broadly divided into two types. Static controls specify precisely such values as the size, position, and other display features of regions such as transparency. Dynamic controls on the other hand put constraints upon the behaviour of regions when affected by user manipulation. Such constraints are graphical containment, selectability, moveability etc. Both types of control information may be updated by the application, or by the user. In addition, the Presenter itself may update the static control information in order to reflect the state of the screen as influenced by device-dependent characteristics such as font size.

All regions except the root have a size with respect to their parent region. Size is expressed as a real proportion of the parent region in both the horizontal and vertical dimensions, and therefore also determines the shape of a region:

SIZES_____

    REGIONSTRUCTURE
    size: REG —|→ ($\mathbb{R} \times \mathbb{R}$)

    ———————————————————

    dom size = allregions − {root}

Similarly, all regions with the exception of the root have a position with respect to their parent region. Each region must in addition have a reference point by means of which it is sited. The value of the position of a region sites its reference point at that position in the plane of its parent region. Both values are expressed in real coordinates:

POSITIONS_____

REGIONSTRUCTURE
position, refpoint: REG —|→ ($\mathbb{R} \times \mathbb{R}$)

_____

dom position = dom refpoint = allregions − {root}

_____

In interpreting these values for screen display, unity
is taken as identity with the parent. Thus a region of size
(1.0, 1.0) is the same size as its parent, and regions of
sizes (0.5, 0.5) and (2.0, 2.0) are a quarter and four
times the size of their parents respectively. Similarly, a
region with reference point (0.5, 0.5) − its centre − and
at position (0.5, 0.5) is at the same position as its
parent (since their centres coincide). The same region at
position (2.0, 1.0) has its centre outside its parent
region and in line with its top edge, and so on. The coordinate origin is the bottom left of all regions. Since any
region may be placed anywhere on the plane, irrespective of
the position of its parent, regions do not capture physical
grouping such as containment. But they do capture logical
grouping, since if a region is moved, all its descendant
regions and leaf objects move with it. Similarly, selection of this group is simply a matter of selecting the owning region.

As an illustration of the usefulness of this model, consider the specification for the display of a box containing
a lengthening horizontal bar, fixed at its left end to the
edge of the box, which may be used to reflect the state of
a terminating process such as compilation. The bar would be
created as a child of the box. If the bar had refpoint
(0.0, 0.5) − halfway up its left side − and position (0.0,
0.5) − fixed to a similar point in the box − then the
length and width of the bar would entirely be determined by
its 'size' value, and simply changing the x-coordinate of
this would be the only action required of the monitoring
process − a value of 0.5 would set the end of the bar half
way along the box, for example. The effect of these values
would be entirely independent of the position or size of
the box itself − it could be left up to the user to place
and shape it as he thinks fit.

'size' and 'position' are therefore relative values.
While this is the primary representation of placement used
within the Presenter, it is also useful, in order to be
able to define further properties of the display, to derive
a measure of the absolute position and size of regions −
that is, with respect to the root of the regiontree (which
represents the full screen). The two functions 'absize' (:
REG —|→ ($\mathbb{R} \times \mathbb{R}$)) and 'abpos' (: REG × ($\mathbb{R} \times \mathbb{R}$) —|→ ($\mathbb{R} \times \mathbb{R}$)), not
defined here, depend on the 'size' and 'position' functions
and return these values with respect not to parents, but to
the root of the regiontree. ('abpos' returns the absolute
position of any point in the plane of a region).

The relation 'contains' records pairs of regions the second of which is graphically contained within the first. This is a dynamic constraint upon the regions within the Presenter: no part of a 'contained' region may be moved outside its 'containing' region either by an application or by the user. No circularity is allowed in this relation: no region may contain itself along any path of the relation:

```
CONTAINMENT_____

    REGIONSTRUCTURE
    contains: REG ⟷ REG
    _____

    dom contains ∪ ran contains ⊆ allregions

    ∀ r: allregions . (r ↦ r) ∉ contains⁺
```

The display layout of the contents of the Presenter is extended by descriptions of the autonomous features of the behaviour and state of regions - that is, features which relate to regions (and their descendant regions considered as a unit) in isolation. These features are represented in the Presenter by a set of attributes of regions. A subset of the full range of Presenter attributes is defined here (text formatting attributes are omitted):

ATTRIBUTERANGE ≙ versizeable | horsizeable | vermoveable | hormoveable | scale | group | clip | transparent | hide | not | selectable | locked | live

The first four attributes permit or prevent sizing and movement of regions by the user in both dimensions independently. This capability can be used for example to display sliding boxes or boxes expandable in only one dimension. 'scale' affects the behaviour of a region and its descendants under sizing: with the 'scale' attribute set, descendant regions will be scaled relative to their common ancestor (in effect, their *relative* size values will not change); without this attribute, sizing a region does not affect the screen size of its descendants. The 'group' attribute has analogous effect with respect to movement of regions: when a region with 'group' set is moved, descendant regions (wherever they are on the screen) will move correspondingly, otherwise not. The effects of the remaining attributes are defined in later schemas.

All regions may have attributes, but character regions, which will ultimately be displayed in a fixed, device-dependent font, may not have their size changed.

REGIONATTRIBUTES_____

REGIONSTRUCTURE
attributes: REG —|→ |P ATTRIBUTERANGE

_____

dom attributes ⊆ allregions
∀ c: dom charlink .
{versizeable, horsizeable} ∩ attributes c = {}

The basic control state of the Presenter, therefore, containing all the information necessary to generate screens on a range of particular display devices, can be encapsulated in a schema:

PRESENTER_CONTROL_____

REGIONSTRUCTURE
CONTENTS
SIZES
POSITIONS
CONTAINMENT
REGIONATTRIBUTES

The state of the specification up to this point totally defines the placement of both text and 'map' regions.

2.3. Screen Generation

From this stage on, for the purposes of display, all regions may be treated alike as simply representing graphical areas of the screen. The screen display is a function of the state represented in PRESENTER_CONTROL. Further display constraints come into effect at this stage. Text, for example, has a complex series of constraints governing alignment of text characters and formatting. This is omitted in this paper. A constraint that may be defined here is the property of containment between arbitrary regions. All the points in a contained region lie within its containing region:

LAYOUT_____

PRESENTER_CONTROL

_____

∀ r1, r2: allregions .
(r1 |→ r2) ∈ contains ⇒
    abpos r2 (POINT) ⊆ abpos r1 (POINT)

Generating a particular screen display from the

information constructed so far is accomplished in three stages. Firstly, character references are converted into graphical character images, so that all contents of the tree can be treated alike as sets of POINTs ('elements'). Secondly, the images of all regions are determined in terms of mappings to absolute screen points ('sheets'), by reference to their sizes and positions, their maps, and attributes such as 'not' and 'clip'. Finally, it is determined, by reference to display layering represented by the ordering of the tree, precisely which subsets of the regions are actually to appear on the screen ('displayed').

A new function 'charmap' is defined (here, informally) which maps character regions to sets of points ('maps') representing their image, by reference to particular fonts on particular devices. Thus all the contents of the region-tree can finally be represented as maps. An element is thus a leaf region which points to a discrete displayable image.

FILLSHEETS defines the images of elements not in the generic 'map' format (where each element is a mapping into POINTs), but in terms of a single display surface of POINTs. Thus the size, position, and attributes of an element region (whether it is transparent, inverted, or hidden) must be taken into account. 'rawsheets' records, for each element, the colours of absolute screen points in the area of the element. The attributes are searched for along the whole path of a region up to the root, and they are thus inherited down the tree:

FILLSHEETS_____

LAYOUT
charmap, elements: REG —|→ ALLPOINTS
rawsheets: REG —|→ POINT —|→ Black | White

_____

elements = charmap ∪ maplink

∀ el: dom elements; p: POINT .
  hide ∉ InheritedAttributes ⇒
    ((p ∈ elements el ⇒
      {abpos el p |→ Col1} ∈ rawsheets el) ∧

    (transparent ∉ InheritedAttributes ⇒
      p ∈ (ALLPOINTS – elements el) ⇒
        {abpos el p |→ Col2} ∈ rawsheets el))

  hide ∈ InheritedAttributes ⇒
    rawsheets el = { }

WHERE
InheritedAttributes = ∪ attributes (parent* el)

not ∉ InheritedAttributes ⇒
  Col1 = Black ∧ Col2 = White

not ∈ InheritedAttributes ⇒
  Col1 = White ∧ Col2 = Black

‘rawsheets’, however, represents the absolute screen image of an element, without taking into account whether the image is clipped or obscured by other regions. A region with the ‘clip’ attribute set restricts the ‘rawsheets’ of all its descendant elements to points within its own extent, giving a new image definition, ‘sheets’. The ‘clip’ping property is not inherited and applies only to those regions in which it is set. Thus the ‘sheets’ of descendant elements of regions which are not clipped are the same as their ‘rawsheets’:

CLIP_____

FILLSHEETS
sheets: REG —|→ POINT —|→ Black | White

_____

∀ r: allregions; el: dom elements | el ∈ descendants r .
  clip ∈ attributes r ⇒
    sheets el = {p: POINT . abpos r p} ◁ rawsheets el

  clip ∉ attributes r ⇒ sheets el = rawsheets el

Finally, the sequencing of the elements ('list') determines their display ordering, and thus which parts of elements will be obscured by others – a later element obscures (notionally: is displayed on top of) an earlier element in the same position. DISPLAY defines two important functions: 'displayed' and 'screen'. 'displayed' gives the final screen extent of an element in terms of those points of the screen at which it will be visible – this is essential for determining the target of a mouse selection, for example. For this reason, the cursor image itself is omitted from consideration – if it were included, the cursor could only ever select itself! Secondly, 'screen' is a precise definition of the total screen image, in terms of assignments of colours to screen POINTs. This is simply a restriction of the sheets to those portions which are actually displayed, the result overwritten by the cursor image.

DISPLAY_____

   CLIP
   displayed: REG $\rightarrowtail\!\!\!\mid\rightarrow$ ALLPOINTS
   screen: POINT $\longrightarrow\!\mid\rightarrow$ Black | White

   $\forall$ list: seq REG | list = oleaves regiontree root $\lceil$ dom elements .
   $\forall$ lel: ran list .
     displayed lel = dom sheets lel –
      $\cup$ {el: leaves – {cursorimg} | [lel]^[el] subseq list .
      dom sheets el}

   screen = $\cup$ {el: ran list .
     displayed el $\lhd$ sheets el} $\oplus$ sheets cursorimg

('oleaves' is a function returning the sequence of leaves of a node in an ordered tree; '$\lceil$' is the Z sequence range restriction operator)

2.4. Processes

The overall state description of the Presenter so far is therefore represented by DISPLAY, which incorporates all the antecedent states. DISPLAY represents a complete specification of the screen appearance of the control information held in PRESENTER_CONTROL on a particular display device. In addition to this, however, the Presenter must be aware of the process origins of each of its regions, so that input may be directed appropriately.

In the Presenter, client processes own discrete subtrees of the regiontree, and it is possible for one process to own a number of subtrees. The roots of these subtrees are all children of the root of the regiontree, so that sets of regions owned by processes cannot be nested. The Presenter records this ownership by means of the 'owner' function, which maps children of the root to processes. All descendants of these children are owned by the same process, and any selection on the regions is sent to this process:

```
PROCESSOWNERSHIP_____
                                                        ⌐

  REGIONSTRUCTURE
  owner: REG —|→ PROCESSES
  _____

  dom owner = children root
                                                        ⌋
```

Finally, in order to echo graphical user input (with a mouse or with cursor keys), the Presenter must own and be in control of a cursor. The specification assigns a region to contain the screen cursor. This region is a child of the root, and is always the last of the root's children. Thus it can never be overlaid by any other screen object. The cursor has zero size, and represents the 'hot spot' of the visible cursor. In addition, the 'cursorimg' region, which is a child of 'cursor', points to the map defining the image of the cursor. This map, and its size, is not specified, so that it may be loaded dynamically by the application or the user:

```
CURSOR_____
                                              ⌐

  REGIONSTRUCTURE
  cursor, cursorimg: REG
  cursorsize: (R × R)
  presenterproc: PROCESSES
  _____

  parent cursor = root
  parent cursorimg = cursor
  cursor = last order root
  owner cursor = presenterproc
  {(cursor |→ (0.0, 0.0)), (cursorimg |→ cursorsize)} ⊆ size
                                              ⌋
```

The final Presenter state, incorporating both control information and the mapping from this to display on a particular device, as well as essential information for the routing of input, is given in the following schema:

```
PRESENTER_____
                                                 ⌐
  DISPLAY
  PROCESSOWNERSHIP
  CURSOR
                                                 ⌋
```

2.5. Initialisation

The specification of the Presenter given above constrains the full module to contain at least the root, cursor, and cursor image regions. Initialising the Presenter upon booting the system establishes the following initial state, including these fundamental regions:

init_PRESENTER_____

Δ PRESENTER
_____

allregions' = {root, cursor}
parent' = {cursor ↦ root, cursorimg ↦ cursor}
order' = {root ↦ [cursor], cursor ↦ [cursorimg]}
textroots' = { }
owner' = {cursor ↦ presenterproc}
charlink' = { }
maplink' = { }
size' = {cursor ↦ (0.0, 0.0), cursorimg ↦ cursorsize}
position' = {cursor ↦ (0.5, 0.5), cursorimg ↦ (0.0, 0.0)}
refpoint' = {cursor ↦ (0.5. 0.5), cursorimg ↦ (0.5, 0.5)}
contains' = {root ↦ cursor}
attributes' = {root ↦ {clip}, cursor ↦ {moveable, locked}
    cursorimg ↦ {transparent, locked}}
screen' = {{POINT} × White}

That is, the Presenter consists at least of the root, representing the screen, a cursor region, and a cursor image region, although the image itself is undefined. The cursor starts in the centre of the screen, and is constrained to be contained within the screen (note that only the zero-sized hotspot is so constrained – the cursor image may overlap the screen edges.) The screen clips all its descendant regions, and starts off totally white. The cursor is moveable, its image is transparent, and neither will accept input. .

2.6. Input

All input from the user can simply be modelled as selection of a region or a set of regions on the regiontree. Selection is also the basis for a number of user operations on the Presenter. For example, deletion or cutting takes place on sets of regions which may be supplied by the user as a selection. There are two types of selection, described in separate schemas. The first takes place by means of progressive ascent of the regiontree from an initially selected screen object at a leaf of the regiontree. The ascent might be marked by the user by successive mouse button clicks, for example, although other means could be implemented. A screen object is potentially selected when the cursor reference point lies inside the 'displayed' portion of an element. If the region has its 'live' attribute set, then a selection is indicated even when no mouse button clicks have been made. In this type of selection, the set of objects selected will be singleton, since this method always returns a single region at some level of the regiontree. Selection is defined on the final schema PRESENTER since information on the displayed appearance of the screen and the position of the cursor must be taken into account:

SINGLESELECTION_____⌐

   Ξ PRESENTER
   selection!: ℙ REG
   noofclicks?: ℕ
   _____

   ∀ el: dom elements | position cursor ∈ displayed el •
   noofclicks? = 0 ∧ live ∈ ∪ attributes ⦇ parent* el ⦈ ⇒
      selection! = {el}

   noofclicks? > 0 ⇒
      selection! = {parent $^{\text{noofclicks?}-1}$ el}

_____⌐

The second type of selection is by (notionally) dragging the cursor over an arbitrary set of screen objects. Thus in this selection a set of regions may be returned since not all sets of screen objects will have a single ancestor region on the regiontree. The information input is a set of points representing the track of the cursor (say while the mouse button is held down) over the screen. The regions returned represent all the objects thus covered. These regions may not be nested: they are the minimal representation for the group of objects and represent a set of discrete subtrees of the regiontree. All regions thus selected must be owned by the same process: selection spanning process boundaries is not permitted:

DRAGGEDSELECTION_____⌐

   Ξ PRESENTER
   selection!: ℙ REG
   cursortrack?: ℙ POINT
   _____

   ∀ els: ℙ dom elements | cursortrack? ⊆ displayed ⦇ els ⦈ •
   selection! = {s, s1: REG | leavesof ⦇ {s, s1} ⦈ ⊆ els ∧
   s ∉ descendants s1 ∧ owner s = owner s1}

_____⌐

These two types of selection can be combined in a single schema which in addition defines the process to which either type of selection will be sent, by reference to the 'owner' of the selected regions:

SELECT_____

SINGLESELECTION
DRAGGEDSELECTION
toprocess!: PROCESSES

toprocess! = owner ⦇ ancestors ⦇ selection! ⦈ ⦈

2.7. Primitive Operations in the Presenter

A number of primitive operations are defined on the Presenter, which may broadly be divided into three types: operations that manipulate the regiontree (OPEN, PASTE, CREATELEAF, DELETE, CUT, READ, WRITE, etc.), operations to set and clear properties maintained in functions and attributes (SETHEIGHT, SETWIDTH, SETATTRIBUTES, CLEARATTRIBUTES etc.), and operations to inquire the values of properties (INQUIRESIZE, INQUIREREFPOINT etc.).

As an illustration, the operation to set the height of a region is defined on the Presenter control state as follows:

SETHEIGHT_____

Δ PRESENTER_CONTROL ▷ (size, absize)
ofregion?: REG
newheight?: $\mathbb{R}$

versizeable ∈ attributes ofregion?

scale ∉ attributes ofregion? ⟹
  ∀ r: allregions │ r ∈ children ofregion? .
    size′ = size ⊕ {r ↦ newsize: ($\mathbb{R} \times \mathbb{R}$)} ∧
    absize′ r = absize r

size′ = size ⊕ {ofregion? ↦ (first size ofregion?, newheight?)}

('first' extracts the first coordinate of a pair). Thus, for a region's height to be changed by the Presenter, the 'versizeable' attribute must be set on the region. If the 'scale' attribute is not set, then all children of the region must have their sizes updated so that their absolute size remains constant over the operation. The operation itself simply inserts a new value for the y-coordinate of the region's size.

3. CONCLUSION

The autonomy of the Presenter puts it in a unique position to assume control of the screen and input devices, and
interpose abstract representations to insulate applications
from device dependencies. The display abstraction
represented by the regions and their properties can be
mapped to different devices via specific drivers. Although
the Presenter has been designed with bitmapped devices in
mind, it could be constrained to a character device, possibly with character-graphic emulation. The control abstraction specified by the attributes and the regiontree, and
maintained by the Presenter process, enables the built-in
generic operations like region movement and sizing and text
editing, but is also extensible, given an environment in
which message-passing objects can exist, to allow the construction of higher-level objects which can handle ever
wider areas of interaction. At an intermediate level these
might consist of menus, valuators, or monitoring objects,
whilst a high level interface manager, determining interaction style and configurable for different users, is conceivable. Even at the level of the Presenter primitives,
this control abstraction is likely to reduce dramatically
the burden of the application programmer, in terms of
amount of code, portability, and the speed of prototyping
of the application's user interface.

4. ACKNOWLEDGEMENTS

Acknowledgements are principally due to Anthony Hall of
System Designers for providing the underlying definitions
of the ordered tree, which are to be found in (1), and for
helpful and fruitful discussions on the structuring of the
Z specification for the Presenter. I would also like to
thank Roy Lakin of ICL for some effective Z sleuthing; Jeff
Sanders of the Programming Research Group at Oxford for
acting as Z guru; and Ian Benest of York University for
more general discussion on interface design issues.

5. REFERENCES

1. Walker, D. I. (ed.), February 1986, 'Specification of
   the Aspect Public Tool Interface',
   aspect/wb/pub/pti/Zspec.1.0, System Designers.

2. Tesler, L., Aug 1981, 'The Smalltalk Environment', **Byte
   vol 6 (8)**.

3. Teitlman W., Masinter L., April 1981, 'The Interlisp
   Programming Environment', **IEEE Computer** , pp 25-33.

4. Beach, J. R., July 1985, 'Experience with the Cedar Programming Environment for Computer Graphics Research',
   Xerox, CSL-84-6.

5. Snowdon, R. A., 1981, 'CADES and software system
   development', in Hunke, H., 'Software Engineering
   Environments', North-Holland, pp 81-96.

6. System Designers, March 1985, Perspective VAX/UNIX target product documentation.

7. Leblang, D. B., Chase, R. P., May 1984, 'Computer-Aided

Software Engineering in a Distributed Workstation Environment', **ACM SIGPLAN notices** : Procs ACM SIGPLAN/SIGSOFT Software Engineering Symposium on Practical Software Development Environments, April 23-25 1984, vol 19 (5).

8. Hill, D. R., Witten, I. H., Neal, R., Lomow, G., 1984, 'JECL and HIDE: Practical Questions for the JADE user interface', University of Calgary Man-Machine Systems Laboratory, IPS Session 84.

9. Fahnrich, K. P., Ziegler, J., 1984, 'Workstations using direct manipulation as interaction mode - aspects of design, application and evaluation', **Interact '84** , **vol 2** , p 203.

10. Hopgood, R. A., Duce, D. A., Gallop, J. R., Sutcliffe, D. C., 1984, 'Introduction to the Graphical Kernel System GKS', Academic Press.

11. GEM AES and VDI user manuals, Digital Research.

12. Shaw, M., Borison E., Horowitz M., Lane T., Nichols, D., Pausch, R., June 1983, 'Descartes: A Programming-Language Approach to Interactive Display Interfaces', **ACM SIGPLAN Notices** , **vol 18 (6)** , pp 100-111.

Chapter 12

Project development in view

P. Reid and R.C. Welland

1. INTRODUCTION

This paper describes the design of the Man-Machine Interface (MMI) for an Integrated Project Support Environment (IPSE) called ECLIPSE which is being funded as part of the Alvey Software Engineering programme and involves collaboration between universities and commercial companies.

ECLIPSE is hosted on a large minicomputer with multiple high-performance personal workstations connected over an Ethernet local area network. The significant feature of this arrangement is the high resolution graphic display of the workstations which supports a windows, icons, mouse and pull-down menus style of interaction (the so-called WIMP interface).

The emphasis of the ECLIPSE programme is on the development of an environment to support the complete project life cycle rather than just programming activities. Thus, ECLIPSE is based on a central database providing configuration management and version control, with a 'cladding' of tools to support design methodologies, the development and re-use of software, cross-development, documentation development, project planning, etc.

The wide variety of tasks involved in project development means that the ECLIPSE Man-Machine Interface has to support many user roles such as project management, secretarial duties, systems analysis, systems design, programming, testing, maintenance, technical authoring, etc. In addition, ECLIPSE users are likely to have a wide range of abilities and expectations, and a highly variable frequency of use. All these factors provide a considerable challenge when attempting to design a Man-Machine Interface which takes advantage of modern WIMP style interfaces and yet is based on a coherent and flexible underlying philosophy.

2. THE WIMP TECHNOLOGY

2.1 Windows

Previous work by Teitelman (1), Herot et al (2) and Rowson and Salama (3) has indicated the effectiveness of a windowed interface in a variety of applications. A windowed interface provides a number of possible advantages. In particular, it allows the user to work in multi-function mode and context may be retained in one window while accessing another function. Also, it is possible to display several different representations of an object simultaneously. In addition, it is claimed that windowed interfaces give a more 'natural' way of working.

However, there are problems with designing a windowed interface, the major one being the lack of display space on a typical screen which, if not fully considered, can lead to a cluttered screen, analogous to a cluttered desk. Even the larger displays (17 or 19 inch diagonal) commonly in use today prove to be rather limited in practice. For example, with many applications it is possible to have no more than three or four open windows at a time. Standard sized displays (12 or 14 inch diagonal) are often limited to only one or two open windows.

It is difficult to design a portable windowed interface because of the lack of standards in the implementation of window management systems. The first major difference between alternative window management systems is the relationship between the window manager and application processes. Some systems assume that the window manager is in control and other processes are 'allowed' to operate under its umbrella. Other systems assume that the window manager is simply a provider of services with the application processes being in control. A further difference is in the style of interface offered to the user. Some systems assume that the user is a novice (and will remain so) and so provide visual details of everything, often leading to a rather cluttered display and reduced working space. Other systems assume that the user is an expert (instantly) and so provide no visual cues to aid the less expert user. A more disconcerting feature of this latter approach is that many such systems make it relatively easy to carry out major actions accidentally.

There are informal reports of a backlash against windowed interfaces, particularly among experienced users who feel that a totally iconic interface is counter-productive. Shneiderman reported such negative feedback during a tutorial at the SIGCHI'85 conference and warned that the current preoccupation with displaying as many windows and as much information as possible on screen could lead to general dissatisfaction with windowed interfaces.

2.2 Icons

Typically, icons are used both for the representation of windows and for the spatial representation of filing systems. However, recent work by Dumais and Jones (4) has cast some doubt on the effectiveness of this latter use. Icons can be used as static representations of closed windows or, more interestingly, they can be used to convey status information. A dynamic icon can be used to show a change of status such as a crash, that the controlling process is awaiting a further input or to indicate progress (using a 'percentage done' indicator). Myers (5) describes such an approach to dynamic icons in the SAPPHIRE system produced as part of the ACCENT operating system for PERQ workstations and discusses the effectiveness of percentage-done indicators in a more recent paper, Myers (6).

2.3 Mouse

The use of a mouse and the number of buttons it should have is the subject of much debate and previous research such as that carried out by Foley, Wallace and Chan (7), Card, English and Burr (8), Price and Cordova (9). Assuming that the use of a mouse is appropriate to the task under consideration, the argument then revolves about the use of a single-button model or a multiple-button model. The deciding factor could be that if each button can have a single distinct use in all circumstances and such uses are non-disruptive, then a multiple-button model can be used. Otherwise, on the grounds of consistency and simplicity, a single-button model should be used, if necessary simulating this model on a multiple-button mouse. Note that an alternative approach to a multiple-button model based upon the user remembering different button usage is to provide 'visual mouse buttons' on screen which may be 'pressed' by picking with the cursor positioned over the required 'button' and pressing any mouse button.

The main arguments against the use of multiple mouse buttons are as follows. Many users are left-right dyslexic, i.e. they cannot consistently mark, or press, left or right without a thinking time delay or visual confirmation. Typical systems often require a mixture of keyboard and mouse input. Therefore the user often has to move a hand from keyboard to mouse and back again. When using multiple mouse buttons the user has to accurately reposition two or three fingers on the mouse. This will involve visual feedback since it is unsafe for the user to use tactile feedback because of the risk of inadvertent selection.

Whatever style of interaction is chosen it is important that all destructive actions should be confirmed by the user supplying an additional non-automatic input. This latter point is strongly supported by Norman (10) who argues that disruptive actions should require 'great mental force' on the part of the user.

It is interesting to note that personal observation and experience has shown that more experienced users will abandon mouse based commands in favour of keyboard based commands in all circumstances except where dynamic graphical interaction or positioning is required.

2.4 Pull-down Menus

The basic selection mechanism in a windowed interface is usually provided via menus. These can be either 'pull-down', appearing as the expansion of an existing label, or 'pop-up', appearing at the current cursor position. Pop-up menus have the advantage that they can be positioned so as not to obscure the current activity but the disadvantage that they are visually discontinuous. Pull-down menus have the advantage that they appear where the user is most likely to be looking at the screen but the disadvantage that they may obscure the current activity.

Many researchers have shown the importance of keeping the number of choices in a menu below a certain threshold, typically less than ten. However, this recommendation tends to assume that the menus in question are being used for command or action selection. In the case of a graphic design system, for example, menus may be used for object selection where the nature of the objects is such that there is unlikely to be any ambiguity of choice. In such circumstances the user will not need to memorise the list since they will read and discard inappropriate choices until the required selection is found.

Recent research by Tullis (11) has indicated that broad rather than deep menus are preferable since users tend to have a lower error rate in such circumstances. This lends support to the use of larger menu lists than would be permissible under the previous general recommendations. Note that a more important factor than the actual number of selections is that the selections have some logical grouping and are ordered appropriately.

2.5 Visual Design Techniques

2.5.1 Cursor Coding. Many windowed interfaces use some form of cursor coding to indicate current mode of input or status. Thus, the two main uses for such coding are first to provide some form of visual cue such that the user is aware of the form of input expected, and second to use change of cursor shape to alert the user to a major change of state such as normal input to erroneous input. However, these two uses can lead to conflicting design decisions since the second use dictates that the coding scheme uses shapes that are immediately and obviously different which may make it difficult to make such shapes sufficiently mnemonic for the first use.

2.5.2 Textual Presentation. Previous work, Hodge (12), has shown that mixed case text is more easily and more accurately read. Some researchers, Marcus (13), quote a 30% increase in reading time for text in upper-case only. Similarly, many practitioners recommend that bulk text is displayed in blocks no wider than 40 to 60 characters and that such blocks are aligned on the left, ragged on the right.

3. DESIGN AND IMPLEMENTATION OF THE ECLIPSE-MMI

The best developed examples of integrated WIMP interfaces are those based on the 'desktop' paradigm, such as the Apple Macintosh and Xerox Star. It could be argued that this paradigm is not relevant for the majority of the user roles identified for ECLIPSE. The alternative facilities provided by powerful workstations, such as the SUN, Whitechapel and Apollo ranges, are tools for expert users and thus would not be suitable in their raw form for the less technical users of ECLIPSE. The ECLIPSE MMI is designed to provide an interface which is suitable for the wide range of user roles identified and which can be implemented on a SUN workstation running UNIX 4.2 bsd.

The implementation of the first version of the MMI for ECLIPSE is limited by the availability of suitable tools on the SUN. The project does not have the resources to develop major interface tools, such as a window manager, specifically for ECLIPSE and therefore some aspects of the interface design are dictated by the facilities provided by SUN tools. Later versions of ECLIPSE will use MMIMS, Smart (14), to provide a consistent interface between the user and the underlying hardware and system software.

The screen details shown in the following figures are mock-ups are produced on an Apple Macintosh. It proved difficult to obtain high-quality output, suitable for inclusion in this paper, directly from the SUN due to inadequate printing facilities.

3.1 Screen Layout

The first major design problem was defining a general screen layout, suitable for a variety of applications. In theory, The SUN's 19 inch screen is capable of holding two A4-size windows side by side. However, this leaves no room for any status display or 'parking' of icons. The prototype screen layout, shown in Fig. 1, has a status display (the ECLIPSE System Control Panel) at the top, an icon park at the bottom of the screen and two main working windows juxtaposed in the centre of the screen.

It was decided to avoid general overlapping windows as far as possible as it was considered these would be difficult for less expert users to handle. Overlapping windows tend to increase the memory load on the user and require the user to be familiar with the window manipulation facilities. Experienced users are not constrained by this approach since they are at liberty to reposition and change the size of the windows to suit their particular purposes.

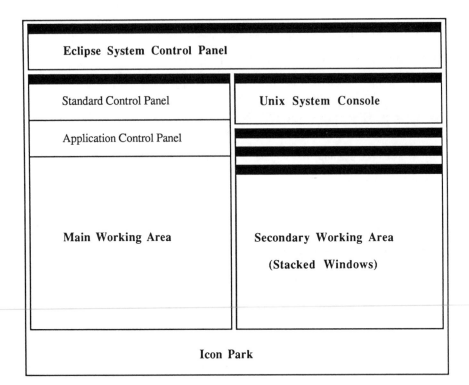

Fig. 1 Screen Layout

Experiments were carried out using a number of different fonts available on the SUN to try and achieve a compromise between a comfortable font size and a usable display area. For the prototype, the possibility of defining a special font was rejected because of lack of resources. However, this is obviously an alternative strategy for later versions of the system after gaining experience with the prototype.

The major problem encountered was that it proved impossible to find a window size which fitted the recommended aspect ratios given in the literature, one to root two or golden rectangle, Danchak (15). An attempt to define landscape windows, in the same orientation as the SUN screen, led to windows which were either too shallow to be usable or so large that only one would fit on the screen! The preferred layout was to have two portrait windows juxtaposed but the only font which would allow this and 'proper' aspect ratios was too small to read. Therefore, a readable font was chosen and windows defined to be the maximum length which can be obtained, producing an aspect ratio of about one to 1.23. These window dimensions are intended as guidelines only since some ECLIPSE applications, especially those of a graphic nature, require a larger working area.

The SUN software automatically includes a name stripe at the top of every window created. In ECLIPSE, this has been used to identify the process associated with the window and, where applicable, the particular version of the software. The text in this name stripe is displayed in upper case to help distinguish it from similar text in the control panel. (Note that this is the only place in which upper-case text is used.)

3.2 Control Panels

The concept of control panels was introduced to provide the unifying paradigm for the ECLIPSE MMI. The objective is to simulate the control panels which are available with many complex pieces of equipment, to provide both status information and controls. An attempt has been made to use analogous concepts within ECLIPSE software control panels. One lesson to be learned from hardware control panels is to avoid information overload, the extreme example of which is probably an aircraft cockpit. Fortunately, much of the information can be hidden within pull-down menus, thus avoiding having a screen full of control and status information.

Five basic control panel objects have been identified: button, menu, state selector, sign and light. Distinctive pictorial representations have been designed for each of them, as shown in Fig. 2.

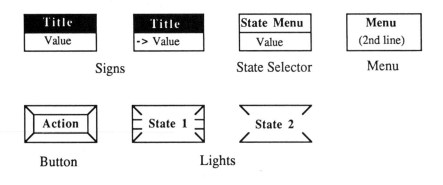

Fig. 2 Control Panel Object Representations

3.2.1 Buttons and Menus. A button is an object which when picked ('pressed') always initiates a single action, such as screen dump. A menu is a straightforward pull-down menu which displays a list of objects one of which can be chosen by the user to initiate some action; a typical use would be command selection.

The following is a series of recommendations regarding the design of menus and the use of buttons in ECLIPSE. Menu options should be centred on a block basis rather than on a per line basis, Marcus (13). The ordering of options within a menu should reflect a logical grouping appropriate to the task at hand, Engel and Granda (16). Frequently used or safe actions should be placed at the top of a menu, less frequently used or unsafe actions should be placed at the bottom. ECLIPSE buttons are provided for both unsafe actions, such as 'quit', and actions which do not fall naturally into a logical grouping, such as 'help'.

Ideally, a user selection from a menu should be confirmed visually by inversion, for example. Unfortunately, a 'feature' of the SUN software is that the user may click on the menu title and make a choice without any form of confirmation. The use of this feature is discouraged in ECLIPSE!

3.2.2 State Selectors. A state selector is a composite symbol consisting of a menu and a value. The value displays the current state while the menu provides a mechanism for changing that state. An example of the use of a state selector, in the ECLIPSE MMI, is for user help levels; the value displays the current help level: brief, summary or in-depth, while the menu provides the title for the state selector and a mechanism for change.

3.2.3 Signs. A sign is a two part object which has a title and a value. The value part may be static, dynamic (changed by the system) or user-changeable. A static sign might be used to display the name of the current user, while a dynamic sign could be used for the display of error messages. A user-changeable sign could be used to display the name of the current file which may be changed prior to some action such as saving the contents of the current window. A user-changeable sign includes the visual cue '->' to indicate that the user may type into the value part of it.

3.2.4 Lights. A light is an indicator with a binary status, either on or off. Lights are commonly used to indicate whether a window is current, i.e. the window to which the keyboard is attached, or a process is busy. In the latter case provision is made for a two state light to reassure the user that the system has not crashed. ECLIPSE lights appear to the right of the control panel, following the recommendations of Danchak (15).

3.2.5 System Control Panel. A system status display is provided via the ECLIPSE system control panel, as shown in Fig. 3, which is always present at the top of the screen. The 'functions' state selector has two states, i.e. display or hide function key assignments. The 'print' button causes a printout of the whole screen to be produced. The 'connected' light is used to confirm that the workstation is connected to the network.

3.2.6 Window Control Panels. Each application window has a standard control panel at the top together with an application-dependent control panel just below it, if required. An example of this combination is shown in Fig. 4.

The 'comment' button allows the user to record comments about the particular application and so provide some feedback to the system developers. In this case, the 'print' button provides a window printout. The 'pilot' button will activate a system navigation aid in later versions of ECLIPSE. The 'help' button activates a context-sensitive help mechanism, producing an associated help window. The 'close' button allows the user to close the window to an icon without having to be familiar with the SUN window manipulation facilities.

The details of the application control panel will vary with the exception that a 'quit' button is always provided. This button allows the user to terminate the application in a controlled fashion. The control panel shown in Fig. 4 is that of the prototype version of the Design Editor being produced at Strathclyde University.

3.2.7 Use of Control Panels. The ECLIPSE MMI uses the concept of a 'control panel' as the primary means of controlling the major functions of both ECLIPSE as a whole and individual applications that run under ECLIPSE. However, the control panel paradigm, like most paradigms, is not the answer to all problems.

The control panel is primarily of use for selecting options, setting contextual information, selecting objects, invoking infrequently used major actions and invoking critical actions. Thus, for example, the general movement and editing commands used within a text editor should be accessed via some other mechanism such as keyboard commands, function keys etc. Conversely, file selection, editing mode, display mode etc. would be suitable actions

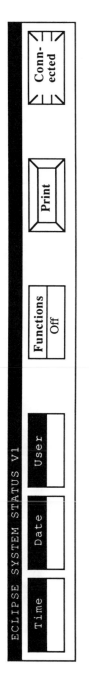

Fig. 3 The ECLIPSE System Control Panel

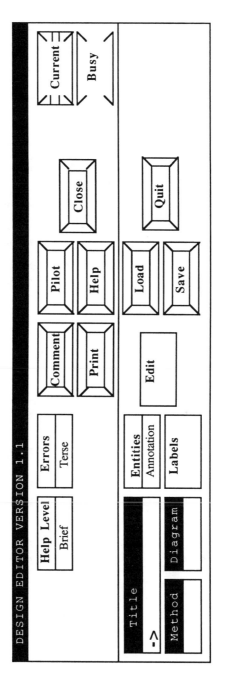

Fig. 4 The ECLIPSE Standard Control Panel and an Application Control Panel

for invocation via the control panel using, for example, menus or buttons. Similarly, actions such as invoking the help system, closing the window, aborting or terminating the application etc. would be provided using control panel facilities.

Frequently used commands that cannot be easily grouped are not sensible contenders for panel buttons since the user would spend a great deal of time 'mousing' around the control panel. This is particularly so in the case of a text editor, for example, where the user is involved in extensive text input via the keyboard.

3.3 Interaction.

The authors' recommendation was to use a single-button model of the mouse. However, the SUN window management software uses a multiple-button model of the mouse and therefore imposes certain meanings on the mouse buttons, for example when moving windows or closing them down to icons. Therefore, it was necessary to compromise by using the SUN mouse button conventions where applicable whilst allowing the single-button model within applications and insisting that all destructive actions be confirmed.

Confirmation of destructive actions is provided via a pop-up selector containing visual targets. The action must be confirmed by positioning the cursor over a target and clicking a mouse button. The wording of the targets must be unambiguous and they must be far enough apart to prevent accidentally hitting the wrong target. An example of such a visual target is shown in Fig. 5.

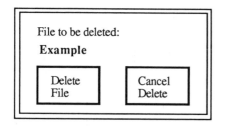

Fig. 5 Example of Visual Target

It is possible that an operation may cause multiple destructive actions to be initiated. It is recommended that in this case each action should be confirmed by a separate pop-up selector containing appropriate visual targets. These pop-up selectors should each appear in a different position to avoid accidentally repeating a previous selection.

Personal experience and observation of regular users of a WIMP interface, has shown that it is highly desirable to provide function key actions equivalent to those provided via the mouse and visual interface. This enables the experienced user, and the user involved in extensive keyboard input, to use function keys to initiate actions. If the functions state selector in the system control panel is 'on', then the function key assignments are displayed in a window at the bottom of the screen, obscuring the 'icon park'. This provides annotation directly above the main function keys.

3.4 Use of Icons

The SUN system provides the basic facilities for creating icons and for changing them dynamically. However, the SUN facilities have been hidden behind a common interface for passing messages to processes controlling windows and this will be able to detect whether a window is in iconic state or not.

Messages can be categorised as normal or urgent. If the window is in iconic state then the effect will be to change the icon for a normal message and to flash the icon for an urgent message. It should be possible for the user to cancel a flashing icon without dealing with the message immediately, Smith and Goodwin (17). If this facility were not available it would be extremely distracting for the user to have a flashing icon on the screen while trying to complete some complex task.

4. DISCUSSION

This paper has presented the design of a Man-machine Interface for an environment being produced to support the complete development of large software systems. It has shown how a control panel paradigm has been used as the unifying concept of an interface designed to support many and varied users.

In addition, it is clear that the WIMP style of interaction does promise to provide the basis of an improved MMI for software developers. An appropriate interface can be developed only by using visual design techniques (supported by prototype development) that take account of generally accepted MMI guidelines and pay particular attention to user roles, abilities and expectations. Thus, the manufacturer-supplied WIMP interface does not, in itself, produce a general purpose interface equally applicable in all circumstances.

It should be noted that the MMI designer is faced with the problem that there are no golden rules which, if followed, will guarantee to produce a 'good' interface. Thus it is necessary to resort to the established engineering practice of building a prototype, or prototypes, and carrying out detailed evaluation and modification until the design of the end product becomes clear, at which time a fully engineered version may be designed and produced.

A major problem which faces all MMI designers is the evaluation of a new interface. It is very difficult to quantify the utility or cost benefit of a particular feature of an interface and often arguments for and against are based on prejudice rather than experiment and measurement. Another aspect of evaluation is timeliness . Hardware technology and software tools and techniques are advancing at such a pace that by the time a system is fully evaluated, it may be obsolete. This problem of technology speed of change versus slowness of evaluation is particularly acute when one is dealing with a complex interface which contains many interrelated factors.

In order to make any meaningful evaluation of an MMI it is essential that it is instrumented as part of its fundamental design, rather than adding instrumentation at some later stage. The prototype ECLIPSE MMI has been instrumented and will be evaluated via a field trial of the whole of the ECLIPSE system at a major test site. In addition, the ECLIPSE programme will use the prototype version to assist in the development of further versions of ECLIPSE.

From the above it can be seen that substantiated advances in the design of Man-Machine Interfaces are not going to occur until either more systematic design methods or rapid evaluation techniques are developed. Thus, in the meantime, extensive prototyping will remain the only approach likely to produce a 'reasonable' result.

5. ACKNOWLEDGEMENTS

The work described here is funded by the Alvey Directorate, UK. Thanks are due to our collaborators Software Sciences Ltd, CAP Group UK Ltd, Learmonth and Burchett Management Systems Ltd, the University of Lancaster and the University College of Wales at Aberystwyth.

The authors would particularly like to thank their colleague Dr Ian Sommerville for his invaluable assistance and advice with this work.

6. REFERENCES

1.   Teitelman, W., 1977, "A Display Oriented Programmer's Assistant", 5th International Joint Conference On Artificial Intelligence, pp. 905-915, Cambridge, Massachusetts.

2.   Herot, C.F., Brown, G.P., Carling, R.T., Friedell, M., Kramlich, D., and Baecker, R.M., 1982, "An Integrated Environment For Program Visualization", in Automated Tools for Information Systems Design, ed. H.J. Schneider & A.I. Wasserman, pp. 237-259, North-Holland.

3.   Rowson, J.R. and Salama, B., 1978, "Virtual Displays", Electronic Displays 1978, London.

4.   Dumais, Susan T. and Jones, William P., 1985, "A Comparison of Symbolic and Spatial Filing", ACM SIGCHI Bulletin, pp. 127-130. (in Human Factors in Computing Systems CHI'85)

5.   Myers, Brad A., 1984, "The User Interface for Sapphire: A Screen Allocation Package Providing Helpful Icons and Rectangular Environments", IEEE Computer Graphics and Applications, vol. 4, no. 12.

6.   Myers, Brad A., 1985, "The Importance of Percent-Done Progress Indicators for Computer-Human Interfaces", ACM SIGCHI Bulletin, pp. 11-17. (in Human Factors in Computing Systems CHI'85)

7.   Foley, J.D., Wallace, V.L., and Chan, P., 1981, "The Human Factors of Graphic Interaction - Tasks and Techniques", , George Washington University, Washington D.C. 20052.

8.   Card, S.K., English, W.K., and Burr, B.J., 1978, "Evaluation of Mouse, Rate-controlled Isometric Joystick, Step keys and Text keys for Text Selection on a CRT", Ergonomics, vol. 21, pp. 601-613.

9.   Price, Lynne A. and Cordova, Carlos A., 1983, "Use of Mouse Buttons", ACM SIGCHI Bulletin, pp. 262-266. (in Human Factors in Computing Systems CHI'83)

10. Norman, Donald A., 1983, "Design Rules Based on Analyses of Human Error", Communications of the ACM, vol. 26, no. 4, pp. 254-264.

11. Tullis, Thomas S., 1985, "Designing a Menu-based Interface to an Operating System", ACM SIGCHI Bulletin, pp. 79-84. (in Human Factors in Computing Systems CHI'85)

12. Hodge, D.C., 1962, "Legibility of Uniform-strokewidth Alphabet: I. Relative Legibility of Upper and Lower Case Letters", Journal of Engineering Psychology, vol. 1, pp. 34-46.

13. Marcus, Aaron, 1985, "Screen Design for Iconic Interfaces", SIGCHI'85 Conference Tutorial 4.

14. Smart, John D., 1986, "A Man Machine Interface Management System for UNIX", 1986 UniForum Conference, Anaheim.

15. Danchak, M.M., 1977, "Alphanumeric Displays for the Man-Process Interface", Advances in Instrumentation, vol. 32, ISA Conference, Niagara Falls, part 1, pp. 197-213.

16. Engel, S.E. and Granda, R.E., 1975, "Guidelines for Man/Display Interfaces", TR00.2720, IBM, Poughkeepsie, NY 12602.

17. Smith, S.L. and Goodwin, N.C., 1972, "Another Look At Blinking Displays", Human Factors, vol. 14, no. 4, pp. 345-347.

Chapter 13

SAGA: A project to automate the management of software production systems

R.H. Campbell

Abstract. Large scale software development is so expensive that new techniques and methods are required to improve productivity. The software development environment is a proposed solution in which software development methods and paradigms are embedded within a computer software system. The goal of an environment is to provide software developers with a computer–aided specification, design, coding, testing and maintenance system that operates at the level of abstraction of the software development process and the application domains of its intended products.

Proposed software development environments range from simple collections of software tools that enhance the development process to complex systems that support sophisticated software production methods. Every environment must include a representation for the eventual software products and a, perhaps informal, notion of the software development process. In the SAGA project, we have been investigating the principles and practices underlying the construction of a software development environment. In this paper, we review our studies and results and discuss the issues of providing practical environments in the short and long term.

1. Introduction

Research into software development is required to reduce the cost of producing software and to improve software quality. Modern software systems, such as the embedded software required for NASA's space station initiative, stretch current software engineering techniques. The requirements to build large, reliable, and maintainable software systems increases with time. Much theoretical and practical research is in progress to improve software engineering techniques. One such technique is to build a software system or environment which directly supports the software engineering process. In this paper, we will describe research in the SAGA project to design and build a software development environment which automates the software engineering process.

The design of a computer–aided software development environment should be guided by the problems that arise in manual software development methods. Many of these problems are reflected in software cost estimation models and measurements (Boehm (4)). A major proportion of the cost of a software system is in its maintenance (60%), and testing (20%). Fairley (13) comments that software costs are very sensitive to mistakes in the early requirements and design phases of development. Sackman et al (37) and Myers (32) have demonstrated that programmers and program testers vary greatly in the productivity and quality of their work. However, high-level languages and software tools to support development may increase the productivity of a programmer by as much as 222% (4). Orders of magnitude improvement in the productivity of software engineers might be achieved in many application areas if the products of software engineering can become reusable, that is, if the requirements, design, documentation, validation, and verification of a software system can be reused in maintenance and in building new systems.

The SAGA project is investigating the design and construction of practical software engineering environments for developing and maintaining aerospace systems and applications software (Campbell and Kirslis (8)). The research includes the practical organization of the software lifecycle, configuration management, software requirements specification, executable specifications, design methodologies, programming, verification, validation and testing, version control, maintenance, the reuse of software, software libraries, documentation and automated management. The research is documented in the mid-year report (Campbell et al (10)). An overview of the SAGA project components is shown in Fig. 1.

In this paper, we will argue for research into formal models of the software development process. Such formal models should aid experimental evaluation of the practical techniques that are used in the construction of software development environments. The SAGA project is developing models of configuration, design, incremental development, and management. The concepts and tools resulting from SAGA are being used to develop a prototype software development system called ENCOMPASS (Terwilliger and Campbell, (41)). Although the research has developed many general tools and concepts that are independent of the application language and domain, we hope to extend ENCOMPASS to support the development of large, embedded software systems written mainly in ADA.

2. The Requirements of a Software Engineering Environment

Practical software development environments will be used by software developers and software managers with several years experience in software development. Although some components of the system may be used as educational tools, this is not a major goal. The requirements for a practical software development environment can be structured into three components:

1. the organization and representation of software products produced by the development process (the configuration management system,)

2. the software development processes (the lifecycle model, software development, management, and methodologies,)

3. the tools by which software development processes interface to, name, and manipulate software products.

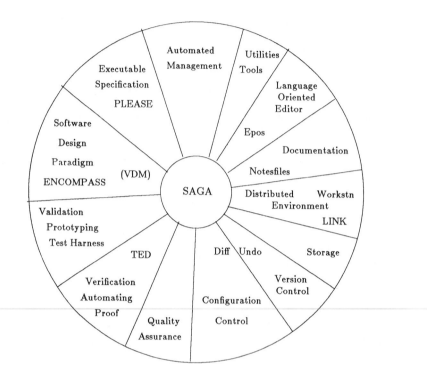

Fig. 1 The SAGA Workbench Components

Guiding the selection of requirements for each of these components, we propose the following principles:

1. A formal basis should be provided for the software environment and its components. This basis should serve to validate the software development paradigms and methodologies used in the environment and also verify the correct operation of the components. The formal basis should allow the specification of such concepts as the model of the software lifecycle in use, the design methodologies, maintenance methods as well as the dependency relationships between products of software development (including requirements specifications, design, tests, documentation, problem tracking, as well as code and versions.)

2. Management by objectives. Each software engineering task should have well–defined goals, participants, and managers. The developers should be able to interact with their managers in refining these goals (Gunther (17)). The task should produce clearly identified software products which may be validated or verified with respect to the goals of the task (Lehman et al (30)) and a method of certifying that the validation or verification has occurred.

3. Automated management aids should provide a project manager with tools which summarize project activity and progress. A project manager should be allowed to review the progress of the project in detail or in summary at any time.

4. Automated development tools should actively support software development and enhance the software developer's abilities. Campbell and Kirslis (8) argue that a software developer must be convinced that a task can be better performed using a tool than without it, irrespective of what other services the tool might provide.

5. Automated quality control tools should permit inspections and audits of the derivation of any software product. This should include examination of any certification process, audits of the software development process, and analyses of the project management. Tools should also support the verification that a software product or development process meets appropriate acceptance criteria and that the configuration management system is kept consistent and up to date.

Many of the principles require further research. In the following sections, we discuss the state of our current research in applying these principles to the construction of software systems.

3. Configuration Management System

The configuration management system is responsible for maintaining the consistency of, integrity of and relationships between the products of software development. In the SAGA project, Terwilliger and Campbell (41) model the configuration management system using a graph in which the nodes represent uniquely named entities or uniquely named collections of entities and the arcs represent relationships between entities. Layers within the graph represent different abstract properties of the software products. The graph also represents the organization of the software products into separate concerns.

The configuration system for ENCOMPASS can be decomposed by organizational relationships into vertical and horizontal structures. The vertical structures form a hierarchy. For example, within a software development *project*, the configuration may be structured into *subsystems*. These, in turn, are decomposed into *modules* which are decomposed into *compilation units*.

The horizontal structures represent attributes of the hierarchy. Thus, each project, subsystem, module, and unit may have an attribute for documentation, version information, requirements specification, shared definitions, architectural design, detailed design, code, binaries, linked binaries, test cases, procedures for generating executable binaries, listings, reports, authors, managers, time and tool certification stamps, development histories, and concurrency control locks. Interattribute relationships specify design, compilation and version dependencies. Depending upon the granularity of the entities, the graph can be represented by the UNIX directory structure, by symbolic links, or by databases. For example, in ENCOMPASS the vertical structure is stored using the UNIX directory structure. Shared definitions are represented by symbolic links. A database at each level in the vertical structure is being built to provide data dictionary capabilities and author manager relations.

Abstractions of the collection of software products are provided by *views*. The "base view" is a complete collection of the software products and other views. A "view" is a layer in the graph which represents a particular abstract property or concern. For example, a "functional test" view might represent the system as a collection of functional specifications, object code, test programs and test data. Other examples of views include a single version abstraction of a system that has many concurrent versions, documentation, and the work of a particular developer.

Fig. 3 shows an example tree traversal program stored in an ENCOMPASS configuration management system (Kirslis et al (26)). It shows a base view, which includes all the details of the software, and a test view, which is a projection onto the base view that abstracts some of the details of the base view and supports the testing of the software. Not all the dependencies and details are shown. The program is presented as a subsystem containing four modules, preorder, stack, tree, and item. Each module contains entities including a makefile (Feldman (14)), specification, body or source code, compiled object code, executable program, test specifications, test body, test makefile, compiled test object, executable test

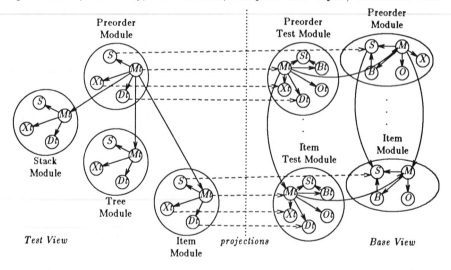

Entities: (S) specification (B) body (M) makefile (O) compiled object (X) executable program

(St) test specification (Bt) test body (Mt) test makefile (Ot) compiled test object

(Xt) executable test program (Dt) test data

Relations: —▷ uses - ▷ projects onto

Fig. 3 A view of the preorder program

program, and test data. Only one type of relationship is shown, the *uses* relationship, which associates an entity with another entity if the former entity references the latter one. Each "uses" relationship should be accompanied by a "used by" relationship, not shown in the figure, which is simply the inverse of of the "uses" relationship, and which permits the references to a module/entity to be determined from that module/entity. Each body within a module references its own specification. The body of *preorder* references the specifications in the other modules. The makefile for each module references the specification and body to be compiled, and the compiled object which will be produced. In addition, the makefile in the preorder module also references the makefiles and objects in the other modules, since it needs these in order to produce an executable program.

A number of benefits are realized if this dependency graph is stored in machine accessible form and if the software tools in use are adapted to refer to the graph. A data retrieval tool can provide information about the hierarchical structure of the program. For a given module, the tool can show its dependencies with respect to other modules.

An editor, adapted to use this graph, can permit a programmer to specify a routine, module, or program to edit. If the programmer specifies a module, that module becomes the locus at the beginning of the editing session. The programmer edits within the context of that layer of abstraction. Only the implementation details of the module are important. The programmer can find and display other modules, routines, or programs which use this module. These references may be checked easily to determine how a change in the current module will affect them. Similarly, other modules which this module references may be located easily and displayed.

Compilation tools, which access the dependency graph, can support automatic, incremental recompilation on a module by module basis. For example since the body of *preorder* depends on the specification for *stack*, if the specification for *stack* has been changed since the time *preorder* was last compiled, then *preorder* will be recompiled. A compilation tool can use the dependency graph to resolve the dependencies at compile time and access all files needed to perform a compilation[1].

Test tools can use the dependency graph to provide incremental, hierarchical testing for modular programs. A test suite and driver may be associated with each module. A program can then be incrementally tested in a bottom up manner, that is, all modules referenced by module A will be tested before module A is tested. If any of the referenced modules fail their tests then the system can print an appropriate message and terminate the testing session. If the test driver, test suite, or module has not been changed since the tests were last run, the system can report the previous results without rerunning the tests.

---

[1]In practice, by using UNIX we can do better than this. By an appropriate implementation of the source dependency information, we can make it appear as though all files needed for a compilation are resident in one place, permitting us to use an existing makefile interpreter program and compiler without modification (26).

Fig. 3 includes a test view which might be used by a quality assurance team to test *preorder* after it has been completed. The test view contains a module corresponding to each code module in the base view. The dashed arrows represent the *projection* relationship which shows the correspondence between entities in the test and base view. Each projection relationship is accompanied by an *abstraction* relationship, not shown in the figure, which is its inverse. Each module in the test view contains the specification of the code module to be tested as well as the makefile, load module, and test data from the corresponding test module in the base view.

4. Software Development Processes

Fairley (13) describes a life–cycle model as the sequence of distinct stages through which a software product passes during its lifetime. There is no single, universally accepted model of the software life–cycle according to Blum (3) and Zave (44). In SAGA, we have investigated several aspects of the software life–cycle.

4.1. Software Design Model

In many models of the life–cycle, a requirements specification of the system to be built is created early in the lifecycle. As the project proceeds, components of the software system are built and *verified* for correctness with respect to this specification. The specification is *validated* when it is shown to satisfy the customers requirements. To help manage the complexity of software design and development, methodologies which combine standard representations, intellectual disciplines, and well–defined techniques have been proposed (Jackson (20), Wirth (42), and Yourdon (43)). In the SAGA project, we are developing a formal model for the development process and using it to study a methodology similar to the Vienna Development method described by Jones (21).

A document describing the function of a software system is called a functional specification (13). Design introduces the algorithms and data structures to implement a functional specification. In this paper, we will argue that there are three separate fundamental issues involved in developing computer–based software design aids. We will assume that the development process consists of a number of refinement steps. The first concern is the design decision to select one refinement step instead of another. Design decisions are difficult to formalize without a better understanding of the development process and the application domain.

The second concern is the documentation and verification of a refinement step or implementation decision. Several researchers have argued the need for rigorous argument or formal verification of a refinement step using proof methods (21). The refinement step can be regarded as a correctness preserving transformation from an abstract program to a more concrete program. Using such an approach, the verification becomes a record of the refinement steps.

The third concern is the development process. We argue that a model for the development process is required in order to reason about different development methodologies and the different methods of verifying refinement steps.

In our model of a development process, a functional specification defines a potentially infinite number of implementations. The development process selects a single implementation from this large set. Each refinement step produces a derived functional specification or "abstract program" which constrains the number of possible implementations. The purpose of the model is to allow a study of incremental program development. Within the framework provided by the model we can compare different development methodologies and investigate subtle problems in a rigorous manner. By separating the development process from the issues involved in performing a refinement step, our approach provides a framework to build tools that support a general notion of a development process and that are independent from particular design methodologies. We hope that the model can also help justify design rules which permit rigorous, but not formal, arguments of correctness by construction.

4.2. Executable Specifications

A major problem arising in the design of software is the accurate determination of the function that the software is to perform. The users of the system being constructed may not really know what they want and they may be unable to communicate their desires to the development team. If a functional specification is in a formal notation, it may be an ineffective medium for communication with the customers, but natural language specifications are notoriously ambiguous and incomplete.

Functional specifications may be introduced as part of the design process (perhaps describing the elements of an abstract program) and should help document the design process as well as enhance the designer's understanding of the design. If a formal notation is used for such specifications, a designer may not be sufficiently well-motivated to document his design with a specification because it does not directly contribute towards the act of creating a program. However, a natural language specification may be too imprecise.

Prototyping (Kruchten et al (28)) and the use of executable specification languages (Goguen and Meseguer (16), Kamin et al (22), Zave (44), (Kemmerer(23)) have been suggested as partial solutions to these problems. Providing the customers with prototypes for experimentation and evaluation may increase communication between customers and developers and enhance the validation process. Executable specifications used in the design process provide stubs that allow experimental evaluation of the algorithms and data structures of a program being developed without requiring the program's completion.

Terwilliger and Campbell (41) describe the design of an executable specification language called PLEASE for use in the SAGA Project. By providing executable programs early in the development process, errors in the specification may be discovered before the internal structure of the system has been defined. We believe that this approach will enhance the software development process. A methodology for using executable specification languages in the software lifecycle is being examined as part of ENCOMPASS (41).

4.3. An Executable Specification Design Method

ENCOMPASS supports program development by successive refinement using a similar approach to that of the Vienna Development Method (Jones (21), Shaw et al (39)). In this method, programs are first specified in a language combining elements from conventional programming languages and mathematics. These *abstract programs* are then incrementally refined into programs in an implementation language. The refinements are performed one at a time and each is verified before another is applied. Therefore, the final program produced by the development correctly implements the original abstract program. The ENCOMPASS software development paradigm is shown in Fig. 4.1.

Terwilliger and Campbell (40) describe how abstract programs may be written in PLEASE and refined into the implementation language Path Pascal (Campbell and Kolstad (9)). In PLEASE, a procedure or function may be specified with pre- and post-conditions written in predicate logic. Similarly, an abstract data type may be specified using an invariant. PLEASE specifications

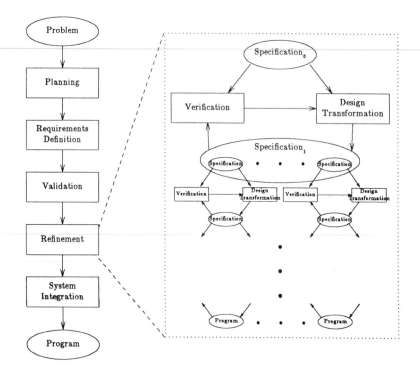

Fig. 4.1 The ENCOMPASS Software Development Paradigm

may be used to argue correctness. They also may be transformed into prototypes which use Prolog (Clocksin and Mellish (11)) to "execute" pre- and post-conditions. These prototypes may interact with other modules written in conventional languages.

Lehman et al (30) propose that software development may be viewed as a sequence of transformations between specifications written at different *linguistic levels*. Neighbors (33) describes the construction of a system that supports a similar development methodology. ENCOMPASS supports this view of software development by allowing abstract, predicate logic based definitions of data types or routines to be transformed into successively more concrete realizations. The use of executable specifications allows prototypes for two or more linguistic levels to be executed using the same input data and the results compared for the purposes of verification or debugging. An executable specification provides a framework for the rigorous development of programs in a manner similar to (21). Although detailed formal proofs are not required at every step, the framework is present so that they may be constructed if necessary. (However, it is our experience that many problems arise in changing a rigorous argument into a mathematical proof.)

Fig. 4.2 shows an example of a PLEASE specification for a SORT program. The specification is given in terms of a pre-condition and post-condition for sort. Two predicates, "permutation" and "sorted", are used by the post-conditions. Terwilliger and Campbell (40) describe the translation of the specification into Prolog. In general, the translation of arbitrary specifications into executable programs is difficult. Theoretically, the guaranteed automatic production of a terminating program from an arbitrary specification written in first order logic is not possible. One aspect of our future research will be to study what is possible in practice.

The specification may be used to validate the user requirements for *sort* or they may be used as a test oracle for the subsequent refinements of *sort* (40). In addition, using rules similar to those provided in the Vienna Definition Method (21), an argument for correctness can be constructed for the sort program based on the refinement steps used to build the program. Examples of some of the rules are given in (40).

4.4. Software Management Model

A management model for software development must identify, control, and record the development process. A management model can be based on a *trace* of the activities within the project. Such a trace can be used to understand the meaning of management in a similar manner to the use of traces in defining the meaning of a programming language (Campbell and Lauer (6)). The trace represents a complete history of all significant events that have occurred in the project. Projections from the trace permit identification of particular sequences of activities. Control can be expressed in terms of the valid continuations of a partially completed trace.

```
program sort (input, output);

#include "integer_list.spec"

var input_list, output_list: integer_list;

predicate permutation (list1, list2: integer_list);
    var front, back: integer_list;
    begin
        (list1 = empty_list) and (list2 = empty_list)
            or
        (list1 = front ¦¦ <hd (list2) > ¦¦ back) and
        permutation (front ¦¦ back, tl(list2))
    end;

predicate sorted (l: integer_list);
    var x: integer;
    begin
        (l = empty_list)
            or
        forall (x ¦ member (x, tl(l)), x >= hd(l)) and
        sorted(tl(l))
    end;

pre_condition;
    begin
        text_to_integer_list(input) <> integer_list_error
    end;
post_condition;
    begin
        (input_list = text_to_integer_list(input)) and
        permutation(input_list, output_list) and
        sorted (output_list) and
        (output_list = text_to_integer_list (output'))
    end;

    begin
    end;
```

Fig. 4.2 A specification of a sort program

In ENCOMPASS, we are implementing a limited set of management functions to record, monitor, initiate activities, and inhibit inappropriate activities. Instead of using a detailed trace model of management, we have adopted a practical approach based on the larger granularity provided by milestones. We structure the management model of a software project into units of work which create well–defined products (Gunther (17)). The management objectives for each activity must define the pre–conditions under which the activity may occur, acceptance criteria for the products produced by the activity, and a procedure for evaluating whether the acceptance criteria have been met. The acceptance criteria evaluation procedure may be invoked at any time during the activity and produces status reports of the software product. Satisfaction of the pre–condition and the acceptance criteria provide "milestone" events. A record of the occurrence of these milestones is stored in a management log. Accounting information may be associated with each unit of work. The log and accounting information can be used to generate reports and, when used with other information such as PERT schedules, to control the project.

Work units form a hierarchical structure. The reports generated by one work unit may satisfy a pre–condition or acceptance criteria for another activity.

In ENCOMPASS, management monitoring, assessment, and control is implemented using makefiles, predicate evaluation, and Notesfiles. Periodic execution of makefiles are used to implement automated management and assessment of the project. The makefiles incorporate automatic evaluation of work unit pre–conditions, the creation of work units, the invocation of acceptance criteria evaluation procedures, and the creation of milestones when a pre–condition or acceptance criteria is met. The Notesfiles (Essick (12)) record milestones and reports and propagate traceable management information to developers and managers.

For example, consider the implementation of a problem tracking system. Bug reports are mailed to the "problem definition" notesfile. They can be created by a user, a developer, or by the execution of a program at a remote or local site. Debugging facilities within a software product can automatically report an internal error by invoking the Notesfiles mailer. Similarly, development tools may report errors, for example the test harness may automatically report the detection of an error.

The problem definition notesfile records the site, author, time, address, and complaint. The "problem tracking manager" may set a timeout on the notesfile sequencer which specifies the acceptable interval within which a "problem definition analyst" should respond to the note. After expiration of the timeout, the notesfile automatically notifies the manager using a "management" notesfile.

The problem definition analyst may respond to the note in several ways. A response may be created that identifies the problem as a user error. Alternatively, the analyst may create a request in a maintenance programmer's "activity" Notesfile to consider possible solutions to the problem.

The acceptance criteria for the programmers task is to assess the practical design issues involved in correcting the problem, provide a cost estimate of the work involved, and produce an implementation plan. While the programmer is considering possible solutions, the problem definition analyst or problem tracking manager may request progress reports. These reports may consist of any milestones accomplished and preliminary documentation generated.

When the problem definition analyst is satisfied that the acceptance criteria for the task have been satisfied, he may then submit a change request note to the project change request board (Fairley (13)). This milestone and the timetable of the change request board determine the conditions under which a meeting of the board is scheduled.

4.5. Project Libraries.

Horowitz and Munson (19) suggest that the *reuse* of software can significantly reduce the cost of program development, and systems which contain libraries of previously coded modules and/or a number of standard designs for programs have been proposed by Lanergan and Grasso (29) and Matsumoto (31). In ENCOMPASS, any software component or group of components can be saved for later reuse. In addition to source and object code, documentation, formal specifications, proofs of correctness, test data and test results can all be stored in the central library and later retrieved. The library can support a number of projects, both accepting and supplying components for reuse in all phases of development. The structure and organization of the library is shown in Fig. 4.3.

A programmer, developing code, will use a view of the project library to access shared code and data, test cases, specifications, design, and other products of the project. The workspace extends the view with local copies of code that are being modified and with new code. Eventually, the programmer will submit his workspace to be placed under the configuration management of the library. The configuration management of the workspace must be consistent with that of the library and acceptance criteria may be applied to the software products before the library is updated. An integration test may be required as a pre–condition to a library update performed on a working version of the software system. A

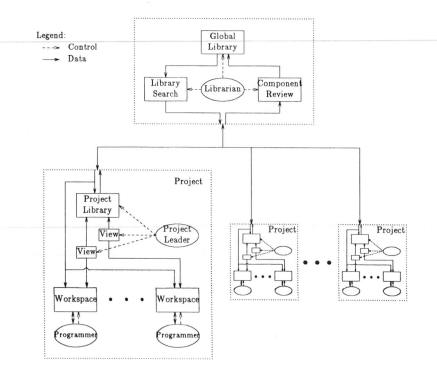

Fig. 4.3 The ENCOMPASS Library Structure

system acceptance test may be required as a pre-condition to a library update performed on a stable version of the software system. The project leader has responsibility for correct library operation including the view and workspace creation and workspace integration.

5. Software Tools

A large number of software tools are required to implement computer-aided software development environment. Rather than build a large number of specialized tools, in SAGA we have chosen to build a small number of tools that can be specialized for specific purposes. Examples of such "generic" facilities are the Notesfiles system (Essick (12), the SAGA language-oriented editor (Campbell and Kirslis (8), the symbol table manager (Richards (35)), tree editor (Hammerslag et al (18)) and the attribute evaluation schemes used for semantic evaluation (Beshers and Campbell (2)). The Notesfile system is used for documentation and management. The editor can be specialized to edit many different languages and specialized editors have been built for Pascal, ADA, PLEASE, and C. In addition to their number, the software tools in a software environment must also have other properties.

Software development environments need to be maintainable for the duration that they are used to support a software development project (Campbell and Lauer (6)). The software tools in the environment must accommodate change and modification of the environment over the lifetime of the software project. In many applications, the software support environment and its tools must be maintained for the duration of the maintenance of the software product; in the case of an embedded system like the space station software system this might be for twenty or more years. Changes in hardware technology may require the environment to be ported to new computer systems. New tools may be integrated into the environment. A solution to the problem of maintaining the environment and tools for a long period of time is to design them as part of an "open architecture".

In such an open architecture, modular tools are built which use standard interface to access other tools. The approach we have adopted in SAGA is to use the UNIX operating system to define a standard interface. UNIX processes become the mechanism to modularize the tools. New software tools built for UNIX can be integrated into the environment and UNIX provides a method of migrating the environment from one computer technology to the next. UNIX UNITED (Brownbridge et al (5)), LINK (Russo (36)) and other distributed UNIX systems permit the support of software development environments on networks of workstations.

Software engineering studies reported by Bauer et al (1) suggest providing the user with a high-level interface which reflects the levels of abstractions in programming. By allowing the user to phrase commands in terms of high-level concepts, the quality of the user's interaction with the computer can be improved. Less time is needed to accomplish a given task, and fewer operations mean fewer errors made during the software development process. Since users spend a large amount of their time using editors, Scofield (38) proposed using an editor as an appropriate program in which to implement a high–level interface.

In the remainder of this section we discuss some of the SAGA tools that have been developed based on these ideas.

5.1. Language–Oriented Editor

Language–oriented editors supply a high–level interface for software development tools (Campbell and Richards (7), Campbell and Kirslis (8)). Since the editor is the primary tool for constructing software products, enhancing the editor with features that aid the editing of specific specification languages and programming languages should be beneficial to the development process. The editors can have semantic and syntactic oriented editing commands and may help the program development process by preventing or providing immediate diagnosis of syntactic and semantic errors in the program text.

Two different approaches may be used to construct a language–oriented editor: the generator, or "template", approach and the recognizer approach. The SAGA project has developed a recognizer–based editor. The editor incorporates an LALR(1) parser augmented for the interactive environment with incremental parsing techniques (Kirslis (25), Ghezzi and Mandrioli (15)). An editor generator (25) allows editors to be generated for a particular language.

The SAGA project has demonstrated (25) that the recognizer approach is a practical basis for constructing language–oriented editors and has several advantages:

1. The recognition approach can be applied consistently to the editing of the lexical, syntactic, and semantic components of the language. This simplifies providing uniform editing commands that manipulate lexical, syntactic, and semantic entities. Template editors are tedious to use if they do not use a recognizer to enter expressions, variable names, and constants. An editing command will differ in operation depending upon whether an entity is recognized or generated.

2. The recognition approach permits arbitrary editing operations on the program. Rectangular blocks of characters may be copied from one part of a screen of program text to another as when initial assignments are being made to array elements. Global string substitutions may be made. Program code may be commented out and comments may be changed into program code. The generator approach cannot handle arbitrary editing commands unless the resulting edit generates text which is reparsed into a form suitable for the editor. Problems occur when such an edit creates a lexical or syntactic error.

3. Program editing during the debugging and maintenance phases of a project will invariably require transforming the program through a number of illegal lexical, syntactic, and semantic constructs. Many editors using the generator approach expressly forbid the creation of incorrect programs. However, the recognition approach permits illegal programs which may have many incorrect semantic, syntactic and lexical errors. The errors may be introduced in any order and may be removed in any order. When a lexical or

syntactic error is introduced, the editor can mark the discontinuity in the corresponding token or parse tree. When an error is removed, the incremental parsing technique will examine the surrounding context of the change only as far as it is necessary to determine that the change results in a lexically and syntactically correct program fragment. The parse tree will be repaired in the local context of the change.

4. The recognition approach allows a lexical or syntactic entity such as a Pascal **while** loop to be incrementally changed into a **repeat** loop whereas the generator approach must include a transformation rule to support such a modification. Although it is simple to generate a set of useful transformation rules, it is not clear whether it is possible to generate all useful transformations of this form.

5. The recognition approach uses existing compiler generation and parsing techniques without major alteration. If standard compiler generation and parsing tools are used, then many existing specifications of the lexical, syntactic, and semantic components of a programming language can be used directly by an editor generator facility to produce corresponding language–oriented editors.

6. Semantic analysis is performed in most language–oriented editors using recognition techniques that extend those developed for compilers. For example, the attribute evaluation schemes proposed by Knuth (27) have been used directly or encoded in a procedural manner to provide semantic evaluation of edited programming languages (Reps et al (34)).

The SAGA editor has been used with various semantic evaluation methods. Beshers and Campbell (2) describe an approach combining the editor with right regular expression grammars, attributed grammars, and maintained and constructor attributes. This method was proposed to overcome some of the overhead that occurs in direct attribute evaluation schemes. A SAGA editor for a subset of Pascal has been built that incrementally compiles Pascal programs using more conventional techniques (Kimball (24)).

One of the major problems in building language–oriented editors is that they provide an unfamiliar interface to the user. To overcome this problem, a new version of the SAGA editor is being constructed using an EMACS editor front end.

5.2. Notesfiles

An important software development tool for any project is a means to record, document and retrieve information. Such a tool can be used to support technical discussions, product reviews, problem tracking, agendas and minutes, grievances, design and specification documentation, lists of work to be done, appointments, news and mail. The SAGA Notesfiles system (Essick, (12)) has been in use for some time to support all these functions within the SAGA project.

The Notesfiles system is a distributed project information base constructed for SAGA on the UNIX operating system. A file of notes can be maintained across a network of heterogeneous machines. Each file of notes has a topic; each notesfile has a title. A sequence of notes is associated with each notesfile. Notes and responses may be exchanged between separate notesfiles. Notes and responses are documented with their authors and times of creation. Updates to the notes and responses are transmitted among networked systems to maintain consistency. Notesfiles use the standard electronic mail facility to facilitate the updates. A library and standard interface permits any user program to submit a note or response to a notesfile. This library has been particularly useful in the construction of automatic logging and error reporting facilities in test harnesses and "beta test" uses of SAGA code.

6. Conclusion

One approach to improving the productivity of large scale software development is to construct software systems that support the software development process. The design of such systems requires an understanding of the principles underlying the software development and maintenance process as well as methods and technologies for building complex design aids. We argue that the experimental research required to build such environments should be based on formal models of the software development process. Much research is required to produce both the appropriate formal models and the methods and techniques of implementation and environment.

In the SAGA Project, we have been studying the construction of an environment to support the software development and maintenance. In this paper, we have outlined some of the models being developed in association with the construction of an experimental environment called ENCOMPASS.

Acknowledgements. The ideas presented in this paper have been summarized from the work of the SAGA Project team. In particular, I would like to thank Bob Terwilliger for his work on PLEASE and ENCOMPASS, Peter Kirslis for building the first SAGA editor, and Carol Beckman–Davies, Leonora Benzinger, George Beshers, David Hammerslag, Dan Laliberte, Craig Neth, Hal Render and Paul Richards for their various contributions to the research described in this paper.

7. References.

1. Bauer, F., J. Dennis, G. Goos, C. Gotlieb, R. Graham, M. Griffiths, H. Helms, B. Morton, P. Poole, D. Tsichritzis, and W. Waite, 1977, **Software Engineering — An Advanced Course**, F. Bauer, Ed., Springer Verlag, New York.

2. Beshers, G. M. and R. H. Campbell, 1985, *Maintained and Constructor Attributes,* **Proc. of the ACM SIGPLAN 85 Symposium on Language Issues in Programming Environments**, pp. 34–42.

3. Blum, B. I., 1982, *The Life–Cycle - A Debate Over Alternative Models,* **Software Engineering Notes**, vol. 7, pp. 18–20.

4. Boehm, B., 1981, *Software Engineering Economics,* **Prentice Hall**, Englewood Cliffs, NJ..

5. Brownbridge, D. R., L. F. Marshall and B. Randell, 1982, *The Newcastle Connection or UNIXes of the World Unite!,* **Software – Practice and Experience**, V. 12, pp.

1147–1162.

6. Campbell, R. H. and P. E. Lauer, 1984, *RECIPE: Requirements for an Evolutionary Computer-based Information Processing Environment*, **Proc. of the IEEE Software Process Workshop**, pp. 67–76.

7. Campbell, R. H. and Paul G. Richards, 1981, *SAGA: A system to automate the management of software production*, **Proc. of the National Computer Conference**, pp. 231–234.

8. Campbell, R. H. and P. A. Kirslis, 1984, *The SAGA Project: A System for Software Development*, **Proceedings of the ACM SIGSOFT/SIGPLAN Software Engineering Symposium on Practical Software Development Environments**, pp. 73–80.

9. Campbell, R. H. and R. B. Kolstad, 1979, *Path Expressions in Pascal*, **Proceedings of the Fourth International Conference on Software Engineering.**

10. Campbell, R. H., C. S. Beckman, L. Benzinger, G. Beshers, D. Hammerslag, J. Kimball, P. A. Kirslis, H. Render, P. Richards, R. Terwilliger, 1985, *SAGA*, Mid–Year Report, Dept. of Comp. Sci., University of Illinois.

11. Clocksin, W. F. and C. S. Mellish, 1981, **Programming in Prolog.** Springer–Verlag, New York.

12. Essick, Raymond B., IV., 1984, *Notesfiles: A Unix Communication Tool*, M.S. Thesis, Dept. Comp. Sci., University of Illinois at Urbana–Champaign.

13. Fairley, Richard, 1985, **Software Engineering Concepts.** McGraw–Hill, New York.

14. Feldman, S. I., 1979, *Make – A Program for Maintaining Computer Programs*, **Software – Practice and Experience**, Vol. 9, No. 4, pp. 255–265.

15. Ghezzi, C. and D. Mandrioli, 1980, *Augmenting Parsers to Support Incrementality*, **Journal of the ACM**, Vol. 27, No. 3.

16. Goguen, J. and J. Meseguer, 1982, *Rapid Prototyping in the OBJ Executable Specification Language*, **Software Engineering Notes**, vol. 7, no. 5, pp. 75–84.

17. Gunther, R., 1978, **Management Methodology for Software Product Engineering**, Wiley Interscience, New York.

18. Hammerslag, D. H., S. N. Kamin and R. H. Campbell, 1985, *Tree-Oriented Interactive Processing with an Application to Theorem-Proving.* **Proc. of the Second ACM/IEEE Conference on Software Development Tools, Techniques, and Alternatives.**

19. Horowitz, E. and J. B. Munson, 1984, *An Expansive view of Reusable Software,* **IEEE Trans. on Software Engineering**, Vol. 10, No. 5.

20. Jackson, M., 1983, **System Development**, Prentice–Hall, Englewood Cliffs, N.J..

21. Jones, C., 1980, **Software Development: A Rigorous Approach**, Prentice–Hall International, Inc., London.

22. Kamin, S. N., S. Jefferson and M. Archer, 1983, *The Role of Executable Specifications: The FASE System*, **Proc. of the IEEE Symposium on Application and Assessment of Automated Tools for Software Development.**

23. Kemmerer, R. A., 1985, *Testing Formal Specifications to Detect Design Errors,* **IEEE Transactions on Software Engineering**, vol. SE–11, no. 1, pp. 32–43.

24. Kimball, J., 1985, *PCG: A Prototype Incremental Compilation Facility for the SAGA Environment*, **M.S. Thesis**, Dept. Comp. Sci., University of Illinois at Urbana-Champaign.

25. Kirslis, P. A., 1986, *The SAGA Editor: A Language-Oriented Editor Based on an Incremental LR(1) Parser*, Ph. D. Dissertation, Dept. Comp. Sci., University of Illinois at Urbana-Champaign.

26. Kirslis, P. A., R. B. Terwilliger and R. H. Campbell, 1985, *The SAGA Approach to Large Program Development in an Integrated Modular Environment*, **Proceedings of the GTE Workshop on Software Engineering Environments for Programming-in-the-Large.**

27. Knuth, D. E., 1968, *Semantics of context-free languages*, **Math. Syst. Theory**, Vol. 2, No. 2.

28. Kruchten, P., E. Schonberg and J. Schwartz, 1984, *Software Prototyping Using the SETL Programming Language.* **IEEE Software**, vol. 1, no. 4, pp. 66–75.

29. Lanergan, R. G. and C. A. Grasso, 1984, *Software Engineering with Reusable Designs and Code,* **IEEE Trans. on Software Engineering**, Vol. 10, No. 5.

30. Lehman, M. M., V. Stenning and W. M. Turski, 1984, *Another Look at Software Design Methodology,* **Software Engineering Notes**, vol. 9, no. 2, pp. 38–53.

31. Matsumoto, Y., 1984, *Some Experiences in Promoting Reusable Software: Presentation in Higher Abstract Levels,* **IEEE Trans. on Software Engineering**, Vol. 10, No. 5.

32. Myers, G. J., 1978, *A Controlled Experiment in Program Testing and Code Walkthroughs/Inspections,* **Comm. ACM**, pp. 760–767.

33. Neighbors, J. M., 1984, *The Draco Approach to Constructing Software from Reusable Components,* **IEEE Transactions on Software Engineering**, vol. SE–10, no. 5, pp. 564–574.

34. Reps, T., Teitelbaum, T., and Demers, A., 1983, *Incremental Context-Dependent Analysis for Language-Based Editors,* **ACM Transactions on Programming Languages and Systems,** Vol. 5, No. 3.

35. Richards, P., 1984, *A Prototype Symbol Table Manager for the SAGA Environment,* Master's Thesis, Dept. Comp. Sci., University of Illinois at Urbana-Champaign.

36. Russo, V. F., 1985, *ILINK: Illinois Loadable InterUNIX Networked Kernel,* M.S. thesis, University of Illinois, Urbana, Il 61801.

37. Sackman, H., et al., 1968, *Exploratory Experimental Studies Comparing Online and Offline Programming Performance,* **Comm. ACM**, vol. 11, no. 1.

38. Scofield, Alan, 1985, *Editing as a Paradigm for User Interaction,* Technical Report 85–08–10, Dept. Comp. Sci., Univ. of Washington, Seattle.

39. Shaw, R. C., P. N. Hudson and N. W. Davis, 1984, *Introduction of A Formal Technique into a Software Development Environment (Early Observations),* **Software Engineering Notes**, vol. 9, no. 2, pp. 54–79.

40. Terwilliger, R. B. and R. H. Campbell, 1986, *PLEASE: Predicate Logic based ExecutAble SpEcifications,* **Proc. 1986 ACM Computer Science Conference.**

41. Terwilliger, R. B. and R. H. Campbell, 1986, *ENCOMPASS: a SAGA Based Environment for the Composition of Programs and Specifications,* **Proceedings of the 19th Hawaii International Conference on System Sciences.**

42. Wirth, N., 1971, *Program Development by Stepwise Refinement*, **Communications of the ACM**, vol. 14, no. 4, pp. 221–227.

43. Yourdon, E. and L. L. Constantine, 1979, **Structured Design**, Prentice–Hall, Englewood Cliffs, N.J..

44. Zave, P., 1984, *The Operational Versus the Conventional Approach to Software Development*, **Communications of the ACM**, vol. 27, no. 2, pp. 104–118.

Chapter 14

Specifying a semantic model for use in an integrated project support environment

A.N. Earl, R.P. Whittington, P. Hitchcock and A. Hall

ABSTRACT

Aspect is an Alvey-supported project concerned
with research into and prototype development of
an Integrated Project Support Environment. At
the heart of the environment being developed is
an information base.
We explain our reasons for choosing the
Extended Relational Model (RM/T) as a modelling
formalism, report on the problems of using RM/T
for this purpose, and describe our solutions to
these problems, including a formal specification
of RM/T.

1. INTRODUCTION

The work reported in this paper has been carried out as
part of the *Aspect* project. *Aspect* is funded by SERC
through the Alvey Software Engineering Directorate, and
involves a consortium comprising Systems Designers, the
Universities of York and Newcastle-upon-Tyne, MARI and ICL.
The project allows the consortium to collaborate on
research and development of an integrated project support
environment (IPSE), called *Aspect*. To be more precise,
Aspect is an IPSE-kit: a collection of facilities by means
of which *Aspect* IPSEs can be tailored. Thus, for example,
there is no single software development methodology with
which *Aspect* IPSEs are associated. The *Aspect* IPSE-kit
provides hooks on which any desired methodology can be
hung. This principle applies similarly to revision and
configuration management, project planning, and other IPSE
functions.
Integration in an *Aspect* IPSE is achieved by means of an
information base: a shared repository of system data
through which development activities communicate and are
controlled. An *Aspect* IPSE offers a tool-writer's interface, the Public Tool Interface (PTI), that permits
developers to extend their environment. Of the facilities
provided by the PTI, some are concerned with information
base manipulation. The selection of an appropriate collection of manipulation operators for the PTI is, in essence,

the selection of a data modelling formalism for *Aspect* information bases.

An *Aspect* information base includes data of a variety of kinds, for example, system configuration details, details of current activities and their resourcing, text corresponding to source code under development, text corresponding to executable code that can be used for development (i.e. tools), and budgeting/planning details. Of these it is useful to distinguish those objects that are relatively small and well defined, and to which access requirements can be expected to be not unlike those found in traditional database application areas, from those objects that are larger, less well structured, and to which access requirements are likely to need a different approach to transaction management.

The latter category includes source and object code for programs, program and system specification documents, and other such (largely textual) kinds of object. The *Aspect* PTI provides facilities for each of these categories of data; the collection of well-structured data in an *Aspect* information base is called an *Aspect* database. That is, in an *Aspect* IPSE, the database is a subset of the information base; the manipulation facilities in the PTI for *Aspect* databases constitute the *Aspect* database engine, a subset of the *Aspect* information base engine (which includes, in addition, facilities for manipulating the larger kinds of object).

This paper concentrates on the *Aspect* database engine. It discusses the reasons for adopting the extended relational model as a modelling formalism (and, consequently, as a manipulation algebra), the difficulties that we encountered with that formalism, and the way in which we specified the facilities that are to be made available at the PTI.

2. CHOICE OF MODELLING FORMALISM

Of the published literature relating to research and development of database management for computer-aided design and engineering applications (see[1] for a good selection of references), much use has been made of the relational model, typically with extensions for handling complex data and orderings. A recent report[2] considers the application of both network-orientated and relational database management systems to traditional engineering applications.

Database modelling formalisms have been an important topic for research for well over a decade now, but, for the most part, these have been considered only in the context of traditional commercial applications. The underlying trend in this research has been in the direction of formalisms that capture as much as possible of the meaning of the application domain, in order best to be able to support the integrity of a database that represents that domain. For this reason, the most recent class of formalisms (which originate from[3] and[4]) are referred to as semantic models (the terminology in this area is slightly confusing: the term model is used to mean both a modelling formalism and a representation of an application, produced by means of a formalism). Surveys of semantic models are given in[5] and,[6] and the application of such models to engineering databases is discussed in.[7]

The choice of an appropriate formalism for *Aspect* IPSEs was influenced not only by the structuring primitives provided by a formalism but also by the power of its manipulation facilities, the level of integrity capture that it supports, and, pragmatically, the maturity of its definition. Initially, the project team considered adopting the basic relational model with a kernel directory (or Catalog) of relations to capture system semantics. This approach is discussed in[8] It was later decided that Codd's extended relational model RM/T[9] offers a preferable approach to semantics capture, and is presented, together with an extended relational algebra, in a reasonably formal manner. These advantages are discussed further in the following section.

2.1. Reasons for Choosing RM/T

Since the function of the database is not only to record details of all information in the information base but also to record the relationships and constraints which hold between such information, our main requirement of the database model was that it should support the capture of relationships and the imposition of constraints in order to maintain the integrity of the database and hence the information base. We chose RM/T because it already contained the following concepts to help with this.

The Catalog

Just as the database holds data concerned with information held outside *it* but within the information base, so the **Catalog** entity types in the database contain full details of the whole database including the Catalog itself. The Catalog can be queried in just the same way as any other entity types in the database.

The latter point is very important within an *Integrated* environment which depends to a large extent upon a uniform interface to the facilities provided.

Integrity Rules

Referential integrity constraints are expressed by the classification of entities into the appropriate types. Entity types in RM/T are partitioned into associative, characteristic, and kernel entity types, all of which may be designative in addition. Integrity rule 6, for example, is association integrity and says that if an associative entity (i.e. one that represents a many-to-many relationship between entity-types) exists in the database, then so must the entities it associates.

Surrogates

A surrogate is a unique, system-generated identifier which is permanently associated with an entity and never reused. We thus overcome the problems associated with naming entities.[10]

Relational Base

Since RM/T is a superset of the standard relational model we have a strong platform of previous work and theory to stand upon. This gives us a well-studied set of query languages.

Extended Algebra

The *Extended* part of RM/T is intended primarily for the database designer to whom the additional operators provided will be very useful, especially when used in conjunction with the Catalog.

Subtype Hierarchy

An important type of relationship that may exist between entity types is the subtype/supertype relationship. The ability to create subtypes of existing entity types is particularly useful in that it not only allows the inheritance of attributes but also enables the solution of the *property inapplicable* problem.

3. PROBLEMS OF EXISTING RM/T DESCRIPTIONS

We currently know of only two English descriptions of RM/T. They are Codd's original presentation[9] and Date's tutorial chapter [6] which attempts to clarify and tidy the model. The model as described in those papers was not immediately implementable as the *Aspect* database. There were problems in three areas. Firstly, we found some discrepancies of a theoretical nature in the descriptions. Our opinion was that neither of the two different Catalog structures presented effectively covered the self-referential requirements implied by the model. Secondly, although a comprehensive set of operators were described for manipulating data, we found the interface enabling data to be updated to be incomplete. And thirdly, the mixture of abstract and concrete concepts, in terms of which the model had been presented, needed to be clarified in order to create a suitable formal specification.

The following sub-sections describe those problems, introduced above, in more detail. The next two major sections will describe how we overcame the specification problems and our whole approach to a formal specification of RM/T, and will also describe both our own Catalog structure and the interface we will provide for updating data.

3.1. Theoretical Problems

Given that our understanding of RM/T comes from the existing descriptions, we found it difficult to accept some parts of those descriptions. The three problem areas are covered in the next three subsections.

3.1.1. Surrogates and naming problems.

Having introduced surrogates as unique system-generated identifiers and stressed their importance, it seems irrelevant (except for pedagogic purposes) to include any naming rules within the model.

Aspect's view of naming is that the database will contain an entity type, the purpose of the attributes of which is to record an entity (surrogate, of course), a namespace (surrogate), and the name (string) of that entity in that namespace. This is flexible but allows a particular IPSE instantiation to adopt a particular naming convention (e.g. the hierarchical approach of the Unix filing system).

3.1.2. Catalog structure problems.

In this section we will point out deficiencies of both the Catalog structure presented by Codd and that by Date.

The main problem with the Catalog structure of Codd was that an attribute could exist without an associated domain. The structure of Date's Catalog did not treat attributes as distinct entities and they could have different domains in different relations. We believe that these problems arose because the Catalogs were designed to hold names rather than surrogates.

Our approach to specifying the Catalog is described later, as is the Catalog structure we chose to provide.

3.1.3. Subtypes of kernels.

Both Codd and Date state that a subtype of a kernel entity type is also kernel. But we can see no reason why attributes which associate entity types cannot be added to a kernel entity type to form a subtype of that which is associative (and hence not kernel).

3.2. Update Interface Problems

Codd defines no operations for adding or updating entity types or entities, and Date only gives a hypothetical syntax for operators to create relations and associations etc. between them. This is surprising since the integrity rules have to be applied at creation, update, and deletion times and most of the rules are expressed in terms of entities and entity types. Our solutions to these problems are presented in the following section.

3.3. Specification Problems

A major set of activities of the *Aspect* project was the formal specification of the Public Tool Interface (PTI) using the notation of Z.[11] A Z document is made up of three languages. The mathematical language is based on strongly typed set theory and first-order predicate calculus. The **Schema** language is a set of operators for manipulating pieces of mathematical text. And English language descriptions allow the mathematics to be more easily followed but do not add semantics to the mathematical statements.

Our major problems with the existing descriptions of

RM/T came from the fact that some statements about the model are expressed in terms of relations whereas others are in terms of entities and entity types. The prime example is the Catalog itself. It is always described as a collection of relations rather than a set of entity types. Our solutions to these problems are presented in the following section.

4. APPROACH TO SPECIFICATION

In this section we use simplified extracts from our complete formal specification [12] to illustrate how we went about formally specifying RM/T. We explain and use Z notation to show how its power and flexibility can be used to build a specification which is not only very precise but can also be documented easily.

Our approach to capturing the features of RM/T can be summarised as follows. We try to express as many of the concepts of RM/T at the level of entity-types, attributes, and entities. We call this the **abstract** level. Our **concrete** level is a collection of Codd's relations, which allow the relational algebra and the extended relational operators to be used. We then need to define a mapping from the abstract to concrete level. Finally, we make the database self-referential by defining a set of special entity-types which together make up the **Catalog**. In the following subsections we describe some of our ideas in more detail with examples extracted from.[12]

4.1. Abstract Structure

4.1.1. Introduction.

This part of our specification deals with the abstract concepts of RM/T. These are: entity types and entities; the attributes of entity types; their values; the subtyping structure; and the classification of entity types into kernel, characteristic, associative, and designative.

4.1.2. Entities and entity types.

We call the objects which are held in our database, entities. The entities in our database can represent or model either objects in the real world or objects in our database. In order to impose some regular structure upon the database we say that every entity is a member of at least one entity type. Thus all entities of a particular type will share the common properties of that entity type.

Suppose then, that we have the set of all possible entity types, **ET**. We do not say anything about the detail of this set. We simply assume that it exists. We call the set of entity types in our database, **entity_types**. We also assume that this set can be partitioned into sets of entity types of different kinds.

[ET]

ETYPES_____

    entity_types,
    kernel,
    associative,
    characteristic,
    designative   : $\mathbb{F}$ ET

_____

    <kernel, associative, characteristic>
           <u>partitions</u> entity_types

    designative $\subseteq$ entity_types

As this is our first Z schema, we will explain its
presentation as well as its content. This schema is called
ETYPES. The schema box is split by a horizontal line into
two sections. The top half is called the **signature** part
which is a list of variable declarations which in turn consist of the variable's name followed by its type. In
ETYPES we have declared five variables, all of the type a
finite set of ET.

The bottom half of a schema box is called the **predicate**
part which consists of a single predicate, but long predicates can be broken at conjunctions and so written on
several lines. The predicate in ETYPES is split into two
parts. The first part says that all entity types in the
database belong to one and only one of the sets kernel,
associative or characteristic. The second says that any
entity type in the database can also be in the set of
designative entity types.

We now introduce the set of all possible entities
called, **E,** and call the set of entities in our database
entities.

Entities in the real world are represented in RM/T by
system-generated identifiers, called surrogates, with some
special properties. When a new entity is added to the
database, it becomes permanently associated with a surrogate whose value is unique with respect to all surrogates
that exist, or have ever existed, in the database.

Formally, because there is a bijection between entities
and surrogates, they can be used interchangeably within our
specification.

[E]

```
ENTS
┌────────────────────────────────────────────┐
  ETYPES
  entities      : F E
  type_of_entity : E —|→ F ET
 ├────────────────────────────────────────────
  ∪ rng type_of_entity ⊆ entity_types

  ∀ e : entities . #type_of_entity(e) ≥ 1
└────────────────────────────────────────────┘
```

This schema, ENTS, shows the use of schema inclusion in Z. The effect of including the schema ETYPES among the declarations in ENTS is that all the declarations in ETYPES are added to those in ENTS, and the predicate in ETYPES is conjoined with the predicate stated in ENTS. In this way, it is possible to build large, complicated specifications in small steps which can be clearly explained at each stage.

In ENTS we have introduced a partial function, **type_of_entity**, which returns the set of entity types of a given entity. The first part of the predicate says that the distributed union of the range of type_of_entity is a subset of the entity types in the database. In other words, if the sets of entity-types for every entity in the database are taken and all unioned together, then the resulting set is a subset of the entity-types known to the database. Hence, an entity will not have an entity-type which does not exist in the database.

The second part of the predicate says that all entities in the database have at least one type.

4.1.3. Attributes and values.

Attributes are the means by which we can hold single-valued pieces of information about an entity type. Instead of using the word *Property*, as do Codd and Date, we use the word **attribute**, so that the relationship with relational algebra is more obvious.

Let us introduce the set of all possible attributes, AT, the set of attributes in our database, **attributes**, and a function relating entity types to their attributes, **attributes_of**.

[AT]

ATTRIBUTES_____

attributes   : $\mathbb{F}$ AT
attributes_of   : ET —|→ $\mathbb{F}$ AT

_____

ATTRIBUTES.1
dom attributes_of = entity_types
ATTRIBUTES.2
∪ rng attributes_of ⊆ attributes

_____

Let us go through the predicate section.

ATTRIBUTES.1 says that the domain of the function attributes_of is the set of entity types in the database. So we say the database only knows the attributes of entity-types in the database.

ATTRIBUTES.2 says that the distributed union of its range is included in the set of attributes in the database. Thus if the sets of attributes of each entity-type are taken and unioned together, then the resulting set is a subset of the attributes in the database. An entity-type cannot have attributes not known to the database.

In our complete specification we go on to describe all the abstract concepts of RM/T. For example, the values which attributes can take, and associative, designative, and characteristic entity types.

4.2.   Concrete Structure and Algebra

This part of the specification deals only with Codd's relations and the set of algebraic operations that can be performed upon them. In both content and specification style we have drawn heavily from the work done in[13] on specifying the relational algebra.

A tuple of a relation is characterised as a finite mapping from attributes to values.

TUP ≙ AT —||→ V

A relation can now be defined as:

REL_____

attributes   : $\mathbb{F}$ AT
tuples   : $\mathbb{P}$ TUP

_____

∀ t : tuples . dom t = attributes

_____

That is, a relation is a set of **attributes**, and a set of **tuples** where the domain of each tuple is exactly the set of attributes.

We can now give some examples of the definition of functions using relations. The operators of the basic relational model have been presented in many different ways. We chose to define the generalised operators defined in.[14] The reasoning behind this decision is that we can have a small number of operators which are general enough to cover all the operators of the basic relational model as defined by Codd with the exception of those dealing with null-values which we consider unnecessary for our application area.

The most useful of those operators is Generalised Intersection. Informally, it is set intersection when the relations are union compatible (i.e. have identical attributes). It is cartesian product when there are no attributes in common. All other cases are equivalent to natural-join.

$\_ * \_ : \text{REL} \times \text{REL} \longrightarrow\!\!\!\!\gg \text{REL}$

$\forall\, r1, r2 : \text{REL}\,.$

$(r1*r2).\text{attributes} = r1.\text{attributes} \cup r2.\text{attributes}$

$(r1*r2).\text{tuples} =$
    $\{t\!:\!\text{TUP}\,|$
       $\text{dom } t = (r1.\text{attributes} \cup r2.\text{attributes})\; \wedge$
       $r1.\text{attributes} \lhd t \in r1.\text{tuples}\; \wedge$
       $r2.\text{attributes} \lhd t \in r2.\text{tuples}$
    $\}$

This is **not** a schema, it is a function definition although the format is very similar. The schema REL has been used as a type, and elements of REL have been accessed in expressions such as *r2.tuples* .

Suppose we have two relations, r1 and r2. The set of attributes of *r1 * r2* is the union of the attributes of r1 and the attributes of r2. The set of tuples of *r1 * r2* is defined as follows. It is clearly a subset of all tuples which map from attributes in *r1 * r2*. We further restrict this set by insisting that a tuple in it has further properties. If we just look at its values for attributes of r1, then it matches a tuples in r1, and if we just look at its values for attributes of r2, then it matches a tuple in r2. The mathematical means to just look at values of particular attributes is **domain restriction**, which has the symbol ◁| .

We also give an example of the specification of one of the extended relational operators. Informally, **partition by tuple**, or **PTUPLE**, promotes each tuple of a relation into an individual relation.

PTUPLE : REL $\rightarrowtail$ $\mathbb{P}$ REL

PTUPLE(r) = {rel:REL |
    rel.attributes = R.attributes $\wedge$
    rel.tuples $\subseteq$ r.tuples $\wedge$
    # rel.tuples = 1
}

4.3. Mapping from Abstract to Concrete

The concrete database represents the abstract database entirely in terms of relations. The mapping of attributes of entities to the attributes of relations is the identity mapping. Each entity type in the abstract database has associated with it an **E-relation** and a set of **P-relations**. The concrete database may also contain other relations, introduced by the user, which are not directly representing concepts in the abstract database. These relations do not form part of the ASPECT data model of course, but may be useful for, for example, holding temporary or derived data.

The database is entirely self-describing. The complete self description method is defined later but we anticipate slightly by noting that every relation in the database is represented by an entity. Furthermore every relation is typed and the type information is also held in the database.

The state of the concrete database therefore includes a set of relations. Obviously, we want to capture all our abstract concepts, and so we include **ABSTRACT DATABASE.**

CONCRETE_DATABASE_____

ABSTRACT_DATABASE
erel   : E $\longmapsto$ REL
relations : $\mathbb{F}$ REL

---

relations = rng erel

$\forall$ r : relations .
  $\forall$ t : r.tuples; a : r.attributes .
  a $\in$ dom domain_of_att
  t a $\in$ domain_of_att a

This introduces the function **erel**, which provides an entity representing every relation in the database. The range of this function, the set of all relations in the database, is also identified for convenience, and simply called **relations.** Note that REL represents the *contents* of relations and that several relations might happen to have the same contents; it is therefore often important to talk about the entity representing a relation rather than the contents of that relation. The second part of the predicate states that the values stored in the relations in the database must all come from the correct domains.

As an example of our style of specification we present the specification of the e-relation function which is considerably simpler than p-relations.

4.3.1. E_relation.

The purpose of the e-relation of an entity type is very simple. It is to record the surrogates of all entities of that type present in the database.

We introduce a function **e_relation_e**, which maps an entity type onto the entity representing its e-relation, and the function **e_relation**, which maps it onto the contents of the e-relation.

We also introduce a function **e_attribute**, which returns the sole attribute of the e-relation of an entity type.

```
E_RELATION_____

    CONCRETE_DATABASE
    e_relation_e : ET >─|─> E
    e_relation   : ET ──|─> REL
    e_attribute  : ET >─|─> AT
    _____

    dom e_relation_e = entity_types
    rng e_relation_e ⊆ dom erel

    e_relation = e_relation_e ; erel

    dom e_attribute = entity_types
    rng e_attribute ⊆ attributes

    ∀ et : entity_types .
       (e_relation(et)).attributes = e_attribute(et)
       (e_relation(et)).tuples =
              {e:entities│ et ∈ type_of_entity(e) .
                   e_attribute(et) |─> e
              }
```

The function e_relation_e gives, for every entity type, the entity which represents its e-relation. The range of this function is of course a subset of all the entities which represent relations, and composing the function with erel yields the e_relation function itself.

Each e-relation has a single attribute which holds the surrogates of the entities of the type.

4.4. Concrete Database

We now include the E and P relations in the concrete database. This is an example of schema *promotion* which is the special case of schema inclusion where the name of the schema also appears within the signature part of the schema. The meaning is that the new schema includes the declarations and predicates of the *previous* schema with that name. Thus a schema with many predicates can be built in understandable subsections without having to invent names for each of the parts.

```
CONCRETE_DATABASE_____
|                                                      |
| CONCRETE DATABASE                                    |
| E_RELATION                                           |
| P_RELATIONS                                          |
| _____                    |
|                                                      |
| rng e_relation ⊆ relations                           |
| ∪ rng p_relations ⊆ relations                        |
|_____|
```

The predicate says that all the E and P relations are included in the database relations. However, these are not necessarily the only relations there.

4.5. The Catalog as Abstract Entity-types

We now describe how we specified the Catalog as a set of entity types in the database whose special purpose is to record details about the contents of the database. This approach is significantly different from Codd and Date who present their descriptions of the Catalog in terms of relations. Of course, our Catalog will exist in relational form via our functions e_relation and p_relations, but our description, and any discussion of it, will be in terms of a set of special entity types.

The importance of this part of the specification is that it allows us to specify not only the structure of the Catalog but also its contents. And, of course, the latter is the most important feature of the Catalog. The contents of the Catalog relations are inherited from our specification of the values of the attributes of the entity types.

The general technique we have used to define the Catalog entity types is to introduce the new entity type along with a function which takes a thing of the type which is to be represented and returns the entity which represents it. The function is not required if the Catalog entity type associates items which already have representatives in the database.

In the following subsections we will demonstrate this technique by means of two examples from our Catalog. Later, there is futher discussion of the complete set of entity types which make up the Catalog.

4.5.1. The relation representative entity type.

In the following schema called **RELATIONS_REPS**, we introduce a kernel entity type, **relation_rep**, the purpose of which is to represent all the relations in the database. Earlier (in CONCRETE_DATABASE) we intoduced a function called erel, which returned the relation an entity represents. Here, we name the (mathematical) relation which is the inverse of erel, **relation_reps**.

RELATION_REPS_____

relation_reps   : REL $\longleftrightarrow$ E
relation_rep   : kernel

_____

relation_reps = erel $^{-1}$

attributes_of (relation_rep) = { }

$\forall$ e : E| e $\in$ dom erel .
    relation_rep $\in$ type_of_entity(e)

We say that the entity type, relation_rep has no attributes, and that there is an occurrence for every relation in the database.

4.5.2. Associating relations and their attributes

We introduce an entity type, **relat**, which records the association between attributes and the relations in which they occur.

RELATION_ATTRIBUTE_REPS_____

RELATION_REPS
relat   : associative
relat_rel,
relat_att   : attributes

_____

attributes_of(relat) = {relat_rel, relat_att}

$\forall$ att:attributes; er:entities; rel:relations |
    erel(er) = rel $\wedge$ att $\in$ rel.attributes
    $\exists$ e:entities | relat $\in$ type_of_entity(e) .
      attribute_value(e) (relat_rel) = (er)
      attribute_value(e) (relat_att) =
       (attribute_reps(att))

The entity-type relat has two attributes, **relat_rel**, which holds the surrogate of the entity representing a relation, and **relat_att**, which holds the surrogate of one of its attributes. We state that there is an instance of relat for every relation/attribute association in the database.

5.   FACILITIES PROVIDED

In this section we give a summary of both the Catalog structure and the operations we provide for updating, creating and deleting entities, and entity types, as well as relations.

5.1.   Catalog Structure

This section presents the structure of our Catalog along with the reasons for choosing such a structure. The Catalog is a set of thirteen entity types. Each is described in a schema of its own as we saw in RELATION_REPS and RELATIONS_ATTRIBUTE_REPS.

```
CATALOG_____

  DOMAIN_REPS
  VTYPE_REPS
  CATEGORY_REPS
  ATTRIBUTE_REPS
  E_TYPE_REPS
  ENTITY_TYPE_ATTRIBUTE_REPS
  RELATION_ATTRIBUTE_REPS
  PROPERTY_GRAPH
  SUBTYPE_GRAPH
  CHARACTERISTIC_GRAPH
  ASSOCIATION_GRAPH
  DESIGNATION_GRAPH
```

We have already presented RELATION_REPS and RELATION_ATTRIBUTE_REPS earlier in this paper. We will give only a very brief description of the other entity types in the Catalog.

Domain_rep is a kernel entity type, has no attributes and represents the value sets in the database. **Vtype_rep** is kernel, designates domain_rep via the attribute, **domain_designator,** and represents the value types in the database.

Categories label the arcs of the entity-type subtype graph of RM/T (i.e. type A is a subtype of type B *per* a category). **Category_rep** is a kernel entity type with no attributes which represents the categories in the database.

Attribute_rep is a kernel entity type with a single attribute, **vtype_designator,** that allows it to designate a value type. This means that an attribute can exist in the database without being associated with any entity type so long as it always designates a value type. Also, if an attribute is an attribute of more than one entity type, it always has the same value type. Thus we have overcome the Catalog structure problems in Codd's and Date's Catalogs which we pointed out earlier in this paper.

Entity_type_rep is the kernel entity type to represent entity types. It has two attributes. **Et_rep_class** indicates that the entity type is kernel, characteristic, or associative. **Et_rep_designative** is a boolean attribute to indicate whether the entity type is designative or not.

Our first associative entity type is **etat** (or entity type attribute representative) whose attributes, **etat_et** and **etat_att** hold information concerning which attributes are associated with which entity types.

The **property_graph** associates e-relations with their p-relations. Similarly, the **subtype_graph** associates a subtype with its parent type and category. And in the same way the **characteristic_graph**, the **designation_graph**, and the **association_graph** associate which entity types are characteristic-of, designate, or associate other entity types via which attribute.

5.2. Manipulative Operators

This section presents a summary of the operators provided and of our reasons for choosing them. Note that these operators are additional to both the basic relational operators and those of the extended relational model.

Firstly, there is a set of operators provided to manipulate the abstract concepts in the database. When using these operators, the toolwriter is guaranteed that the built-in integrity rules will be applied for him or her. the information does **not** have to be thought of in terms of its relational representation, but in terms of entities and attribute values.

o   Create Value set

o   Create Value Subtype

o   Create/Delete Attribute

o   Create Category

o   Create Entity Type Kernel/Characteristic/Associative

o   Create/Delete Entity

o   Update Entity

There are three forms of **Create Entity Type** because different information is required for each class of entity type (but all three allow the entity type to be designative in addition). It is important that there is an **Update Entity** operation, in addition to **Delete** and **Create Entity**, because, in the case of an update, we do not want the surrogate of that entity to change. We have not yet defined a delete version of all the operators in order to simplify the specification.

Secondly, there is a set of operators to be used in conjunction with the extended relational operators for the manipulation of relations.

o   Create Relation - given a set of attributes and tuples.

o   Delete Relation - given a surrogate.

o   Assign Relation - given a surrogate and a set of attributes/tuples, put the given tuples in the relation with that surrogate.

o   Overwrite Relation - given an existing relation (surrogate), a set of attributes (surrogates), and a second relation, the first relation's tuples are updated to the values in the second relation wherever the given attributes' values match.

o   Delete Tuples - in the same fashion as Overwrite Relation, the first relation loses any tuples whose attributes' values match those of the second relation for the given attributes.

The **Overwrite Relation** operator allows, not only tuples in a relation to be updated, but also tuples to be added to a relation. The important feature of this operation, shared by **Delete Tuples**, is that it allows the whole relation to be updated at once, rather than looping one tuple at a time.

6. CONCLUSION

We have described part of the work being carried out within the *Aspect* project. We have concentrated on the information base and, in particular, on the requirement for that information base to contain a structured section called the *Aspect* database. We have given reasons for choosing the Extended Relational Model as the foundation of this database.

We have described the problems which arose from that choice and the methods we used to overcome them. Of particular importance has been the activity of formally specifying the Public Tool Interface of *Aspect* in Z. This has enabled us both to clarify RM/T and to state precisely the interface to the database which will be provided to the users of *Aspect,* especially toolwriters.

The formal specification of RM/T has been completed, and implementation of a prototype has been started which will enable other parts of the project to experiment, and therefore to gain experience in using the RM/T database to satisfy their information management requirements.

7.   ACKNOWLEDGEMENTS

The authors wish to acknowledge the financial support given by SERC through the Alvey Software Engineering Directorate, and the many discussions with other members of the information base team, especially Dave Robinson, Ray Weedon, Alan Brown and Ben Dillistone, which have resulted in the ideas reported in this paper. We also owe a special debt to the members of the Programming Research Group in Oxford who have helped immensely with our specification work, especially Bernard Sufrin and Jeff Sanders.

8.   REFERENCES

1.   Vernadat, F. A., "Selected Bibliography with Keywords on Engineering Databases," *IEEE Database Engineering* 7 (2), pp. 55-63 (June 1984).

2.   Boerstra(ed.), M. L., *Engineering Databases,* Elsevier, Association for Applications in Engineering, Zoetermeer, The Netherlands (1985).

3. Chen, P. P., "The Entity-Relationship Model - Toward a Unified View of Data," *ACM Transactions on Database Systems* 1(1), pp. 9-36, Massachusetts Institute of Technology (March 1976).

4. Smith, J. M. and Smith, D. C. P., "Database Abstractions: Aggregation and Generalization," *ACM TODS* 2(2) (June 1977).

5. Tsichritzis, D. C. and Lochovsky, F. H., *Data Models*, Prentice-Hall (1982).

6. Date, C. J., *An Introduction to Database Systems VolumeII*, Addison Wesley (1983).

7. Hartzband, D. J. and Maryanski, F. J., "Enhancing Knowledge Representation in Engineering Databases," *IEEE Computer*, pp. 39-54 (September 1985).

8. Hitchcock, P., Whittington, R. P., and Robinson, D. S., "Modelling Primitives for a Software Engineering Database," in *Proc. of 4th British National Conference on Databases (BNCOD4)*, ed. A. F. Grundy, Cambridge University Press (10th-12th July 1985).

9. Codd, E. F., "Extending the Database Relational Model to Capture More Meaning," *ACM Transactions on Database Systems*, IBM Research Laboratory 4(4), pp. 397-434 (December 1979).

10. Kent, W., "The Entity Join," *Proc. 5th International Conf. on Very Large Data Bases* (October 1979).

11. Sufrin, B., Morgan, C., Sorensen, I., and Hayes, I., *Notes for a Z Handbook Part 1 -- Mathematical Language*, Oxford University Computing Laboratory, PRG, July 1985.

12. Walker(ed.), D. I., "Specification of the Aspect Public Tool Interface," aspect/wb/pub/pti/Zspec.1.0, System Designers (February 1986).

13. Sufrin, B. and Hughes, J., *A Tutorial Introduction to Relational Algebra - Draft copy*, Programming Research Group, Oxford, July 1985.

14. Hall, P. A., Hitchcock, P., and Todd, S. J, "An Algebra of Relations for Machine Computation," pp. 225-232 in *Proceedings of 23rd ACM Symposium on Principles of Programming Languages* (1975).

Chapter 15

Some practical aspects of software reuse

M. Stanley and S. Goodenough

1. INTRODUCTION

With the current high cost of developing new software and the concomitant risk that any new software component may not be adequately tested, it is usually agreed that re-use of well established software components is a desirable aim. We shall consider some of the factors in programming support environments which may affect the desire or ability to re-use components in a new context and describe how these problems are tackled in the Flex programming support environment.

We define re-use of software to be any way in which previously written software can be used for a new purpose or in a new context, to avoid writing more software. Product re-use is re-use of a program or procedure normally called from the command interpreter. Component re-use is re-use of existing components (procedures, programs, compiled units or source text) in new software products. Product modification is another form of software re-use in which either some source code is taken as a model from which a new component can be created or a product is modified by replacement of some part of the product by a new part.

We do not address the problems of the specification of software for reuse, or those aspects that are independent of the support environment such as legal responsibilities, protection of the Intellectual Property Rights or the difficulty of locating a suitable candidate component for re-use in a specific task. We concentrate on some practical issues in relation to the RSRE Flex system.

2. PROBLEMS

Various factors in software development environments affect the ability and desire of programmers to re-use existing software.

2.1 Component Re-use

A major problem with software re-use is ensuring that the interfaces between components always match. Non-matching interfaces are a hazard not only when a product is initially assembled from its components but throughout the life of the product. Corrections to components can give rise to non-matching interfaces. Users must have confidence that they will always know when an interface has been changed so that they can take appropriate action to correct the using software, or at the least to prevent the using software from being run with a non_matching interface. The separate compilation and software construction facilities must therefore ensure matching interfaces between components at all times. Choice of language and of separate compilation facilities will affect the clarity of the interface definition. A language such as Algol68 or Ada that enforces adequate type checking of interfaces is probably essential before a software component can be re-used with confidence. It should not be possible to run a program in which some interface does not match.

Configuration management facilities are needed to allow a component supplier to propagate corrections to all users of a component with a minimum of effort while also being able to make trial changes to his version without affecting other users. He needs to prevent users from changing issued components. A user may also wish to prevent changes to a component from being applied to his copy. It may be easier to live with an error than to accomodate the corrections, particularly if these involve changes to the interface.

Components are not always self sufficient. They may depend on the availability of other associated components.

Software products made available only as executable programs are not usually regarded as candidates for component re-use because of the difficulty of including them in any new software product. The compiled units and source text from which a program was derived are sometimes withheld for commercial reasons. Often the components that one would like to re-use, for example components of the editor, are embedded in monolithic systems and cannot be extracted.

Some languages and systems impose an artificial restriction on component re-use because procedures are partitioned into two groups, those (main programs) that can be formed into programs and called from the command interpreter and those that can be called from other procedures. Main program procedures are not direct candidates for component re-use because they cannot be called from other procedures. They can be invoked only from the command interpreter. Another artificial restriction on component re-use is imposed by systems that do not support mixed language working.

Some conventional systems allow a main program to be called from another procedure but such calls are often subject to certain restrictions particularly with respect to communication between caller and called. Re-use of main programs by spawning a new process to run the program is relatively complex, may still only allow communication in a restricted fashion and may give rise to other problems and so is likely to discourage potential users.

Some components that could be useful for re-use are restricted to privileged users because they have a considerable potential for abuse. System suppliers are rightly cautious about issuing components which, if misused, could cause filestore corruption or system crash. Similarly components that contain critical values or data structures which a supplier wishes to hide from his customer are not made available for fear that the customer will gain unauthorised access to values, perhaps through the debugging facilities of the machine.

2.2 Product Re-use

Product re-use is encouraged if each individual product performs a single isolated function. Individual functions can then be combined in different ways to achieve new objectives. On many systems there is insufficient separation of concerns. Monolithic programs are provided to perform a sequence of distinct operations that could usefully be separated into different programs or procedures. Users are forced to have a whole program or nothing. In fact the programs often consist of a set of procedure calls but the component procedures cannot be taken in isolation because they share common data areas. Even where the procedures do not rely on shared non-local data they are not supplied as separate programs because they pass complicated data structures between them which cannot be handled as program input/output by the command interpreter. Complicated data structures often have to be passed between programs by writing them to backing store sometimes as characters. If all inter-program communication must go via the backing store, there is a strong disincentive to providing complex functions as a sequence of separate programs. Furthermore it will probably be necessary to ensure that the format of this data is correct.

2.3 Product Modification

Product modification by replacement of an existing component by a different component having the same external interface is sometimes permitted only by complicated manipulation of build files or component libraries which thus discourages this form of re-use. Product modification by re-coding using some existing source text as a model is usually easier provided the necessary source text is accessible.

With these factors militating against re-use of software components and products it is sometimes surprising that any re-use occurs.

The Flex programming support environment (Currie et al (1, 2)) has some features which specifically encourage re-use of software components. One of these is the treatment of the procedure as a "first-class" value (Landin (3) and Currie (4)), another is the Flex separate compilation and software construction system, and a third is the ability of the Flex command interpreter to handle arbitrarily complex data structures. We shall briefly discuss each of these.

3. FLEX

The Flex Programming Support Environment (PSE) built on the Flex capability architecture (1,2) developed at RSRE, Malvern, supports the efficient use of procedures as "first-class" values in the sense of Landin (3,4, and Stanley (5)). Flex is an interactive PSE in which re-use of operating system and other software components is the norm. It relies

on procedure values to provide a high integrity, reliable PSE that is
noticeably different from other PSEs.

The Flex capability computer architecture has (so far) been
implemented in microcode on four hardware configurations including one
multi-user implementation in which 3 Flex computers share a common
filestore and common peripherals. The most recent implementation is on
the ICL Perq.

A full description of Flex is beyond the scope of this paper, which
will discuss software re-use and how this is encouraged in the Flex PSE.

4. PROCEDURE VALUES

"First-class" or "context independent" procedure values are vital to
software re-use on the Flex PSE. In most conventional computer systems a
procedure is not a context independent value. The procedure code needs a
context (its non-locals) to make it executable. Procedure values,
supported by the Flex architecture, are highly re-useable because they
have their non-locals bound into them.

4.1 What is a Procedure Value?

A procedure value is an executable value that consists of the
procedure code, constants and a set of non-local values. A local
workspace is supplied when the procedure is called. The non-local values
are those values (including any values declared in a separately compiled
unit) that are used in a procedure but declared outside it. Procedures on
conventional machines are represented not by a value but by the address
of the procedure code. The assumption is made that the procedure can
find its non-locals during execution using suitable pointers on the stack
frame. On Flex the non-local values are preserved by the existence of the
procedure value, whereas on most conventional systems the non-local
values are not bound to a procedure, they are associated with a procedure
only when it is called. The run-time system must then search the various
scopes to find the correct non-locals to associate with the procedure. A
procedure can be executed only while its non-local values remain in
existence.

For example, consider a procedure defined by:

```
DECS proc_m:
   INT counter:=0;
   PROC proc=(INT input_parameter)BOOL:
   BEGIN
      .......
      counter:=counter+1;
      ........
      counter< input_parameter
   END
KEEP proc
FINISH
```

Counter is a non_local value of proc which is incremented every time proc is executed. When proc is executed on a conventional system, the run-time system must find the environment in which proc was declared to find the correct value of counter.

On Flex every procedure is a context independent, executable value. It is created in mainstore (with code, constants and non-local values bound together) when the procedure declaration is elaborated (i.e. when the declaration is encountered). In the example given above, proc exists as an executable value independent of any enclosing environment, with its non-local value, counter, bound to it as soon as it is declared. When a procedure is called on Flex the run-time system already has the correct non-local values. There is no need to set up a complex mechanism to find the values.

The procedure value can be treated like any other value in that it can be passed to other users, used as a parameter to other procedures or even delivered as a result from other procedures without taking special steps to ensure that the non-local values can be found.

4.2 Main Programs and Other Procedures

A procedure value can be called from within a user procedure or, because the value is context independent, it can be executed directly by calling it from a command interpreter. The effect is exactly the same.

On conventional systems main programs are often represented as executable images that often cannot be called from other procedures. Any potential software re-use has to take into account the difference between main programs and other procedures. To be executed a main program must be called from the command interpreter. On the Flex system with procedure values any procedure can call any other. Privilege is not needed to make a system procedure or utility callable from another procedure.

A procedure value is an executable value in mainstore but values that are to be retained long term need to be written to backing store. Although a procedure value is not normally held on backing store, an analogue of a procedure value, called a filed procedure, can be retained on backing store. A mainstore procedure value is created from its filed analogue when it needs to be loaded for execution. This is done automatically on Flex when the filed procedure is called from the Flex command interpreter. The Flex user need make no distinction between calling a mainstore procedure value and calling a filed procedure value. Note that any procedure can be held as a filed procedure provided its non-locals can also be held on filestore.

A Flex filed procedure is not the same thing as an executable image. An executable image on filestore usually has its own copy of the code of all its procedures and its own copy of all non-local values of those procedures, with all links resolved and with a single entry point. Each program loaded from an executable image normally contains its own copy of all its procedures except for a few privileged procedures which can be shared between programs. In contrast a Flex filed procedure does not contain copies of all the separately compiled units; it contains references to the required separately compiled units. The values kept by such units will be created during loading. A filed procedure can be loaded from the command interpreter, or if the filed procedure value is a value within another procedure it can be explicitly loaded from the using procedure. Since the Flex filed procedure does not contain copies of all its constituent procedures, the loading process can take advantage of this to re-use code already in mainstore. Code sharing is entirely automatic. In addition, because the filed procedure only contains references to the other modules used, it will use the most up to date version of such other modules. Re-use of modules in several products therefore saves both filestore and mainstore space. The same copy is shared by each product.

5. COMPONENT RE-USE

Why are procedure values relevant to component re-use? With procedure values the artificial distinction between main programs and other procedures disappears. We are not hampered by the notion that some kinds of procedure are unsuitable for component re-use. Any procedure, including one such as a system utility that would be regarded as a system program on a conventional system, can therefore be re-used in new contexts.

The unit of separate compilation on Flex is the Flex module. Compilers on Flex check that the interfaces of all used modules match their use so a user can have confidence that he is not using non-matching interfaces. Multi-language working is possible. A module gives access to the compiled code resulting from a compilation, to its external specification (the data and procedure types and source text names that are visible to users of the compiled unit) and to the source text from which it was derived (unless the source text is explicitly hidden, see below). Every module includes references to all the components that it uses, so if a component is accessible for re-use, the components it needs come with it.

A component supplier can supply a module while denying the user access to the source text from which it was derived. A product supplier may be unwilling to allow the modules from which a filed procedure was created to be made available. Unlike most conventional systems Flex has facilities that allow products supplied as filed procedures to be treated as components and incorporated in new software products without making the compiled code or source text generally available. The user can load the filed procedure from within his program without being able to access its text or compiled code.

Normally a user who wishes to call a procedure from his own code will pick up the module that defines it and include a reference to that module in his own source text. The modules used to create the Flex system, the command interpreter, editor, compilers and other utilities are easily accessible to the ordinary Flex user. They are held in the general documentation file together with their documentation. (Editable files on Flex can contain arbitrary values in addition to lines of characters.) A potential user can browse through the set of modules to find one that provides the function he needs. It is normal on Flex to re-use system procedures such as the editor and the command interpreter to interface with the user. This leads to a much more consistent user interface than is usual, as well as reducing the number of new procedures written by users to interface with the screen.

6. CHANGES

A common problem in software development is to ensure that, when an error is corrected in a component, the correction is propagated to all users. This is particularly important if component re-use is to become a normal way of working. Although some systems provide automatic propagation of changes in compiled units to all dependent units, the propagation is not always extended to cover programs or executable images including the changed units.

Changes to Flex modules have immediate system wide effect. This means that a change is automatically propagated to all users of the module, to all programs or filed procedures that involve the module and across all Ada libraries that contain the module. Changes are so propagated because the user of the module (be it a module or a filed procedure) does not incorporate the code of a module until it is loaded at run time.

If a module is widely used by other users, it may be desirable to try out changes to the owners' version that are not propagated to other users and this is also possible. A procedure is provided on Flex that permits selective replacement of chosen modules used within a procedure. It can be used to replace a module locally without propagating the replacement. The replacement has no effect on the old version of the procedure and it is unnecessary to alter any source text to achieve the replacement. Module replacements can be made only if the replacement has the same external specification as the replaced module. This facility can be used to test proposed changes before propagation of the change or to construct multiple versions of a piece of software by merely replacing certain modules. The remainder of the modules will be common and corrections to those will be reflected in all versions of the software. Replacement of modules with altered external specification is achieved by replacing the using module, altered as necessary to match the altered used module specification.

Modules are protected from unauthorised change. Only the creator of a module will normally be able to change it. Sometimes a user may wish to protect a re-used component from all changes propagated by the component supplier. Flex has facilities for this if, as is usually the case, a re-used component was a module rather than a filed procedure. The programmer re-using the module can create a new module from the old one. The new module will not receive any of the changes propagated to the module from which it was derived. Obviously to prevent any changes to anything would require creating a whole new set of modules. However, in practice this rarely seems necessary.

Users of components supplied by another programmer will not wish to be involved in any unnecessary recompilation just because the owner has decided to change a module. If a Flex module is changed without changing its external specification it is not necessary to recompile any module that uses it. If however the external specification has changed, this invalidates all existing use of the module. To prevent the use of modules whose interfaces no longer match, components involving invalid modules cannot be loaded. Thus any programmer re-using a module whose external interface has changed will know that the change has occurred when he tries to use the procedure involving the changed module even if not formally notified of the change. He will never be subject to the undefined results that can occur if accidentally using a procedure whose specification no longer matches the call. It is easy to locate invalid modules and to recompile their users, making any necessary changes. This will enable everything to load correctly again. Indeed a procedure is provided on Flex that scans a module and all used modules, automatically recompiling any that use an invalid module, calling the editor and inviting change to a using module where non-matching interfaces are involved. This will not work, however, if the using module has also been supplied from elsewhere. Modules can be amended only in the environment in which they were created. For this reason suppliers of components for re-use should have a responsible attitude about making changes that alter external specifications.

It is possible to arrange that all changes to modules are automatically recorded within a log file accessed through the module. The procedure to change the module records the change in the log file inviting the amender to add a comment explaining the change. Other relevant information, such as the name and address of the author and even source text of the superseded version may also be included. A Flex module automatically gives access to the source text from which it was derived unless steps are taken to hide the text. Similarly anyone re-using a module has access to the log file although only the owner can update the log file.

7. PRODUCT RE-USE

Because Flex supports procedure values all tools or programs in the Flex PSE whether system provided or user provided, are just procedure values. There is no distinction on Flex between a procedure value and a program or tool. The effect of calling a procedure from the Flex command interpreter, "curt" (Currie and Foster (6)), which is itself a procedure, is the same as that of calling it from any user procedure. Any programmer can, without privilege, call procedures such as the system utilities from his own procedures. System utilities such as the Flex editor and the Flex command interpreter are procedures that can be (and are) used by other procedures to communicate with the user.

When a procedure value is called from curt the data required by the procedure are the parameters of the procedure, and the result of obeying the procedure is delivered to curt in the same way as the result is delivered to any other calling procedure at the point of call. In the example of section 4.1, "proc", supplied with an integer parameter, will deliver a boolean result whether called from another program or from the command interpreter. Each call of proc will increment counter. If proc were always called with the parameter "5" then the fifth call of proc would be the first to deliver the result 'FALSE'.

7.1 Flexible communication between programs

A command interpreter that can call any procedure directly must be capable of handling procedure parameters and results of arbitrary complexity. The Flex command interpreter does not impose any artificial restriction on the data types of the parameters or of the results of procedure calls (Stanley (7)). Arbitrarily complex values can be delivered from a procedure directly to the command interpreter for direct input to another procedure or for retention for future use without the need to resort to filestore. This is in contrast to systems where a procedure that is a main program must have only very simple values (such as a single integer, or a file) as input parameters and can deliver only simple data structures as results. Some systems handle more complex values, by reading from or writing to backing store.

The Flex command interpreter not only handles arbitrarily complex data structures; it also provides type checking such as is usually provided only within programming languages. Every object or value handled on Flex, whether on filestore or in mainstore, has an associated Flex mode (type) that is used to indicate how the value is to be interpreted, and the operations that are valid on it. Values vary in type from simple integers to complicated structures with many fields including pointers or references. The Flex mode system is more general than that of most programming languages and includes generic procedure types, and facilities for handling objects of any type. The user can also invent additional modes (that are composed of the basic modes) to suit his problem. This type system extends to filestore, so that boundless varieties of objects may be held permanently giving much greater flexibility than with conventional filestore.

7.2 Mode Checking

Because procedures (or programs) on Flex are values like any other value, every procedure has an associated Flex mode. The mode of a procedure defines the mode of its input parameters and the mode of the result of obeying the procedure. Curt will not call a procedure on values of the wrong mode. This encourages product re-use. Having selected a procedure for re-use a programmer can call it from curt with confidence that curt will reject the call rather than allow him to apply a procedure to an unexpected data structure. The implicit re-use of the mode checking software automatically provided by curt limits the need to write explicit software to check the validity of the input data for procedures that are main programs.

A mode can also be regarded as a value (of Flex mode Mode) that can be passed into and out of a procedure. Re-usability is enhanced if a single procedure has the ability to handle correctly any data structure it may receive. Different procedures are not then needed for the different data structures. To achieve this a procedure needs access to the mode of the data structure. A special Flex mode, called "Moded" is available in which any value, V, of any mode, M can be expressed as a moded value. The representation of the Moded value contains both V and M. Thus the mode of a value can be passed into and out of procedures together with the value. Curt can, when appropriate, convert a value V of mode M into a Moded and it can untangle a Moded to deliver the value V in mode M.

For example, consider a procedure "show" that takes any Flex value and displays it on the screen in a form appropriate to its mode. The Flex mode of "show" is: Moded -> Edfile. The procedure "show" untangles the Moded (V, M) and displays V in appropriate form. If "show" is called from curt the input may be of any mode, because curt will convert the value to Moded form. It delivers as a result an editable file that contains a copy of the display.

Consider a procedure "find" which takes a name and searches a dictionary for a value associated with the name. Dictionaries on Flex hold values of arbitrary mode, not just files. The procedure delivers the value together with its mode, as a Moded value. The Flex mode of "find" is: Vec Char -> Moded. Curt will untangle the Moded and deliver the value in the correct mode.

One result of embedding the mode information with the value in the Moded mode is that an existing procedure to handle any mode can (and does) handle new modes created since the procedure was written.

7.3 Separation of Concerns

One consequence of calling procedures directly from a command interpreter able to handle arbitrarily complex data structures is separation of concerns. Single purpose procedures can exist as executable entities no matter what non-local values or parameter structures are involved. They do not have to be embedded in programs. There is no need to combine different procedures into a single program to enclose the non-local values; to pass results from one procedure to the next or to perform a complex function. Complex functions are achieved by applying single purpose procedures in sequence, each performing one simple function. Each procedure is applied to the result delivered by its predecessor.

For example, consider four distinct procedures:

```
PROC line=(FILE edfile)VECTOR [] CHAR:
        (extracts a character string from an editable file)
PROC convert=(VECTOR []CHAR line)VECTOR []INT:
        (converts the character string to a vector of integers)
PROC mean⇒(VECTOR []INT ints)INT:
        (calculates the mean of a vector of integers).
PROC sd=(VECTOR []INT ints)INT:
        (calculates the standard deviation of a vector of integers)
```

A user wishing to discover the mean of some integers held in character form in an editable file would call the first three procedures in turn from the command interpreter, delivering the result of each call as input to the next call. If he later decided he also needed the standard deviation he would need only to call the last procedure on the result delivered by the second. It is unnecessary to combine the procedures into a single program to allow them to pass the result of each call to the next procedure nor need the results be written to filestore to be passed between the procedures.

The separation of concerns applies equally to system utilities. The Flex editor processes only editable files. If a user wishes to change the text of a module (a value giving access both to compiled code and to the text from which it was derived), he first applies a procedure to the module delivering the text as an editable file and then applies the editor to the result. Similarly, he may apply a procedure to the module delivering its external specification as an editable file and then apply the editor to the result in order to display the specification. It is unnecessary to merge the distinct functions into a single tool. The separation of concerns into distinct procedures makes it easy to re-use them.

8. USING PROCEDURE VALUES

Procedure values can be used to solve a number of common problems associated with component re-use. The facilities provided are not privileged. They can be used by any programmer.

8.1 Abstract Data Types

Component suppliers may be more willing to issue a set of procedures to handle a data structure if they can hide from the user the details of the structure itself. One of the many uses for procedure values is to create abstract data types or packages in a very flexible way. For example a procedure can be provided that will create a private data structure and then deliver to the user other procedures which manipulate it. However these other procedures will not have the data structure as a parameter, it will be a non-local bound to the set of procedures. This ensures that the user cannot tamper with the data structure because there is no way in which the user can get hold of it. The only mechanism for manipulating it is the set of procedures supplied. This is more general than the package mechanism in some languages. It is quite clear that as many structures are created as the number of times that the "generating" procedure is called, and each of these has its own set of access procedures.

For example, consider the familiar example of a stack of integers. The effect of a call of the procedure make_stack is to create a stack and provide a structure of two procedures for manipulating it. The stack itself is completely hidden from the Flex user. The variable "space" has been bound into the delivered procedures and there is no way in which a Flex user could get at it directly. Furthermore at a later time the implementor of the stack procedures could change the operation of the procedures or the representation of the stack, but provided that the modes of the procedures remained the same (i.e. that make_stack took no parameters and delivered a STACKPROCS and that STACKPROCS remained the same) users would not need to recompile.

```
MODE STACKPROCS = STRUCT(PROC(INT)VOID push, PROC INT pop);

PROC make_stack = STACKPROCS:
(HEAP REF VECTOR[]INT space := HEAP VECTOR[0]INT;
                    {this declaration will be available
                     only inside the delivered procedures}

  PROC push = (INT e)VOID:
  (HEAP VECTOR[UPB space + 1]INT new space;
   new space[:UPB space] := space;
   new space[UPB new space] := e;
   space := new space);

  PROC pop = INT:
  (INT result = space[UPB space];
   space := space[:UPB space - 1];
   result);

  (push, pop))
```

Given a suitable language (such as the Ten15 - an algebraic abstract machine upon which most of the future Flex development work will be based) the above example could be extended to be generic and create stacks of a variety of types.

This can be compared with Ada, where one needs to invoke packages, private types and even generics to achieve a similar effect. For example:

```
package STACKS is
  type STACK is limited private;
  procedure PUSH(S : in out STACK; E : INTEGER);
  procedure POP(S : in out STACK; E : out INTEGER);
private
  type STACK is ...
end;
```

This allows the user to declare objects of type STACK and the "limited private" prevents tampering except by the procedures PUSH and POP. However the disadvantage is that a change in the type of STACK will inevitably lead to recompilation by users.

A second choice might be to hide stack away:

```
package STACKS is
  procedure PUSH(E : INTEGER);
  procedure POP(E : out INTEGER);
end;    -- actual stack declared in body
```

This might solve the recompilation problem but unfortunately leads to our program being able to have only one stack, since the package is only going to get loaded into the program once.

Finally we are led to use generics to achieve multiple stacks:

```
generic   -- no parameters!!
package STACKS is
  procedure PUSH(E : INTEGER);
  procedure POP(E : out INTEGER);
end;   -- actual stack declared in body
```

Each instantiation of this will produce a pair of procedures bound to a new stack. In effect each instantiation corresponds to a call of "make_stack" in the original example.

A system with "first-class" procedures subsumes packages and some of the uses of generics. It is arguably much easier to understand what is happening.

The abstract data types created as in the make-stack example may involve mainstore or filestore values. Consider a procedure of Algol68 mode:

```
PROC make_read_file=(INT disc) STRUCT(PROC INT read_next_int,
                                      PROC BOOL read_next_bool,
                                      PROC BOOL is_empty);
```

The delivered procedures (all giving access to the same file parameter of make_read_file) may be stored on backing store because all the non-locals can be stored on backing store. Different procedures may be issued to different users, providing communication through the shared data structure. No user need know the structure of the stored data, nor need they have access to every value in the structure.

The facility to create abstract data types in such a flexible way encourages software re-use by enabling suppliers to hide the structures from users and by allowing easy creation and use of structures such as stacks without the need to redesign them. Procedures such as make_read_file and make_stack can be issued to any user and delivered procedures that can be held on backing store can also be issued to other users.

8.2 Binding Critical Values

It is possible using procedure values to permit free re-use of critical operating system procedures without the risk that they will be abused by supplying them with wrong parameters. Suppliers can embed critical values in procedures both to prevent unauthorised access and to prevent the use of wrong parameters where the correct use of parameters is crucial. This is achieved by hiding the critical value inside an access procedure in the same way as the stack is hidden in push and pop in the make_stack example. In particular critical parameters to system procedures can be embedded in the procedures supplied to users, so they cannot be changed. The same kind of protection can be applied to any procedures.

For example, procedures that operate on the vdu screen need the identity of the current vdu. Each user can be supplied with procedures containing the basic code for displaying on a vdu. The pointers identifying the current vdu are bound to them when the procedure values are created at run-time. The supplied procedures all use the same basic code but they will only affect the vdu to which they are bound. The user does not need to have the pointers identifying the vdu. Indeed he has no access to them and cannot replace them with other values to gain access to another vdu.

Flex procedures to access a dictionary do not have the dictionary as a parameter. They are delivered to the user with the dictionary bound into them. They can be retained on filestore because the bound in value (the dictionary) is a filestore value. They cannot operate on another dictionary, or on any other filestore object. A user is thus prevented from accidentally or maliciously modifying a dictionary to which he has no right or even from reading it. He does not need to know the internal structure of the dictionary, since all access is through procedures. Different functions such as modifying the dictionary, delivering a named value from a dictionary, adding a named value to the dictionary or displaying the content of the dictionary will all be bound to the same dictionary. Another user will get a similar set of procedures bound to a different dictionary.

8.3 Privilege

Most conventional operating systems have to allow certain privileged users to break the normal access rules to allow access to operating system values. Privilege is needed to access the special values needed in order to archive or to access peripherals. It is sometimes risky to allow programmers to re-use privileged procedures or procedures that use operating system values (normally protected from general access) as parameters. However, procedure values allow a supplier to provide normally privileged operations in an unprivileged way thus enabling normally privileged software such as operating system procedures to be made available for re-use. Privileged values are made available only within procedures that allow them to be used only in the authorised way.

Procedure values allow the same code to be bound to different non-local values before being delivered to users as procedure values. The bound in values can neither be accessed nor changed by the user. These could of course be sensitive data structures, which must not be tampered with, or peripherals such as the current vdu, the data structures for which are bound in to the procedure so that the user cannot tamper to get access to another vdu.

Any Flex user can have access to the archive procedure, which has bound to it, hidden from the user of the procedure, the values needed to achieve the archive. As already mentioned procedures to communicate with a vdu and keyboard have the pointer to the specific vdu bound into them.

9. EXCEPTIONS

Software that is being re-used will sometimes fail and this may allow a user to gain access to information about a component or product that the supplier would rather keep hidden. Failed procedures in any language on Flex deliver a value of Flex mode Exception, containing information on the situation at the point of failure. A procedure can process the exception value internally or it can pass it out to the calling procedure adding its own information to the exception value on the way. A diagnostic procedure uses the exception value to provide a list of procedures called before reaching the failure point, the names and values (displayed in appropriate format) of all local variables in each called procedure and the source text of each procedure with a marker at the failure point. The owner of a procedure issued to other users may wish to prevent the use of diagnostic tools for unauthorised examination of the internal working of a failed component. Flex allows the programmer to include instructions in his program that prevent any trace of selected procedure calls from appearing in the exception value available to diagnostic tools. It is also possible to deny access to the source text of modules used by a procedure. Thus suppliers of components and products for re-use on Flex can be protected from unauthorised prying by customers.

10. CONCLUSIONS

The Flex PSE encourages re-use of software in several ways. The main characteristics of Flex that encourage component re-use are context independent procedure values, the separate compilation and software construction system, a command interpreter that handles typed values of arbitrarily complex structure and checks appropriate use of procedures, and facilities for suppliers to protect their software from unauthorised examination.

Procedure values have many consequences. The uniformity of a system in which there is no distinction between use procedures and main programs or system programs eases re-use of system utilities such as the editor and the command interpreter in user programs.

The separation of concerns necessary to product re-use is fostered by the ability of the command interpreter to call directly procedure values with parameters and results of arbitrary types. The fact that procedures values can share non-local data, thus communicating without involving either the command interpreter or the filestore also assists separation of concerns.

Every procedure called directly from curt implicitly re-uses the mode checking provided by curt, thus making it unnecessary to provide mode checking internally in each procedure. The facility to pass the mode of a value into procedures with the value assists in re-use of software by enabling a single procedure to handle any mode it may receive.

Complex data structures can be re-used by issuing only the procedures that handle the structures. The structures themselves can be hidden from users. They can even be modified without affecting the user of the issued access procedures, provided that the issued procedures retain the same external specification.

Facilities to protect commercially sensitive information include the ability to re-use procedures, not only through their modules but also as filed procedures whose modules are not accessible. Modules that are released may have the source text issued with them or the source text may be hidden. The same applies to the log file. Particularly sensitive information can also be hidden from the diagnostic tools.

The configuration management facilities on Flex include automatic propagation of authorised change to all users while still giving the supplier the opportunity to modify without propagation and the user the opportunity to cut himself off from module updates. The fact that the source text and the log file are part of the module (unless explicitly excluded) gives confidence that the supplier (and user if permitted) will always know what source text was used to create the current version of a module. No-one except the supplier can modify an issued module. No product can be loaded with non-matching interfaces between components. The software construction facilities allow not only modules but also filed procedure values to be incorporated into new products. They do not impose artificial constraints preventing mixed language working.

A PSE such as Flex demonstrates that it is possible to achieve a high degree of software re-use, both product re-use and component re-use, with minimal risk. Future work on Flex is aimed at making the PSE more widely available, and at improving the facilities. The body of software available for re-use on Flex is constantly growing.

11. References

1. Currie, I.F., Edwards, P.W., and Foster, J.M., 1985, 'PerqFlex Firmware', RSRE Report 85015.

2. Currie, I.F., Edwards, P.W., and Foster, J.M., 1982, 'Flex: A working computer with an architecture based on procedure values', RSRE Memorandum 3500.

3. Landin, P.J., 1964, 'The mechanical evaluation of expressions', Computer Journal, Vol 6, No 4, pp308-320.

4. Currie, I.F., 1982, 'In praise of procedures', RSRE Memorandum 3499.

5. Stanley, M., 1986, 'Using true procedure values in a programming support environment', RSRE Memorandum 3916.

6. Currie, I.F., and Foster, J.M., 1983, 'Curt: The command interpreter for Flex', RSRE Memorandum 3522.

7. Stanley, M., 1985, 'Extending data typing beyond the bounds of programming languages', RSRE Memorandum 3878.

Chapter 16

Some experience from the design of an integrated programming environment

N.H. Madhavji and L. Pinsonneault

ABSTRACT

Integrated programming environments have recently received considerable attention, as they seem to provide some hope in improving the process of software construction and, possibly, also improving the quality of the software produced. This paper describes some experience gained by the authors in the design of the MUPE-2 programming environment. The system is aimed to support the development of Modula-2 programs, and is being implemented in this same language. Issues discussed in this paper include: the distributed design of the system, implementation language support, integration of operations, extensibility and the bootstrapping process, and portability of the system.

1. INTRODUCTION

A large software system is generally recognised to be difficult to build. In order to simplify this construction process, there is currently a considerable effort that is being invested in the design of suitable environments for software development [2, 4, 5, 6, 7, 17, 21, 22]. Unfortunately, this task can be even more challenging. Several reasons for this may be:

- An environment needs to capture the software development *process*, which may not be well understood.

- New software development concepts and methods proposed by environment designers often induce unexpected complexity in the design and implementation of the supporting software.

- Software environments themselves are often large systems, and therefore present the kind of difficulties, in their design, that are experienced in the development of large user software systems.

This paper describes some experience gained by the authors in the design of MUPE-2, a programming environment for Modula-2, which is currently under development at McGill. In particular are discussed the architecture of the system, and the design and engineering issues, such as: distributivity of major system functions; implementation language support; integration of environment features; portability and extensibility of the system, and bootstrapping the environment.

MUPE-2 is a *fragment-based* integrated programming environment, i.e., software is developed in fragments. However, these fragments are well-defined structures, and their types are called *fragtypes*. Example fragtypes are: Expression, Statements, Declarations, Procedure, Module, System-layer, and Subsystem. As can be seen from this, these fragtypes cover both programming in the small and programming in the large structures, in varying granularity. This enlarged scope is called *programming in the all*.

Along with fragtypes, are fragment *construction rules* and fragtype *transitions*. These guide the underlying machinery in constructing well-formed program fragments. Such fragments may be stored in the system's library, called Fraglib, and may be re-used in the construction of new fragments. Fragments may be brought in the environment from the outside, and vice versa. This system is being developed on the School's VAX 11/750 that runs under the UNIX operating system.

It is important to note that, in general, this paper does not describe the functionality of MUPE-2, as this has appeared in several related papers on this environment [12, 11, 13, 14, 15]. Rather, the paper concentrates on the rationale behind the design decisions and system level issues that the authors find interesting in the design of the environment.

2. THE MUPE-2 PROCESSES

MUPE-2 is being designed as a distributed system, such that its parts: the Screen Manager, the General Manager, the Edit-Compile System, the Run-Time System, the Host Operating System Interface and the Fraglib Manager, are independent but co-operating processes. Inter-process communication among these functional units takes place via message passing facilities. This is illustrated in Figure 1.

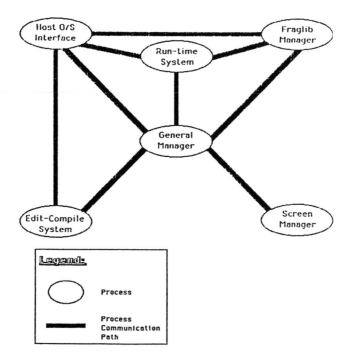

Figure 1 - The MUPE-2 processes

Screen Manager (SM)

The Screen Manager is in charge of the user interface. It accepts user input from the keyboard and the *mouse*, and displays textual and graphical responses from the system. This process communicates messages with the General Manager via input-output buffers. Since these two processes run asynchronously, it is possible for a process, say SM, to generate messages faster than the other one can respond to them. Thus, it was necessary to implement the message queue as a ring buffer, where the sending process has to wait if the ring is already full.

In addition, the SM accesses graphics procedures to interface with the terminal primitives. Because of the monitor-cpu communication, and input-output routines, this process is hardware dependent. Furthermore, the SM is terminal dependent as well, but a terminal capability data base mitigates this dependency.

General Manager (GM)

The General Manager manages all system activities in a manner similar to an operating system kernel. It initialises all other system processes, command menu routines and operand compatibility checking routines for the operations. This process also receives user input, which is first analysed and then transmitted to the appropriate process. For example, the decoding of command and menu selection messages deposited, into the input buffer, by the SM would result in gathering operand information, until the operation is fully specified. The GM then communicates to the appropriate core function, such as the editor or run-time system, in order to execute the operation. In addition, the GM has access to program fragments that are present in RAM, so that it can carry out user tasks of fragment selection; calls to display routines, and mapping of actual/virtual coordinates.

Edit-Compile System (ECS)

The Edit-Compile System contains editing and compilation routines for program fragments. Editing operations, both top-down and bottom-up, can be carried out on fragments of small granularity (e.g., expressions, statements and declarations) and of large granularity (e.g., procedures, modules, system-layers, and subsystems). Thus, both programming in the small and in the large is accommodated into a single scope, called programming in the all [11].

This subsystem of MUPE-2 also contains a *fragment* parser and code generator, which are currently being implemented. The parser is normally used to incrementally parse fragments of code inserted from the keyboard. However, program fragments of various types may be brought into the programming environment from the host operating system file storage. For this reason the ECS needs to communicate with the HOSI process.

The ECS also communicates with the GM. When the GM has completed the full specification of an editing command, the ECS performs the necessary editing operation. The GM then sends appropriate messages to the SM to update the display screen.

Run-Time System (RTS)

The Run-Time System is aimed at providing both interpretation and code execution facilities for a given program fragment. Along with these facilities is planned a *fragment-based* symbolic and graphics debugger. These tools are a departure from conventional run-time tools, since they need to cope with program fragments of various kinds.

Clearly, in order to run a fragment, it must have a run-time data structure environment tied to the fragment. Such structures may be artificially created from the user interface, or may be a result of executing another fragment. In addition, a fragment may be dynamically bound to another one. This is particularly useful for making calls to procedure fragments stored in the library of fragments, called Fraglib. The RTS also communicates with the HOSI process; particularly when fragments need to access the host operating system facilities, such as system calls.

Host Operating System Interface (HOSI)

The host operating system interface is between MUPE-2 and the host system. This interface is used for several purposes:

(a) To provide full access to the low-level facilities (e.g., input-output, system calls, etc.) of the host system, from within MUPE-2.

(b) To provide the full host operating system functionality to MUPE-2 users, via a window into the host system. Thus, users do not need to log out of MUPE-2 in order to use utilities such as mail, text editor, and documentation tools.

(c) To up-load and down-load program fragments to and from the host file system. For up-loading, the fragment parser in the ECS is utilised; for down-loading, the unparser from the GM is used.

(d) To communicate with the Fraglib Manager during the system initialisation phase and during an interactive session, to load/store library fragments.

Fraglib Manager (FM)

The Fraglib Manager manages the data base of program fragments in MUPE-2. Normally, the whole Fraglib, i.e., its hierarchical ring directories and program fragments are stored on the host file system. At initialisation time, the minimal library structure (i.e., super user, project, group, and home ring directories) is loaded. Thereafter, whenever a user wants to access a fragment which is not memory resident, the FM arranges to access the required fragment from the host file system. This scheme is analogous to the well-known operating system concept of paging [3].

Fragments in the host file system are stored as ASCII files. But since they are represented as abstract syntax trees in MUPE-2, they need to be parsed for loading and unparsed for storing. With a persistent data base environment [1] many of these mapping routines between abstract syntax trees and the host system files would be unnecessary, resulting in a more efficient implementation of the system.

3. DESIGN AND ENGINEERING ISSUES

There are several desirable features that could be considered in the design of a programming environment. Some of these are: *integration* of environment features, so that software development may be simplified; *modularity* of the whole system, for simplicity in its design; *adaptability*, for versatility of the system; *portability*, so that the system can be made available on varying hardware systems; *extensibility*, so that new features can be easily added to the system, possibly via the *bootstrapping* process; the *distributed* nature of major system functions, so as to speed up processing and system responses; and adequate implementation language support. This section discusses several of these points in the context of MUPE-2 design.

3.1. Integration

In batch environments, the independent tools often provided limited capabilities to the user and, in comparison to integrated tools, were less flexible to use. This is because the separate tools had their own specific representations of data, thereby causing inter-tool communication to be prohibitively expensive and their usage inflexible.

Integration has brought together different utilities of a system, and has put them at the user's disposal in a given context. Thus, in integrated programming environments such as MUPE-2, it is possible to *edit* a program fragment, *merge* parts of another fragment with the current one, *fold* or hide selected parts of the fragment from screen display, perform simultaneous operations on selected structures from the fragment, *save* the fragment in the library, *find* more information about a desired structure in the fragment, etc., in a series of actions, without painfully invoking these different utilities as one would in a batch environment.

There are several issues that may be examined when considering integration:

(i) **Increased program space**. This means that various pieces of program information and operations are available to the user simultaneously. For example, multiple windows containing program fragments, data structures, commands and menus, library of fragments, etc., on a display screen contribute to increased program space. Availability of multiple pieces of information simultaneously, almost certainly encourages the user to carry out varying operations on different program structures. Thus, the environment needs to be receptive to any of several possible inputs at a given time. This leads to integration of environment features.

(ii) **Distributed environment**. A network of processors may be utilised to perform several programming tasks in parallel. The task of the environment here, is to assign processes to available processors. But in order to maximise the usage of the underlying hardware, integration of programming activities can be helpful. Note that this is in contrast to user processes in the UNIX operating system, which runs on a single processor.

(iii) **Centralised data base**. A common data structure, e.g., an abstract syntax tree, which is accessed by several programming utilities provides a powerful mechanism for integration of the utilities. Through increased program space, tools such as a tree editor, interpreter, debugger, and a program inquirer, may be accessed in an interactive manner. Since these tools *understand* the common data structure, their responses to the user can be intelligent. Also such responses can be input to some other utility. For instance, a program inquiry may result in a program fragment, which may then be edited or interpreted.

(iv) **Operation states**. In conjunction with increased program space, the degree of integration in an environment can be made higher by providing *escape points* at each intermediate state of an operation. In general, an operation is of the form $S_0, S_1, ..., S_i, ..., S_n$, where S_0 is the start state, S_n is the termination state, and S_i is an intermediate state. The intermediate states request further input. Clearly, atomic operations, such as **Delete**, have no intermediate states, since the operation is immediately applied to a chosen program structure. On the other hand, non-atomic operations, such as **Insert** and **Move**, may have one or more further inputs, e.g., a menu selection and source or destination program structures.

In order to facilitate high degree of integration in MUPE-2, a user may *freeze* an operation in any state S_i and invoke a new operation, possibly on another fragment. Thus, any state is an escape point. The frozen operation is tied to the program structure concerned, thereby permitting integration of many incomplete operations on program structures. Resumption of a frozen operation is simply achieved by clicking the mouse on the program structure concerned.

There is inherent complexity in designing an environment to provide integration of utilities. In the design of MUPE-2, we needed to examine different possible actions on a given structure in a particular context. The number of such actions can at times be difficult to comprehend, and therefore, a methodology such as Wasserman's transition diagrams [24], or Lingard's process script [8], can be helpful.

As mentioned in the introduction, program structures in MUPE-2 range from a simple expression to a sub-system of modules and procedures. Hence, both programming in the small and programming in the large are facilitated in an integrated manner. Because of the high degree of sensitivity integrated operations need to provide to the user, this wide range of program structures are classified internally into several *domains*. Example domains are: several kinds of sub-systems in Modula-2, with several possible root nodes (e.g., compilation units, modules, procedures, units, etc.); several kinds of layers of sub-systems, with clear indication of boundary conditions and types of nodes in the layers; solitary node types; declarations, with details about *opaque types* of Modula-2, export/import features, etc.; statements, with indications on the use of abstract phrases for later refinement; and so on.

These domains give *contextual* information that affect compatibility checks when operands and operations are selected. For the *cursor* structure, the enclosed, adjacent and enclosing program structures need to be taken into account in providing contextual information. Domain descriptions may also contain conditional or other related pieces of information for a given context.

Once the domain of the cursor structure is known, together with the chosen *operation*, then the operation analysis phase begins so as to check the compatibility of other selected operands. During this process, domain descriptions are particularly useful, although there may be inherent complexity in the conditions associated with the domain.

The benefit of the domain scheme for program structures is that often users can be provided with advanced responses that were not possible in batch environments. In some cases, users can be *warned* not to select a particular structure because of compatibility reasons. Such checks may seem computationally expensive, but in powerful workstations a considerable amount of machine cycles are wasted during programmer *think-time*. With increasingly powerful hardware, highly integrated software can provide visual responses based on operation/operand checks described above.

3.2. Modifiability and Extensibility

A prime concern in the design of MUPE-2 is *modifiability* and *extensibility* of the system. The authors believe that these two desirable system characteristics should be considered from the outset, and not as an afterthought, in the design of a system. These design goals are particularly important in the construction of programming environments because:

(a) the initial implementations of such systems may not have captured the process of software development as desired;

(b) parts of such systems (e.g., the user interface) may not be quite acceptable to some users, the way provided by software engineers, and

(c) new features become apparent, or some existing ones become obsolete, after gaining some experience with the system.

In order to aim for a high degree of flexibility in MUPE-2 design, our implementation strategy is to build only a minimal subset of the system that will be self-supporting. Subsequently, further development of the system will be carried out in stages using the previous stage of development. This cyclic process of development, which we term *environment bootstrapping*, is likely to ensure extensibility and modifiability of the system.

There has been considerable concern in the past about how to achieve flexibility in system design. Some proposed solutions to this problem include module decomposition and top-down refinement techniques for software development [25, 19, 18]. They permit a part of a system to be changed or extended without affecting most other parts of the system; indeed a desirable quality. However, these techniques do not help in breaking away from conventional programming techniques. Software is still *hard-coded*, i.e., programming knowledge is retained in algorithms. As a result, modifications and extensions to systems are carried out largely by using textual or structured editors.

It is highly desirable to automate this process as much as possible, by developing specialised *installation* tools. This goal would ensure that new modifications or extensions take place in a consistent manner. However, for such tools to be programmed, there are certain requirements from the implementation language in which the software system is written. These requirements entail *binding* of procedures, or action routines, to variables, tables and dynamic data structures. Action routines may then be invoked by accessing data structures instead of explicit calls to procedure names. Also, modifications to data structures imply changes to system design.

Table-driven Technique

One method of achieving some degree of flexibility in programming environment design is to use table-driven techniques for user interface and for action routines. For efficiency reasons, in most languages in the Pascal family, table dimensions are generally statically determined. Each table element, say, represents a programming command or an item of menu, in a bit mapped interface. The table elements are then statically bound to their corresponding command and menu action procedures. Invocation of the action routines than take place via table entries.

Here, the user interface knowledge is represented, in part, in table data structures, rather than algorithmically in selection statements. The table elements can only be bound to action routines provided the implementation language supports *procedure types*. The programming language Modula-2, which is the implementation language for MUPE-2, supports this method of programming adequately.

With the table-driven approach, modifications to table sizes and procedure bindings are generally quite simple compared to those required in selection statements. Besides, tables are susceptible to automatic loading by specialised installation tools. The basic algorithms for searching tables need not be modified. Thus, this technique permits isolation of the modification and extension problem in software.

However, early in the design of MUPE-2, we realised that while the table-driven technique is more desirable than hard-coding, it does not support repeated modifications in a simple manner. This requirement is particularly important in MUPE-2 design, as we expect to bootstrap the environment. In this process, we expect to add incrementally new features of the environment. Thus, we discarded our table-driven software and started implementation all over again with a new technique which we term *soft-coding*.

Soft-coding Technique

The soft-coding technique uses dynamic data structures, built at system initialisation phase, to hold the programming environment knowledge in linked structures. These structures correspond to the static tables of the table-driven approach, but are readily modifiable, since they are dynamic. Such modification can be safely carried out by installation tools which bind action routines to linked structures.

A major advantage of this technique over the table-driven approach is that, modification by soft-coding can be performed at *run-time* of the system to be modified. For example, to add a new command and its menu of items, the command installation tool should be invoked instead to editing the source code of the programming environment. This tool is part of the programming environment, and therefore, the environment need not be taken out of service during the modification phase. The operation of the tool proceeds by obtaining, possibly interactively, the names of the command and menu items to be installed. These are then added to the dynamic structures of previously installed features. The new structures are then bound the the appropriate new action routines.

While the soft-coding technique is attractive from modification and extension point of view, it has two main drawbacks. Firstly, the programming environment knowledge structures may not be comprehended as easily as algorithmic structures. This is because the dynamic data structures, as provided in Pascal-like languages, are not as visible as static structures [10]. Secondly, testing a soft-coded programming environment is considerably harder than testing a hard-coded environment. In particular, the familiar control flow path analysis and testing largely do not exist in soft-code. Hence, run-time monitoring of the system has to be carried out on dynamic data structures.

3.3. Distributivity

Two of the most important considerations in the design and implementation of a distributed system are the target underlying system/hardware configuration and the proposed implementation language. We are currently carrying out implementation of MUPE-2 on the school's VAX 11/750, running under the UNIX operating system, and we plan to change to the new version of Modula-2, described in [26], as soon as compilers become available. The compiler we use currently is Decwrl [20].

Our plans for the near future are to port the environment to one of the school's MASSCOMP 5500 computers. These are dual processor machines with an optional third, graphics, processor. The graphics processor that is available for MASSCOMP is user programmable, and hence in that configuration, the computer can be considered as a three processor machine. MASSCOMP machines run under a variant of UNIX. The main reason why this environment migration is being considered is that we would like to conduct experiments in a truly concurrent environment.

3.3.1. Concurrency

Each of the six functional units, described in section 2, is being implemented as a UNIX process rather than as a Modula-2 PROCESS such as that described in [26]. There are two main reasons for this choice. Firstly, UNIX processes offer a better approximation of true concurrency, or parallelism, than that which can be achieved using Modula-2 PROCESS facility, as is described below:

(a) True concurrent processes run independently of each other, in an asynchronous mode, even though it is some times necessary to synchronise them, as in the case of database processes. Modula-2 PROCESSes always run in a synchronous manner, because the act of releasing control of the 'processor' has to be made explicit by the use of the TRANSFER call. Such a call indicates, to the run-time system, the process which is to be given control of the 'processor' next. UNIX processes do not suffer from this explicit control transfer: it is performed implicitly, some times randomly, by the UNIX operating system.

(b) Although true concurrent processes can physically share some memory space if the computer architecture permits it, they are not dependent on this for their communications with other processes. Modula-2 PROCESSes have no alternative but to use common global memory area to pass messages. On the other hand, UNIX processes are like true concurrent processes, and the UNIX system provides *pipes*, which are dedicated communication channels for inter-process communication.

(c) Finally, the Modula-2 PROCESS implementation is that of a coroutine, which is local to the program which defines it. Thus it is impossible to have coroutines running on separate processors not sharing memory, since the PROCESS should have access to all the global data area. UNIX processes are, conceptually, separate programs which do not share common data areas, so that they could, possibly, run on separate processors.

The second reason for selecting UNIX processes over Modula-2 PROCESSes is that, an extensive amount of modifications is required, in the Modula-2 system, in order to provide genuine concurrency. According to [26], individual implementations of Modula-2 compilers have the freedom to modify the PROCESS implementation to support genuine concurrency.

Support for genuine concurrency involves extensive modifications to both the back-end of the compiler and to the run-time system. The modifications required to implement MUPE-2 are as follows:

(a) Since the PROCESS facility is not part of the Modula-2 language, but is defined in the SYSTEM module which is part of the compiler, it would be necessary to modify the PROCESS definition as well as the functions and procedures that can be applied to it. This involves modifying the parser, code generator, and that part of the compiler that deals with the SYSTEM module.

(b)   The run-time system would need to handle inter-process communication via some kind of protocol, possibly using something similar to UNIX pipes. The existing Modula-2 TRANSFER function which is used for transferring *control* between co-routines, could now be used to transfer *data* between processes.

(c)   In order to solve the busy-wait situation, the run-time system, like an operating system, should be able to *block* a process upon call to a WAIT function. A blocked process would remain inactive until it is unblocked, and therefore, it would not receive the time slices it would receive otherwise.

(d)   The loader should be able to assign PROCESSes to processors if there are many available. Otherwise, UNIX-like processes should be created.

(e)   In the current implementation of Modula-2, a program must end on termination of one of its PROCESSes. For genuine concurrency, this would need to be slightly modified to read: on termination of the main program, all processes must terminate.

Other interesting points are that process initiation and termination could either be implicit,   or   be   made   explicit   by   the   use   of   functions NEWPROCESS/DISPOSEPROCESS, which are analogous to Pascal's NEW/DISPOSE functions on dynamic data structures, or the **fork/kill** calls of UNIX on processes. These functions, NEWPROCESS and DISPOSEPROCESS, make it possible to dispose of specific running processes without shutting down the whole system, so as to upgrade the environment. For example, in MUPE-2, it is conceivable to install a new version of one of the processes, say the editor or the run-time system, without affecting the other processes. This idea is not new, as operating systems already operate in this manner with respect to device drivers.

The implementation of these features does not require syntactic modifications to Modula-2. However, semantic changes involve a run-time process administrator, which breaks off communication links between the terminated processes and other processes which can potentially communicate with the now inactive process. This could be implemented with exception handling facilities [9, 23], that would trap illegal communication attempts and take appropriate action, or by simply terminating the program when such an illegal attempt is made.

3.3.2. Inter-Process Communication

Processes need to communicate among themselves in order to cooperate. We have examined several communication methods and have retained the most promising. The following gives a description of three different methods and compares them.

The first method relies only on message passing in order to achieve the required level of cooperation among MUPE-2's processes. This implies that the processes are not allowed to share any memory. Thus, the structures that are operated upon by the different processes must either exist in every process, or belong to only one of the processes.

In the case where copies of the data structures exist in each process, the problem that occurs is that, in order to avoid possible inconsistency between the different copies, we would have to *echo* every modified structure, or modification operation, to all the processes. For this purpose, these processes would have to share a major portion of the code needed to modify and operate on these structures. Clearly, this defeats the reason for requiring processes in the first place.

On the other hand, where only one process is the 'owner' of all the data structures, every time an operation on a given structure is to be performed, the structure would need to be sent to the correct process through the message passing mechanism and, subsequently, returned to the owner the same way. In this respect, the UNIX message passing mechanism is specialised in passing *textual messages*, and therefore it is not suitable for passing structures. Its use would entail unparsing the whole structure before sending it, and reparsing it upon receiving it. As structures to be modified can be large, this scheme is also not considered suitable.

The second communication method lies in the other extreme. Processes are permitted only to share memory, and no message passing mechanism, such as UNIX pipes, is made available. This implies that messages should now be deposited in the shared area, and that the processes should examine this area to determine whether or not there are messages for them. On existence of a message, it is decoded and the appropriate action performed. This method is similar to that available to Modula-2 PROCESSes, which have no message passing mechanism.

While the performance of this method may be acceptable on parallel hardware, the fact that processes must continuously check for message arrival may degrade the overall performance of the MUPE-2 system on a uni-processor machine. This degradation occurs due to the fact that each process that is busily waiting receives a time-slice from the operating system, and exhausts it by repetitively checking the shared memory area. Instead, if it was *blocked* by the operating system when attempting to read a not yet arrived message, the time-slices that this process might have received will now be allocated to processes that actually need them in order to perform computations.

Finally, the third communication method is a compromise between the first two: certain processes can share the data structures in memory area, while providing a message passing facility. Here, processes that share data structures (see Figure 2) can directly operate on these structures when required, and all the processes can communicate through the established communication channels (see Figure 1) which are now used only to pass commands and textual data.

	Shared Store
GM	YES
SM	--
ECS	YES
HOSI	--
RTS	YES
FM	YES

Figure 2 - Storage sharing between MUPE-2 processes.

This method is the best of the three that we have examined. By sharing storage, it eliminates the need for duplicating considerable amount of code in each of the processes. By having a message passing facility, it eliminates the need for busy waiting. Thus, even though this method will work only on machines where processes, or processors in parallel architectures, are allowed to share memory, it is the one we decided to use for the implementation of MUPE-2.

3.4. Implementation Language Support

The programming language Modula-2 has been chosen as the environment's implementation language for several reasons:

(a) Like Pascal, it is a simple language, but it is powerful enough to carry out systems implementation.

(b) The environment is for Modula-2, and hence its construction in Modula-2 gives an improved understanding of the character of the environment for the target language.

(c) As the target language is the same as the implementation language, the environment need not be fully hand-crafted. As soon as minimal features of the environment have been implemented, the bootstrapping process can begin so that further development of the environment can be carried out using earlier versions of the environment.

In the course of our research, we noted some interesting conflicts and coherences between the programming language Modula-2 and the MUPE-2 environment. These observations are described in [16], and they address issues largely pertaining to the software development *process* using MUPE-2. However, this section discusses how well Modula-2 supports the design of MUPE-2.

The programming language Modula-2 provides a number of advanced features, in comparison to Pascal, that make it a realistic system programming language. In addition to Pascal's various control structures, procedure mechanism, user defined structured data, enumerated types, sets, and linked data structures, Modula-2 provides modularisation, separate compilation facility, *opaque* types, procedure types, and low-level facilities to perform type transfers, address specific storage locations, and simulate concurrency.

Modularisation

Modula-2 facilitates system development in modules. The interface part of a module is called the *definition module*, and the implementation part is called the *implementation module*. Both these modules are separately compilable, and therefore, they are suitable for large system development work.

A definition module[†] *is* the *export* list of the module, i.e., items programmed in this module are available to other modules for importation. Besides this controlled usage of items, Modula-2 facilitates *opaque* types. An opaque data type is defined in the definition module by indicating only the type name. The inner details of this data type, which is restricted to pointer types in Modula-2, appears in the implementation module. Thus, importing modules cannot inadvertently access the inner details of this data type; this is done in the implementation part of the exporting module.

An implementation module, on the other hand, encapsulates local procedures and modules, which operate on related data structures. The language is particularly powerful here, as local modules in the implementation part provide further protection. Items cross module boundaries by indicating so in the export/import lists of the local modules concerned. Also, variables can be of procedure types, the benefit of which in MUPE-2 design has already been described in an earlier section.

These high-level language features have proved to be helpful in MUPE-2 design. Error cases tend to be localised to the modules in which they originate; modularised software forms its documentation, since related functions are encapsulated; and the use of the language has given us an insight into software development using Modula-2.

Low-level facilities

The main low-level facilities in Modula-2 are the type transfer functions, explicit addressing of storage locations, and co-routines. As the last of these has already been considered in conjunction with UNIX processes, in an earlier section, it is not discussed here any further. A type transfer function, on the other hand, transfers the value of a given type into the corresponding value of the type specified by the function identifier. For example, a record or array can be treated as a sequence of storage locations. This is particularly useful for storage management.

Most of the functions in MUPE-2 do not use type transfer functions and the explicit addressing mechanism of Modula-2. This is because the environment functions are largely user, or high, level. However, specific major MUPE-2 functions that would need to use these low-level language facilities are the run-time system, the host operating system interface, and the loader.

These low-level facilities of Modula-2 would be increasingly useful in the environment bootstrapping process. Through the host operating system interface, the initial,

---

[†] For the benefit of some readers, in the previous (second) edition of the language as defined by Wirth, an export list was required in the definition module.

hand-crafted, minimal sub-set of the environment would be represented internally as program fragments. The fragment editor and the library would then be used to add new features to the source fragments. This would be followed by code generation of the new features, and the whole process repeated. It is during each such cycle that there would be a need to use the low-level facilities of Modula-2, in order to interface with the UNIX operating system.

4. CONCLUSIONS

The distributed design of MUPE-2, and studies in language-environment interactions and implementation techniques, have given the authors insight into integrated environment design. An overall remark that can be made from this experience is that designers may need to compromise, perhaps temporarily, theoretically best solutions in the presence of practical constraints.

Modula-2 implementations available to the authors treat the PROCESS feature as a co-routine. Therefore, in the current design of MUPE-2, UNIX processes are favoured, since they are a closer approximation to genuine concurrency. Modula-2, in the opinion of the authors, has one of the highest power/complexity ratio. However, building an environment for this language in the same language has surfaced a number of conflicts and coherences between the language and the environment [16].

With several differing implementations of Modula-2 and UNIX, and the changing definition of Modula-2, it is important to take extra care in the design of MUPE-2. Therefore, for portability reasons, we decided to shield the environment from the host operating system by creating a buffer-layer for items interacting with the outside. This leaves the environment largely intact.

The initial implementation of user interface and action routines used the table-driven approach. This was later discarded all together in favour of the new implementation technique, which is termed here as *soft-coding*. In retrospect, this was a wise decision because this technique will enable us, and the users of the environment, to modify and extend the system in a much simpler manner using installation routines.

Finally, soft-coding has two main drawbacks. Firstly, the implementation of the environment using this technique is a lot more difficult than conventional hard-coding or table-driven techniques. This is because the programming environment knowledge has to be captured in internal structures. On the other hand, the algorithms manipulating these structures are much simpler than in other implementation methods. Secondly, the soft-coded structures are difficult to test. But it is expected that the encapsulation feature of the language would be of help here, as it tends to localise errors.

ACKNOWLEDGEMENTS

The work described in this paper was in part supported by FCAR, Quebec, and NSERC, Canada research grants.

5. REFERENCES

[1] Atkinson, M.P., et al.: *An Approach to Persistent Programming*. Computer Journal, Vol. 26, No. 4, 1983, pp. 360-365.

[2] Delisle, N., Menicosy, D. and Schwartz, M.: *Viewing a Programming Environment as a Single Tool*. Proc. ACM SIGSOFT/SIGPLAN Soft. Eng. Symposium on Practical Software Development Environments, ACM Sigplan Notices, Vol. 19, No. 5, May 1984, pp. 49-56.

[3] Denning P.J : *Virtual memory*. ACM Computing Surveys, Vol. 2, pp153-189, 1970.

[4]   Donzeau-Gouge, V., Houet, G., Kahn, G., Lang, B.: *Programming Environments Based on Structured Editors: The MENTOR Experience*. In Interactive Programming Environments, Barstow, D.R., et. al., McGraw-Hill, 1984.

[5]   Goldberg, A.: *Smalltalk-80: The Language and its Implementation*. Addison-Wesley Publishers, 1983.

[6]   Hood, R.T., Kennedy, K.: *A Programming Environment for Fortran*. Proc. 18th Hawaii Int. Conf. on System Sciences, Vol. 2, January 1985, pp. 625-637.

[7]   Lewerentz, C. and Nagl, M.: *Incremental Programming in the Large: Syntax-aided Specification Editing Integration, and Maintenance*. Proc. 18th Annual Hawaii Int. Conf. on System Sciences, Hawaii, Jan. 1985, pp. 638-649.

[8]   Lingard, R.W.: *A Software Methodology for building Interactive Tools*. Proc. 5th Int. Conf. on Soft. Eng., San Diego, CA., March 1981, pp. 394-399.

[9]   Liskov, B. and Snyder A.: *Exception Handling in CLU* IEEE Trans. on Soft. Eng., Nov. 1979, pp. 546-558.

[10] Madhavji, N.H.: *Visibility Aspects of Programmed Dynamic data structures*. Comm. ACM., Vol. 27, No. 8, August 1984, pp. 764-776.

[11] Madhavji, N.H.: *Operations For Programming in the all*. Proc. IEEE 8th Int. Conf. on Soft. Eng., London, U.K., Aug. 1985, pp. 15-25.

[12] Madhavji, N.H., Choudhury, S., Robson, R. and Friedman, N.: *On Commands for an Integrated Programming Environment*. In Press. Proc. IFIP WG 2.7 3rd Int. Working Conf. on The Future of Command Languages, Rome, Sept. 1985, North Holland Publishing Co.

[13] Madhavji, N.H., Leoutsarakos, N.: *A Dynamically Self-adjusting Structured Editor*. Proc. ACM SIGSMALL Symposium on Small Systems, Denvers, MA, May 1985, pp. 101-116.

[14] Madhavji, N.H., Leoutsarakos, N. and Vouliouris, D.: *Software Construction using Typed Fragments* Proc. TAPSOFT Int. Joint Conf. on Theory and Practice of Software Development, Berlin, March 1985, Springer-Verlag LNCS No. 186, pp. 163-178.

[15] Madhavji, N.H., Pinsonneault, L., Choudhury, S., Friedman, N.: *The MUPE-2 Programming Environment Project: An Overview*. Proc. CIPS Session'85, Montreal, June 1985, pp. 372-382.

[16] Madhavji, N.H., Pinsonneault, L., and Toubache, K.: *Modula-2/MUPE-2: Language and Environment Interactions*. Internal Report SE-86.1, Jan. 1986, pp. 34, available from the authors.

[17] Medina-Mora, R. and Notkin, D.S.: *ALOE users' and implementors' guide*. Tech. Rep. CMU-CS-81-145, Dept. of Comp. Science, Carnegie-Mellon Univ., Pittsburgh, Pa., Nov. 1981.

[18] Myers, G.J.: *Reliable Software through Composite Design.* Petrocelli/Charter, New York, 1975.

[19] Parnas, D.: *On the Criteria to be used in Decomposing Systems into Modules.* Comm. ACM., Vol. 15, No. 12, Dec. 1972, pp. 1053-1058.

[20] Powell, M.L.: *A Portable optimising Compiler for Modula-2.* Proc. ACM SIG-PLAN'84 Symposium on Compiler Construction, Sigplan Notices, Vol. 19, No. 6, June 1984, pp. 310-318.

[21] Reiss, S.P.: *Graphical Program Development with PECAN Program Development Systems.* Proc. ACM SIGSOFT/SIGPLAN Soft. Eng. Symposium on Practical Software Development Environments, ACM Sigplan Notices, Vol. 19, No. 5, 1984, pp. 30-41.

[22] Teitelbaum, T. and Reps, T.: *The Cornell Program Synthesizer: A syntax directed programming environment.* Comm. ACM, Vol. 24, No. 9, Sept. 1981, pp. 563-573.

[23] U.S. Department of Defense: *Reference Manual for the Ada Programming Language.* ANSI/MIL-STD 1815A-1983, Washington, D.C., Feb. 1983.

[24] Wasserman, A.I.: *User Software Engineering and The Design of Interactive Systems.* Proc. 5th Int. Conf. on Soft. Eng., San Diego, CA., March 1981, pp. 387-393.

[25] Wirth, N.: *Program development by Stepwise Refinement.* Comm. ACM., Vol. 14, No. 4, April 1971, pp. 221-227.

[26] Wirth, N.: *Programming in Modula-2.* Springer Verlag, 1985.

Chapter 17

Where software production is going

M.E. Falla

1 Introduction

This paper is an attempt to look some little way into the future and to guess at how we, or our successors, will go about the production of software.

Any such attempt is of course fraught with difficulties, but rational planning implies trying to see where evolution in the state of the art is leading us so that we can position ourselves to take advantage of opportunities - or at least avoid disasters. In putting these thoughts before you I am conscious of how wrong, particularly in timescale, they may be, but I am emboldened by the observation that they may at the least help to crystalise your own thinking on where software production is going.

2 The drivers for change

The principal drivers which will lead to changes in the way software is produced are:

A. Hardware push, coming from:

- continuing reduction in the cost (and physical size) of hardware delivering a given level of computing power.

- new computing configurations, such as dataflow and graph reduction architectures, and very large numbers of linked processors.

  (New terminal devices and sensors will extend the range of application of software but not, I think, its structure or the way in which it is produced.)

B. User pull, which takes three forms:

- a demand for `user friendliness´: ie a good human/computer interface. Increasingly a system which is comfortable to use will succeed over one that is not.

- a demand for reliability: computing systems are increasingly expected to work reliably like any other piece of office or domestic equipment without any esoteric operations on the part of the user. Beyond this, there are some, and there will be many, situations where human lives could be lost or massive social disruption caused if a computer system fails or behaves incorrectly.

- a decreasing willingness to adapt the `problem´ to the solution: ie computing systems are expected to fit in with and serve the (changing) needs of the organisation rather than the other way about; and these needs are being seen with greater clarity.

C. Growing ambition, as users are prepared to contemplate, and suppliers to attempt to produce, systems of ever greater complexity and sophistication. The Icarus complex.

D. The desire on the part of the producers to reduce the cost of production, maintenanace and enhancement.

3. <u>Trends</u>

A very noticeable trend is the split between the production of systems on the one hand by the IT system professional, and on the other by the end user. The methods and tools provided for the former are getting increasingly sophisticated, and will get more so, in an effort to meet targets of useability, reliability, production cost, etc.

Evolution in the support of end-users who in a sense produce their own systems has moved from FORTRAN compilers through spreadsheets and database query systems into the `4-th generation languages´. There will be a continuing evolution here as tools are developed which will allow the software non-specialist to formulate systems of increasing complexity to meet his own specific needs. Eventually we can expect a system which behaves much as a human assistant would: accepting general rules for information processing and asking the `boss´ about unspecified cases. For a small system (or a user´s interface into a large one) the `boss´ is the immediate user, for large systems the `boss´ is the organisation which owns the system, which of course has to act through some agency such as a `Management Services Department´.

At the moment, most end-users are remarkably tolerant of poor ergonomics: people seem to expect computers to be hard to use. That will change and design of an IT product will involve much more attention to the user interface. The example which is often quoted is that of the car which has evolved from a bare-bones, hard to drive, machine to an easy

-to-use consumer durable with most of the sales packaging
going into the `user interface´. In contrast to the car,
however, IT products have a much wider range of function and
have to address, often within the same product, a range of
users from the totally unfamiliar through the occasional
user to the person who uses the system for several hours
every day.

On the IT professional´s side there is already a trend
towards software-as-glue. Software has always been the magic
ingredient which turns a lump of computing hardware into
something useful. Software is increasingly being seen as the
glue which holds together a dispersed aggragate of computing
and communications equipment plus - and this will be of
growing importance - pre-existing software components. If
what you are basically doing is wielding a glue-pot than you
need rapid and detailed appreciation of the shapes of the
pieces you are gluing together - and a deft hand with the
brush.

Perhaps the most potent, and for many in the UK the most
threatening, trend is the growing capitalisation of the
production of software. Until recently one could go a long
way in producing software with pencil and paper. Software
houses were renowned for owning nothing but their coding
sheets. We are now firmly in the age of a terminal per desk,
backed by computing hardware, software tools, occasional
libraries of reusable components, standards and procedures
manuals, etc., and at least some professional training. This
conference is part of a trend to heavier capital investment
in workstations and tooling, and much more extensive component libraries and professional training.

4 <u>What will IT system production be like in 2006?</u>

In this section I have tried to take a look forward at
what IT system production might be like in 20 years time.
The choice of twenty years is fairly arbitrary but can be
justified as follows. I want to look at problems which
researchers are just begining to tackle. It seems to be
generally true that from the first gleam of an idea
through to general commercial application takes between ten
to fifteen years. If we allow a little time for the idea to
happen, and a little time for pessimism, then a sensible
time scale for prediction is 15 - 20 years.

4.1   Firstly to look at the end-user systems:

a) Physically small but with very large memory capacity,
   including a capacity for large programs. Selectiveness
   among buyers will put pressure on vendors to satisfy a
   wide range of demands. The systems will therefore be
   `adaptable´ in the sense that the user can adapt them to
   his own particular needs. This will mean changing not
   only minor things like formatting, but more substantial

things related to the way the user does his job or runs
his business. This in turn means very large and potentially complex systems to cater for all the options which
a user might select. Where major adaption is needed, eg.
to adapt to new tax laws, the user will expect to get a
software update which expresses the new regulations and
smoothly incorporates all his personalised adaptions, as
well as accommodating existing data.

b) Computer systems are already an integral part of the
administration of many large companies. Already the lack
of software effort is proving a brake on the speed with
which a company can adapt to changing circumstances. As
this trend continues purchasers will demand systems which
can be adapted cheaply and safely to meet changing
circumstances.

With these large systems, adaption will not mean just
adding a new rule of procedure or changing formatting,
but rather a mechanically assisted version of what we now
call systems analysis.

c) Systems (even small ones) will not run on single processors or even collections of similar processors. Some
functions will be implemented directly in electronics
(the equivalent of VLSI), some in distinctive harware
architectures such as inference machines or dataflow
structures. Systems designers will therefore have to
master a wide range of target expressions for their
designs. I dont believe that logical inference machines
will take over the world. But I could be wrong - is ICOT
the future or a feint?

d) The applications for end-user systems will, of course, be
wide, one assumes much wider than today. This is not an
area I intend to speculate much on since it is not, as
such, particularly relevant to the question of how
software is produced. One can, however make some general
points about the typical application system of the year
2006:

- its behaviour will be more intelligent

- it will make fewer demands that the world should be
   drilled into straight lines for the sake of the
   computer

- it will interact far more comfortably with the user

- there will be a growing tendency to look on, and
   expect a computer to behave as, a `brain amplifier´

- a computer will also frequently be a communications
   device, so that even personal IT systems will linked
   by wire or radio to national and international services.

(I take it for granted that systems will include the handling of speech, vision, etc. These are significant problems, but in this paper I am attempting to concentrate on how software is produced rather than on the development of specific software-based tchniques.)

4.2   From the need to produce these sorts of systems, and the pattern of evolution implied in sections 2 and 3, we can deduce, as implications for the IT supplier that:

a) There will be a much stronger user orientation. The requirements for large systems will emerge out of much more scientific (and computer assisted) analysis of the information processing needs of the organisation to be served. The user interface in all systems will be subjected to greater experimentation and analysis in order to fit it to the prospective users.

b) There will be a strong emphasis on formal methods and on sophisticated specification and design techniques - I see no other way in which systems which are so complex, adaptable, and yet reliable can be produced.

c) The huge investment in such design work will not be thrown away to match the marketing needs of the hardware manufacturer; instead, either hardware will be coerced to be compatible with the software or, more likely, the human (and therefore expensive) part of software production will stop at a level well above differences of hardware, the gap being bridged by a `super compiler´. Thus the systems professional will produce and verify `meta-systems´ built out of verified meta-components. These meta-systems will then be converted to `code´ or circuit design by compiler-like technology.

d) Similarly, new systems will be built out of the verified meta-components. These meta-components and the associated support environments (the `super compilers´, information management systems, prototyping and test environments, etc) will form a major capital investment and asset for IT system vendors.

e) All the principle `new´ techniques for expressing required behaviour will survive:

- functional and declarative programming (to promote provability)

- object-oriented programming (to control complexity)

- rule-based programming (for self-consciousness in a program and for the expression of users´ rules)

as will many of our current notations for expressing algorithms, dataflow and data structures.

These techniques will be joined fairly early by sound notations for expressing organisation ("programming in the large") and later (much later?) by programming by general logical inference at system generation time as well as at run time. We can expect to see these forms of expression linked to each other and to notations based on various forms of logic (model building, algebraic and temporal) in such a way that different forms can be used where each is most appropriate. This implies harmonisation at both the surface level, so that the engineer does not get lost, and at the deepest level to maintain logical coherence.

f) The general style of system development (by the IT professional) will embrace both the classic `software engineering´ approach of formal progression from requirement through to implementation, and the `experimental´ or iterative approach much favoured by the AI community - this latter will be used in a pathfinder role to explore new problem areas and particular subsytems. A consequence of the heavy investment in flexible, but not infinitely flexible, reusable (meta-)components will be a very large cost differential if a system is required which falls outside the limits of flexibility of existing components. The talents of the `fixer´ who can put together existing components in a new and attractive combination (in the style of current IC use) will not be lost.

g) There will be a class of IT professional who will never write (or cause to be written) anything remotely like conventional programs. They will interact with sophisticated generators for the large scale systems referred to in 4.1(b) above. These `generators´ will be capable, within their sphere of competence, of accepting new requirements, analysing the implications, pointing out the pros and cons of several solutions, posing demands (eg for new classes of input or assistance in an area outside its competence) and eventually of producing an upward compatible modified system.

4. How do we get there from here?

How do we acquire the sort of capability which I have described above?

Obviously it would not be wise to set up some massive project tasked with reaching that position in one step. Nor is it necessary. Current work contains the seeds of most of the capabilities we need. (Or, possibly to be more accurate, the future that I am predicting is an extrapolation of the growth of some of the seeds we see around us.)

It is possible to see an evolutionary path in which we start with the capability of the current IPSEs, tools, languages and methodologies, and integrate in the more advanced features step by step as our understanding of them is completed. It may even be possible, if we plan with care, to carry forward much of the investment in actual software components.

Index